Degrees of Difference

Degrees of Difference

Reflections of Women of Color on Graduate School

Edited by
KIMBERLY D. McKEE and
DENISE A. DELGADO

Foreword by
KAREN J. LEONG

**UNIVERSITY OF
ILLINOIS PRESS**
Urbana, Chicago, and Springfield

Publication of this book was supported by
Grand Valley State University's Center for
Scholarly and Creative Excellence.

Cataloging-in-Publication Data available
from the Library of Congress

ISBN 978-0-252-04318-5 (cloth : alk)
ISBN 978-0-252-08505-5 (paper : alk)
ISBN 978-0-252-05206-4 (ebook)

For women of color and indigenous women

Contents

Foreword

Karen J. Leong

Since this project began in 2014, numerous student demonstrations at public and private colleges and universities have demanded the hires of male and female faculty from underrepresented groups, particularly African American but also Native American and Alaskan Native and Latinx.[1] Greater undergraduate diversity has only highlighted the small numbers of faculty with diverse experiences *and* the lack of diverse perspectives and knowledge in the curriculum. Thus, while most institutions of higher education and academics profess a commitment to diversity and inclusion, students recognize that actual investments in hiring and structural change tell a different story.[2] Meeting these demands also requires successfully recruiting and retaining racially diverse graduate students.

Enrollment data demonstrate that the pipeline has greater numbers of nonwhite graduate students, but these numbers may not be translating to tenure-track faculty hires. Indigenous women and women of color (IWWOC) graduate students who identify as Hispanic/Latina, American Indian/Alaskan Native, Asian, Black/African American, Native Hawaiian/Other Pacific Islander, and Two or More Races[3] now outnumber IWWOC men, representing slightly more than 14% of all U.S. graduate students who are U.S. citizens and permanent residents in Fall 2017[4]; 17% of doctorates awarded to U.S. citizens and permanent residents in 2016 were awarded to IWWOC.[5] In 2017, IWWOC constituted about 9.7% of all tenure-track faculty and less than 6% of professors.[6] Nonetheless, Martin J. Finkelstein et al. observe that African American women's "proportionate presence among all full-time faculty has remained virtually unchanged (6.6.% in 1993, 6.9% in 2013) . . . while their proportionate presence among tenured full-time female faculty has actually *declined* from 6.3% to 5.8% between 1993 and 2013."[7] They note that, "the most robust growth [for IWWOC] in the academy has been among full-time non–tenure-track appointments (177.4%) and part-time appointments (238%)."[8] Alarmingly, the proportionate presence of African American women among tenured full-time female faculty has not increased since 2013, still remaining at 5.8% in 2017, with a drop in the proportionate presence among all full-time women faculty to the 1993 levels of 6.6%.[9] Thus, structural changes driving the casualization of academic labor have further entrenched existing hierarchies of gender and race.

These hierarchies continue to negatively and differentially affect women of color in graduate school. IWWOC undergraduates and faculty are all too familiar with specific racial and gendered microaggressions, which render women of color hypervisibly different but intellectually invisible, and the devaluation of family responsibilities and community obligations.[10] Experiencing this violence and dehumanization in graduate school, however, can be especially jarring. After IWWOC are encouraged by some faculty to pursue graduate work and assured by graduate programs that they value diversity, the differences between expectation and reality can be stark. Graduate school is much more political than undergraduate education, with funding, research opportunities, and mentoring tied more closely to interpersonal relations between faculty and graduate students. Departments may have only recently hired faculty women, much less IWWOC faculty, and greater resources may be had by working with senior faculty who are not be as invested in diversity initiatives.[11] Graduate students may find themselves tangled up in these lines of power without even knowing that they exist or without fully understanding the political landscape at the graduate level.[12]

Such challenges for scholars of color in graduate school have been documented. Research from at least the past two decades reveals how a hidden curriculum in graduate training maintains the status quo of what knowledge is valid and who is legitimized as a knowledge producer.[13] This research also provides empirical evidence of specific programming and training needed for graduate students as well as administrators, faculty, and staff.[14] Instead of implementing these recommendations, however, U.S. universities often look to faculty of color, indigenous faculty, and women faculty to socialize and support marginalized graduate students.[15] A combination of neglect as well as sexism and racism contributes to students of color, indigenous students, and first-generation students leaving their graduate programs or not pursuing faculty positions after completing their graduate degrees. Those who do acquire full-time faculty positions will likely already be prepared for the disconnect between statements affirming diversity and the lack of institutional action because of their graduate school experiences.[16]

A roundtable addressing how these broader issues affect IWWOC graduate students took place at the 2015 National Women's Studies Association national meeting. "Experiences of Women of Color in WGSS Graduate Programs: An Open Discussion" featured Sierra Austin, Krista Benson, Denise Delgado, Tay Glover, all enrolled in The Ohio State University's program, along with alumna Dr. Kimberly McKee. The frank discussion by these women of color, and a white woman who identified as an ally, about their experiences in OSU's Women's, Gender and Sexuality Program presented a stark contrast to other roundtables organized by and featuring faculty discussing the future of graduate education in the field. The students shared how they sought to bridge the demands of family and community—who may be unfamiliar with academia's idiosyncrasies—with those of their graduate program, as well as the code-switching required when acculturating oneself to certain, classed ways of interacting and performing in the academy. As the panelists made clear, indigenous women, women of color, and first-generation women graduate students in the academy face unique challenges based on their intersectional locations and the ongoing hidden curriculum of graduate training in academia.

This roundtable was organized by Dr. Kimberly D. McKee, a new assistant professor in the Liberal Studies Department at Grand Valley State University and Dr. Denise A. Delgado, then a doctoral candidate. Kim and Denise and their cohort of IWWOC and allies were aware of how intersections of racism, sexism, classism, ableism, and heterosexism could work together to limit opportunities and support for IWWOC junior scholars in academia. Their own experiences convinced them of the need to openly address the challenges IWWOC face as graduate students. The response to these honest discussions and calls for participation indicate a deep-seated, ongoing need for IWWOC junior scholars to collectively name and challenge the structural barriers they face in academia.

Kim, Denise, and their colleagues' efforts to create a larger, sustained conversation about the systemic violence and neglect—the simultaneous hypervisibility and invisibility—that IWWOC graduate students currently experience in institutions of higher education resulted in additional publications. Kim and another graduate school colleague, Dr. Adrienne Winans, assistant professor at Utah Valley University, proposed a special issue of *Feminist Teacher* focusing on the experiences of IWWOC graduate students in the classroom; they subsequently coedited for that journal a special section, "Women of Color in the Academy."[17] This manuscript, completed after Denise successfully defended her dissertation and chose not to pursue a faculty career, also is the outcome of conversations that began among women of color graduate students at the Ohio State University and grew to include other IWWOC graduate students and junior faculty across multiple fields and institutions. It is appropriate that this anthology was helmed by two successful women of color scholars who are pursuing diverse careers, because completing graduate school can support career paths both in and beyond the academy.

Denise and Kim shared with me their ideas for this collection and invited me to write this foreword in Fall 2014. As coeditors, Denise explained that she and Kim envisioned a collection that would center "the lived realities of graduate women of color . . . and serve as a tool of women of color doctoral and masters students as well as of their peers contemplating entering the academy." They sought personal narratives from junior scholars that highlighted their experiences in graduate school, with "special attention to the class issues that often coincide with women of color entering the academy, and the struggles faced by first generation students."[18] Their conviction about the need for a collection that prepared IWWOC for graduate school was matched only by what I already knew of their commitment to feminist intersectional analysis in all aspects of their scholarship and activities as junior scholars. It is not a coincidence that these original discussions initially took place within Women, Gender and Sexuality Studies, Asian American Studies, and Latino/a Studies, units that often have women of color faculty who engage in interdisciplinary, intersectional pedagogies and encourage junior scholars to identify and transform those conditions that maintain the elitism and homogeneity of the academy.[19]

Kim and Denise assembled narratives from the sciences, professional schools, education, and social sciences that have been missing from the conversation about IWWOC graduate student experiences. As Dian D. Squire and Kristin McCann observe, "there is limited research on the experiences of [women of color] doctoral students specifically, and no literature to date specifically examines women of color with critical worldviews."[20] Importantly, this collection does not flatten differences among IWWOC junior scholars but instead encourages readers to engage these stories through the lens of women of color feminism which, Grace Hong explains, "emerged precisely to enable such a political analytic able to articulate coalitional practice based on, rather than in spite of, historical and material differences between and within racial groups."[21] The editors include the voices of Asian American women (often excluded because Asian Americans are overrepresented in terms of national population, even though marginalized in academia as women of color), Native Americans (often not even visible in quantitative studies about higher education because their numbers are so small), Arab women, and multiracial women, as well as specific narratives that address navigating motherhood or transnational distinctions for certain fields. The practical strategies provided in this collection will assist future IWWOC graduate students as well as other students marginalized due to various social factors, specific departmental cultures, and institutional climates.

The most valuable contribution of this book for IWWOC junior scholars may be the knowledge that what they are experiencing has been survived by others before them. The authors in this volume soundly reject the deficit mentality that equates different skills and knowledge as being unprepared or not good enough. Some share how they reframed internalized feelings of inadequacy to understanding the *imposter syndrome* as symptomatic of the problems with academia itself.[22] Several emphasize the need for IWWOC junior scholars to draw upon their already developed navigational and resistant capital, evoking the important role that collectivism historically has played in resisting deficit-based assumptions.[23] Besides resulting in greater retention, IWWOC junior scholars who seek out community with each other and with allies can affirm for each other that academic knowledge and their community worldviews do not have to be in opposition but may complement each other in energizing and ethical ways.[24] This book provides the opportunity for IWWOC across multiple professional and graduate degree programs to share with each other what is unique to their personal circumstances and disciplinary contexts, while also building coalitions to demand institutional change and accountability on the part of universities, units, and faculty. Five years in the making, this collection is a labor of love, an affirmation of collectivism and community, and a promise for the ongoing survival of indigenous women and women of color in the academy.

Notes

1. Tanya Washington, "Students' Demands for Diverse Faculty Is a Demand for Better Education," *The Conversation, The Conversation US*, December 2, 2015, https://theconversation.com/students-demand-for-diverse-faculty-is-a-demand -for-a-better-education-50698; Kimberley A. Griffin, "Reconsidering the Pipeline Problem: Increasing Faculty Diversity," *Higher Education Today*, American Council on Education, February 10, 2016, https://www.higheredtoday.org/2016/02/10/ reconsidering-the-pipeline-problem-increasing-faculty-diversity/; and Hollie Chessman and Lindsay Wayt, "What Are Students Demanding?" *Higher Education Today*, American Council on Education, Jan. 13, 2016, http://www.higheredtoday .org/2016/01/13/what-are-students-demanding/.

2. Bridget Kelly, Joy Gaston Gayules, and Cobretti D. Williams, "Recruitment without Retention: A Critical Case of Black Faculty Unrest," *The Journal of Negro Education* 86, no. 3 (2017): 305–317.

3. For history of "women of color," see Marjorie Spruill, "Women Unite! Lessons from 1977 for 2017," *Process: A Blog for American History*, Organization of American Historians, Jan. 20, 2017, http://www.processhistory.org/women-unite-spruill/. However, the women of color as a political identity based on racialized identities erases the political sovereignty of indigenous women; my use of IWWOC to refer to indigenous women and women of color is informed by the University of Minnesota Women's Center. See "Reflection: This World Is Ours to Build," *University of Minnesota Women's Center Blog*, The University of Minnesota, Apr. 24, 2018, https://mnwomenscenter.wordpress.com/2018/04/24/reflection-this-world-is-ours -to-build/.

4. Hironao Okahana and Enyu Zhao, "Graduate Enrollment and Degrees: 2007–2017." Table B.10: First Time Graduate Enrollments by Citizenship, Race/ Ethnicity, and Gender, Fall 2017, *CGS/GRE Survey of Graduate Enrollment and Degrees*, 2007–2017, 2018, 31.

5. They were 4% Hispanic/Latina, 7% Black/African American, 3% Asian American, 1% more than one race, and less than 1% each for American Indian/ Alaskan Native and Native Hawaiian/Other Pacific Islander. U.S. Department of Education, National Center for Education Statistics, Integrated Table 7–8: Doctorates Awarded to U.S. Citizens and Permanent Residents by Sex, Field, Ethnicity and Race, 2016 (NSF 19–304).

6. U.S. Department of Education, National Center for Education Statistics, Table 315.20. Full-time Faculty in Degree-granting Postsecondary Institutions, by Race/Ethnicity, Sex, and Academic Rank: Fall 2015, Fall 2016, and Fall 2017 (Table was prepared November 2018), https://nces.ed.gov/programs/digest/d18 /tables/dt18_315.20.asp.

7. Martin J. Finkelstein, Valerie Martin Conley, and Jack H. Schuster, "Taking the Measure of Faculty Diversity," April 2016, Advancing Higher Education, TIAA Institute, New York, N.Y., 13.

8. Ibid.

9. U.S. Department of Education, National Center for Education Statistics, Table 315.20.

10. Earlier narratives include Patricia J. Williams, *The Alchemy of Race and Rights. Diary of a Law Professor* (Cambridge: Harvard University Press, 1991); chapters from bell hooks, *Ain't I a Woman: Black Women and Feminism* (Cambridge, Mass.: South End Press, 1991); and *Talking Back: Thinking Feminist, Thinking Black* (Cambridge, Mass.: South End Press, 1999).

11. Tamara Bertrand Jones, JeffriAnne Wilder, and La'Tara Osborne-Lampkin, "Employing a Black Feminist Approach to Doctoral Advising: Preparing Black Women for the Professoriate," *The Journal of Negro Education* 82, no. 3 (2013): 334; William H. Robinson, Ebony O. Mcgee, Lydia C. Bentley, Stacey L. Houston II, and Portia K. Botchway, "Addressing Negative Racial and Gendered Experiences that Discourage Academic Careers in Engineering," *Computing Science and Engineering* (March/April 2016): 34–35; Mignon R. Moore, "Women of Color in the Academy: Navigating Multiple Intersections and Multiple Hierarchies," *Social Problems* 64 (2017): 200–205.

12. Darla J. Twale, John C. Weidman, and Kathryn Bethea, "Conceptualizing Socialization of Graduate Students of Color: Revisiting the Weidman-Twale-Stein Framework," *The Western Journal of Black Studies* 40, no. 2 (2016): 80–94.

13. See, for example, Elvia Ramirez, "¿Qué Estoy Haciendo Aquí? (What Am I Doing Here?)": Chicanos/Latinos(as) Navigating Challenges and Inequalities during Their First Year of Graduate School, *Equity & Excellence in Education* 47, no. 2 (2014): 167–186.

14. Eric Margolis and Mary Romero, "This Department Is Very Male, Very White, Very Old, and Very Conservative": The Functioning of the Hidden Curriculum in Graduate Sociology Departments," *Harvard Educational Review* 68, no. 2 (Spring 1998): 1–32. Additionally, Christine V. Wood, Patricia B. Campbell, and Richard McGee, "'An Incredibly Steep Hill': How Gender, Race, and Class Shape Perspectives on Academic Careers among Beginning Biomedical PhD Students," *Journal of Women and Minorities in Science and Engineering* 22, no. 2 (2016): 159–181; and David L. Brunsma, David G. Embrick, and Jean H. Shin, "Graduate Students of Color: Race, Racism, and Mentoring in the White Waters of Academia," *Sociology of Race and Ethnicity* 3, no. 1 (2017): 1–13, draw upon studies from the mid-2000s about graduate school socialization and mentoring in their analyses about providing better mentoring models for graduate students of color.

15. Relying on this invisible labor to address invisible needs reproduces the gendered and racialized hierarchies of the academy that devalue the work of marginalized bodies, particularly those of women of color. See Patricia A. Matthew, "What Is Faculty Diversity Worth to the University?" *The Atlantic*, Nov. 23, 2016, https://www.theatlantic.com/education/archive/2016/11/what-is-faculty-diversity -worth-to-a-university/508334/; M. Kevin Eagan Jr. and Jason C. Garvey, "Stressing Out: Connecting Race, Gender, and Stress with Faculty Productivity," *The Journal*

of Higher Education 86, no. 6 (Nov./Dec. 2015): 928–929; and Laura E. Hirschfield and Tiffany D. Joseph, "'We Need a Woman, We Need a Black Woman': Gender, Race, and Diversity Taxation in the Academy," *Gender and Education* 24, no. 2 (Mar. 2012): 215, 221–222.

16. Women students of color already in graduate programs are likely to be more cynical about departmental and university commitments to diversity. See Wood, Campbell, and McGee, "'An Incredibly Steep Hill.'"

17. *Feminist Teacher* 27, no. 2–3 (2017).

18. Personal email, Denise Delgado and Kimberly McKee to Karen J. Leong, Nov. 4, 2014.

19. Even so, it is critical to heed and reflect upon Grace Hong's caution: "What happens when we who study race and gender ourselves champion a limited notion of 'excellence,' and in so doing, constrain ourselves from recognizing, as [Barbara] Christian suggested, how 'narrowly defined our own definition of scholarship might be?'" Grace Hong, *Death beyond Disavowal: The Impossible Politics of Difference* (Minneapolis: University of Minnesota Press, 2015), 143.

20. Dian D. Squire and Kristin McCann, "Women of Color with Critical World Views Constructing Spaces of Resistance in Education Doctoral Programs," *Journal of College Student Development* 59, no. 4 (July–Aug. 2018): 405.

21. Hong, *Death beyond Disavowal*, 8.

22. Graduate programs assuming a common type of student evokes the misfit theory articulated by Rosemary Garland-Thomson. Alison Kafer argues that crip theory allows for alliances and coalitions to develop without flattening the distinctions between forms of difference. Rosemary Garland-Thomson, "Misfits: A Feminist Materialist Disability Concept," *Hypatia* 26, no. 3 (Summer 2011); and Alison Kafer, *Feminist, Queer, Crip* (Bloomington: Indiana University Press, 2013).

23. Tara J. Yosso, "Whose Culture Has Capital? A Critical Race Theory Discussion of Community Cultural Wealth," *Race Ethnicity and Education* 8, no. 1 (2005): 77; also cited in Susan K. Gardner and Karri A. Holley, "'Those Invisible Barriers Are Real': The Progression of First-Generation Students through Doctoral Education," *Equity & Excellence in Education* 44, no. 1 (2011): 80. Rejecting a deficit model of cultural capital for first-generation students and students of color, Yosso identifies the cultural wealth of communities of color as "aspirational, navigational, social, linguistic, familial, and resistant capital."

24. Danielle L. Apugo, "'We All We Got': Considering Peer Relationships as Multi-Purpose Sustainability Outlets among Millennial Black Women Graduate Students Attending Majority White Urban Universities," *Urban Review* 49 (2017): 347–367.

Acknowledgments

This collection is for the hundreds of women of color and indigenous women in graduate school and the professoriate that we've come across since we both began our academic journeys. The generosity of mentors, colleagues, and friends benefited this project as we moved from graduate school to our current careers. Conversations at conferences, in hallways, over coffee or drinks continue to fuel the reasons why this volume is needed in the lives of women of color and indigenous women, as well as their mentors and allies. Our deepest gratitude to Dawn Durante and the University of Illinois Press who believed in this project when it was in its earliest days as a book manuscript. Additionally, our thanks go to the *Feminist Teacher* editorial board whose interest in this work resulted in a special section of Vol. 27, No. 2–3 on "Women of Color in the Academy" coedited by Kimberly McKee and Adrienne A. Winans. A few of the essays in that special section first originated in this collection. We also want to recognize the work of our contributors, whose investments in sharing their experiences make this collection possible. Without their commitment to sharing our collective truths, we would not be here.

The Women's, Gender, and Sexuality Studies department, Asian American Studies program, and Latina/o Studies program at the Ohio State University were formative spaces as we conceived of this project. Our collective time together in graduate school laid the foundation for why we wanted to have an open and frank conversation about what it's like to be a woman of color in graduate school. And, we recognized then that our disparate and different experiences have common similarities due to the ways in which women of color negotiate the academy. We appreciate and value the mentorship of Judy Tzu-Chun Wu, Mary Thomas, Lynn Itagaki, and Guisela Latorre. We also recognize that graduate school would not have been the same without the friendships with Sierra Austin and Kate Livingston, as well as membership in Colorful Women in the Academy. And a special thanks to Karen Leong, who supported this project early on.

Kimberly also would like to thank members of the community she formed throughout her career. The mentoring from Carolyn Herbst-Lewis and Karla Erickson along with friendships with other non–tenure-track junior faculty sustained her as a Consortium for Faculty Diversity post-doctoral fellow at Grinnell College. It was while there she learned the value of building a strong community of people in diverse disciplines. As she transitioned to her current position at Grand Valley State University, Kimberly appreciates the mentors, sponsors, and colleagues who provided valuable guidance and feedback in the last six years. Those individuals believed in the value of her and her work. A special thanks to the Kutsche Office of Local History Advisory Council, Wendy Burns-Ardolino, Anne Hiskes, Melanie Shell-Weiss, and Courtney Sherwood. It also goes without saying that there are many additional individuals from GVSU who supported Kimberly along the way. Gratitude goes toward the Center for Scholarly and Creative Excellence and the book subvention fund, which supports this endeavor. Thank you also to the undergraduate students who demonstrated why this volume is so needed, in particular Dionna Cheatham and Kendra Garcia.

At the same time, conversations with mentors and friends in the broader interdisciplinary fields of Asian American Studies, Adoption Studies, and Women's and Gender Studies contributed to Kimberly's trajectory as a scholar. Thank you to Cathy Schlund-Vials who made the space for Asian American Studies early career women faculty to seek advice and support. A special thanks to Sarah Park Dahlen, Elizabeth Raleigh, Kim Park Nelson, Emily Hipchen, Cynthia Callahan, and the broader Adoption Studies family, as well as the communities she forged through the Association of Asian American Studies, American Studies Association Korea, American Studies Association, National Women's Studies Association, and Alliance for the Study of Adoption and Culture. Kimberly appreciates the countless opportunities that generated conversations concerning mentoring and building networks. Her conceptualizations of mentoring were shaped by casual and formal conversations with Douglas Ishii, Tom Sarmiento,

Genevieve Clutario, Mai-Linh Hong, Meghan Cai, Krista Benson, Krupal Amin, among others. Yet, this intellectual community are not the only people who sustained Kimberly over the years. A special thanks to her parents—all of them, as well as York, Ashley, Max, and Parker.

Denise would like to thank the Graduate Association of Latin@/Latin America Students, Theresa Delgadillo, Brena Tai, Breanne Fahs, Hilda Perez, and Deema Kaedbey who were always ready with advice and support. Peggy Solic who was a coworker, colleague, friend, and sounding board, and Dana Friez who listened and encouraged and pushed me to be more practical, thank you so much. To her family, thank you for your support, encouragement, and love. Her grandfather, Jesse Delgado, had enough faith for the two of them, and her mother taught Denise to stand up for herself. She could not be more grateful.

More importantly, we would like to thank the countless women of color, indigenous women, and our allies who tirelessly work to diversify the academy and support the next generation. This book is for you.

Degrees of Difference

Introduction

Kimberly D. McKee and Denise A. Delgado

Gather together a group of women of color and indigenous women graduate students and our stories are often similar. Nearly all of us will have that faculty member who regularly makes racist statements, the faculty member that dismisses the scholarship of people of color and indigenous peoples or the value of Ethnic Studies, and if one's work is on nonwhite communities, there will inevitably be the faculty member that believes there are more worthy topics of study. Men will dominate the texts of most classrooms, with the occasional writing of a woman, who will almost inevitably be white, included in the syllabi. When women of color and indigenous women disagree with these scholars, perhaps noting their androcentric or white-oriented worldview and presumptions, it will be assumed that it is because we failed to grasp some key concept or are too focused on our own identity, rather than a legitimate criticism. Our use of women of color and indigenous women is deliberate—a call to recognize the role of settler colonialism in addition to understanding that indigenous women are not a racialized group; rather, the term recognizes their sovereignty.

We are asked invasive and inappropriate questions (*Where are you from? What are you?*) or some variation that begins with *your people* and ends with our frustration. Many of us have sat in courses where women of color are belittled for their accents or pronunciation, where we are the only people of color among a sea of white faces, where speaking up and pointing out sexism and/or racism (often both simultaneously) feels necessary but also exhausting.

Encountering sexism, racism, homophobia, and classism among other graduate students is distressingly commonplace. It is not uncommon to hear economically privileged graduate students make jokes about those who went to community or state colleges or have assumptions made about what your family is like, as well as your beliefs. We know that we must perform at a certain level—upper-middle class, whiteness—to be taken seriously. We must prove our intellect in our classes, not seem angry with colleagues even when given ample justification and do additional work to support and encourage other women of color scholars that are so often dismissed and marginalized.

Many of us are subject to unfair scrutiny from faculty, students, and colleagues. Knowing that this scrutiny is biased does not necessarily stop us from feeling like imposters masquerading in a place not meant for us. If we are lucky, we find other people of color in our cohorts, senior scholars willing to guide us, and white allies that are actually willing to do the work to be effective, meaningful allies. Oftentimes, we must leave our programs, departments, or even the university to find places where we can be comfortable, where we can see people opening their mouths to speak without tensing in anticipation of what they will say.

Despite the commonplace nature of these narratives, they are rarely mentioned to those seeking to enter graduate school. While the accounts of women of color and indigenous women faculty continue to prolifer-ate, the voices of their successors in graduate school are unheard. Yet, these women's voices must be located within a broader discussion of the intersection of gender, race, and sexuality in the academy. By centering the lived realities of this recent generation of junior scholars, *Degrees of Difference: Reflections of Women of Color on Graduate School* serves as a tool for women of color and indigenous women doctoral and masters students, as well as their peers contemplating entering the academy. We feature feminist analyses that combine radical critique of the current model of higher education with work toward progressive social change from within and outside of the Ivory Tower. These women reflect on how departmental and university-level commitments to diversity and inclusivity often do not translate to an understanding of how intersectional experiences impact nonwhite women graduate students' work differently than their white peers. Yet even within this environment, women of color and indigenous women find ways to overcome these difficulties. Each essay in this collec-tion acknowledges the resistance and lack of understanding contributors faced within their cohorts, departments, and families as well as the friends, colleagues, and mentors that offered support along the way.

Like so many others in *Degrees of Difference*, the struggles the editors faced as graduate students were surmountable, at least in part, because of the support of women of color and indigenous women colleagues and mentors in graduate school. We joined a number of organizations on campus and off, some for people of color and others specifically for nonwhite women. We engaged in service directed at helping our communities and junior scholars. We found mentors and likeminded colleagues who became friends. Academia is not a safe space, but we made a place for ourselves in it. The stories of women of color and indigenous women successfully navigating graduate school and overcoming obstacles need to be shared, so others know that they are not alone in their struggles.

As women of color we feel a responsibility to contribute to a body of knowledge that will ensure that those that come after us have more resources and are better prepared for what they will encounter in academia than we were. This collection should also be seen as a tool to educate men of color, Native men, white allies, and family members on the experiences of women of color and indigenous women in graduate school. A common thread weaves together these narratives: the sense of alienation and of being an imposter, and the struggle to balance personal and professional obligations. Yet while our contributors discuss their struggles as graduate students, the essays also touch upon the comfort, support, and mentorship found within their academic community that helped them succeed personally as well as professionally. *Degrees of Difference* unfolds in a manner that not only acknowledges the struggles of current and former women of color and indigenous women graduate students, but also helps other women overcome these obstacles and shows them the means through which other women of color have successfully completed their degrees.

Creating a Pipeline of Women of Color in the Academy

Women of color in the United States and abroad represent less than 10% of all full-time faculty in degree-granting postsecondary institutions.[1] The percentage decreases when accounting for women of color as full professors versus untenured, tenure-track faculty. And while the conversation to ensure that women of color move from the tenure-track to tenured faculty member and perhaps transition into an administrative role is necessary, we must be cognizant of pipeline building from graduate student to faculty member. And as Regina Emily Idoate highlights in this volume, this number is lower for indigenous scholars. Research demonstrates that nonwhite, poor, and queer professors are more likely to spend their time on invisible labor such as classroom preparation, mentoring, and service than other faculty. These activities, though key to marginalized and underrepresented populations in academia, are not considered crucial to the attainment of tenure.[2] In departments where there are few women of color, such as law, clannishness paired with racism and sexism make recruitment of women of color a low priority, and with low retention, fewer women of color are in the position to become tenured faculty.[3] The last ten years also has seen a decrease in faculty tenure-track hires across the humanities, the adjunctification of higher education, and more graduate students contemplating academic adjacent careers.

And, women's increased participation in a discipline does not translate to immediate equality. The Modern Language Association's Committee on the Status of Women in the Profession found that although women entered the fields of English and foreign languages in large numbers at the end of the twentieth century, this did not result in more tenure-track positions or salary parity with their men counterparts. Rather, the Committee discovered that even as white women and women of color are playing larger roles in the profession, "men continue to occupy tenure-track positions at a rate that is disproportionate to their actual numbers among new PhDs."[4] The higher number of women in the field rarely leads to greater respect for their scholarship or prominence.

In the fields of science and engineering, according to the 2008 National Science Foundation Survey of Doctorate Recipients, Latina and Black women are 5.1% of non–tenure-track faculty and only 2.3% of tenure-track or tenured faculty.[5] Absent from these statistics are indigenous women faculty. What is also troubling is the erasure of Asian women faculty as women of color; rather, Asian women are accounted for in statistics under "other" with white women faculty even as their numbers are as negligible as Black and Latina women. Asian women are 3.8% of non–tenure-track faculty and 2.6% of tenure-track or tenured faculty.[6] It is also unclear whether these statistics account for Asian or Asian American women, or both. We mention the exclusion of Asian women from the category of women of color to highlight the erasures of women of Asian descent as a result of the pervasiveness of the model minority stereotype.[7]

Given this landscape, it is imperative that we build a sustained network and pipeline of encouragement for women of color and indigenous women to thrive in graduate school and enter a career path that nourishes them and does not diminish their experiences because of their intersectional identities. Part of this conversation includes accounting for past and current efforts to recruit and retain women of color and indigenous women. And, it is important to underscore that these efforts are often discipline-specific. Within the humanities and social sciences, universities may adopt diversity hiring practices to add new perspectives and scholarship to departments, but as some scholars discuss, these practices are derided as "affirmative action" hires, and the nonwhite women who benefit from them have sometimes found themselves ostracized from their departments.[8] The fields of science, technology, engineering, and math have scholarships and programs aimed at attracting women of color and indigenous women to the disciplines and supporting them throughout their academic journey from undergraduates through graduate school. Yet, these programs have their own struggles as many nonwhite women within those fields experience isolation from peers paired with a type of hyperawareness of their gender and race.[9] Instead of ignoring or deemphasizing the seriousness of these issues, we believe that it is important to illuminate the various struggles in these fields and encourage women to speak out about their experiences within their cohorts, departments, and universities.

Embracing Our Inner Feminist Killjoy

Degrees of Difference seeks to accurately portray the lived realities of women of color in graduate school. In doing so, we actively engage in disrupting singular notions of a graduate school experience. We are invested in upholding and recognizing the ways in which women of color and indigenous women are often seen as, what Sara Ahmed terms, feminist killjoys—"spoilsport[s] because [they refuse] to convene, to assemble, or to meet up over happiness."[10] In doing so, the feminist killjoy unnerves moments of perceived solidarity as she fails to be in agreement with the rest of the community. The notion of the feminist killjoy relates directly to the concept of "airing the dirty laundry." Many of the experiences the women discuss are around topics they are encouraged to not express. The killjoy moniker is a sign that someone is telling an uncomfortable truth, drawing attention to oppression and hypocrisy. Academia, a space that often prides itself on its progressive meritocracy, needs the killjoy as they work to bring to light harsh truths and areas of much needed improvement. At the same time, we believe this volume discusses the importance of allies, mentors, and communities of color that support our contributors as they engage in successful careers.

We both embrace the moniker of feminist killjoy. As killjoys, we recognize the power to transform narratives about graduate school and the academy. We can contribute to rewriting what it means to be a nonwhite woman in graduate school and work to transform the pipeline for others. *Degrees of Difference* is rooted in our desire to facilitate an open conversation of the joys and frustrations of being women of color and indigenous women in a space that was not designed for us to thrive let alone succeed. And yet we did, as well as countless others, some of who are in this volume.

Our paths to becoming feminist killjoys were different even though we entered graduate school in the same cohort. While one of us entered our program midway through a doctorate she began at another institution, the other was a new direct-to-PhD student that had taken years off prior to completing her undergraduate degree and then moving on to graduate school. Asian American and Chicana, respectively, our class circumstances, sexualities, and ages were different. Our individual and shared challenges of being women of color in graduate school influenced our commitment to centering women of color and indigenous women's voices and facilitating avenues for us to speak back to the academy.

Consistent across class lines were assumptions of labor—that graduate students engage only in intellectual labor with theoretical texts and other scholarly works. This ignores the other labor—emotional, maternal—that women often are primarily responsible for as well as the invisibility of nonwhite women's service to our communities. White graduate students failed to realize that in addition to service to the department, we also contributed significantly to the Asian American and Latina/o Studies programs and Asian American and Latinx communities on campus as well as to other diversity and identity studies collective programs. This was work that sustained and nourished us—work that reminded us why we loved our positions in the academy. We could integrate our pedagogical investments, research, and service into a fluid narrative that overlapped with our commitments to social justice. But when a white, female colleague notes that, "Next time you need to go to an [insert ethnic community event here], let me know and I will go in your place," and fails to realize you're going because you are a member of that particular community, whose body encompasses multiple identities, you cannot help but be infuriated at her ignorance. The ability to be able to *not realize, not recognize* that women of color negotiate the academy in fundamentally different ways is a privilege—a privilege that we as women of color often lack. In fact, as a good friend later told Kim, "the desire to help, but offering the wrong things, is a privilege that white women have in academia." This statement is entirely true. The white woman graduate student's interest in better supporting her women of color peers cannot go unnoticed; however, her white privilege obstructed her ability to not only understand why women of color are routinely called upon to serve in multiple spaces because of their raced identities, but also to why her offer of support fell short.

Another example underscores the ways our white peers overlook the labor of women of color. After joining a graduate student organization, Denise found herself at the receiving end of a white colleague dumping a project on her because she felt overloaded with course work. Never mind that Denise was involved in more organizations and picked up a second graduate assistantship. In many ways this single incident exemplifies how Chicanas, and women of color more generally, find themselves relegated to the background *doing the labor* with little fanfare or recognition.

Yet what brought the two of us together was when we found ourselves engaged in negotiating what it meant when a white peer and someone we believed was an ally demonstrated that she was not in fact an ally but rather out to prove that she, too, experienced oppression—and, she claimed, in often more difficult circumstances. It was as if her whiteness was some-how made unimportant to her, something that we found troubling in a supposed ally. Her lack of awareness concerning her white privilege was startling as she claimed to stand with women of color. It was this particular relationship that led us to become skeptical of who to trust in graduate school, especially of white women colleagues who claim themselves to be feminist and antiracist. We wrongly assumed that the academy would be a place where our intersectional identities could come together and work in conversation with one another in meaningful and intentional ways. We found ourselves drawn to each other because of our shared interest in social justice, work ethic, and encounters with racism and sexism within the academy.

We share these anecdotes because we want to call attention to what happens if we remain silent about these incidents. In voicing our truths, we underscore how our experiences may look different than our white peers and how our white colleagues may be complicit in these negative encounters. And while we are grateful for the privilege to gain entry into the academy and recognize that many women of color lack these opportunities due to structural and institutional racism, as feminist killjoys it's imperative to intervene when the conditions for our survival result in an uncritical perspective toward racism, as well as other oppressions. When these stories are told only in whispers, off the record, and on the phone, we grasp at the intangible and seek the affirmation in dark corners. *Degrees of Difference* desires to open these whispers to a call to action for women of color and indigenous women in graduate school to find one another, to see one another's experiences as their own and to urge our allies inside and outside the academy to account for the lived realities of nonwhite women as we transform higher education to truly be inclusive. The narratives explored in this collection encourage readers to find their voice and empower them to inform allies of the struggles experienced by women of color and indigenous women so that they can better help their colleagues and friends create stronger communities.

Writing Ourselves In and Mentoring as We Go

First-person narratives are important when understanding the experiences of women of color in higher education as it joins a long history of women of color and indigenous women *writing in* their experiences from the margins, or as Kia Lilly Caldwell and Margaret Hunter argue, it is a form of community building as oppressions are recognized through the sharing of stories and become a joint struggle.[11] These women use their personal narratives as way to highlight their struggles and create a sense of community with their readers. More broadly, nonwhite women scholars discuss struggles within the classroom, the difficulty in attaining tenure, balancing work and a personal life, racism and sexism within their departments and universities, and tokenism within their fields of study, as well as their strategies for overcoming these obstacles.[12] The existence of women of color and indigenous women on the margins of academia often necessitates the creation of separate spaces that privilege women's voices, whether that space is physical or metaphorical.[13] Too frequently our voices are absent from dominant discourse or excluded from scholarship.

This collection complements recent works that critically examine the position of women of color in the academy. *Unlikely Allies in the Academy: Women of Color and White Women in Conversation* (2012) highlights the need for a productive dialogue that addresses how race and racism function within higher education. Likewise, *From Oppression to Grace: Women of Color and Their Dilemmas within the Academy* (2006) provides a voice to an often voiceless population through the deployment of a critical race, feminist lens. Essays in these two edited volumes capture the realities of women of color across diverse fields and disciplines. Yet it was only in *Presumed Incompetent: The Intersections of Race and Class for Women in Academia* (2012) that a deeper discussion concerning the women of color and indigenous women in the academy occurred throughout the academy-at-large. Cataloging the experiences of more than forty women, this collection provides a comprehensive understanding of the complexities that nonwhite women encounter due to their intersectional identities. In addition, we find that while a selection of books exists to support faculty of color once they join the ranks of junior faculty and negotiate the job market process (e.g., *Mentoring Faculty of Color: Essays on Professional Development and Advancement in Colleges and Universities*, 2012; and *The Black Academic's Guide to Winning Tenure: Without Losing Your Soul*, 2008), a dearth of resources exists for graduate students of color and indigenous graduate students. In engaging with this body of scholarship, *Degrees of Difference* expands the knowledge of women of color and Native women outside the ranks of established faculty to speak about the experiences and struggles of those with less power within the academy. This scholarship focuses on how women of color doctoral and master's students participate in formal institutional avenues for research support and mentoring.[14]

Degrees of Difference contributes to an expanding genre of women of color and indigenous women integrating the personal and professional as they reflect on their lived realities within higher education. For example, Patricia Sánchez and Lucila D. Ek reflect on their lives as graduate students and the importance of communities of women of color within higher education as well as conferences like Mujeres Activas en Letras y Cambio Social (MALCS) in supporting them and their scholarship. Underscoring the value of cultivating supportive spaces for women of color is Mary Romero's examination of sociology departments. Romero highlights how curriculum that often excludes women of color scholars contributes to the sense of isolation and imposter syndrome experienced by women of color graduate students.[15] Similarly, Mariana Souto-Manning and Nichole Ray discuss their challenges as graduate students and classroom instructors.[16] Donna J. Nichol and Jennifer A. Yee echo their interventions as they reflect on their careers as graduate students, staff, and faculty.[17] Capturing the experiences of women of color in the STEM fields, Joretta Joseph explores the challenges African American women experience when getting their PhDs at primarily white institutions and their struggles to stay within these programs.[18] Many of Joseph's concerns are echoed in Vakalahi et al.'s discussion of women of color masters of social work students and the strong feeling of isolation and exclusion experienced at predominately white institutions.[19] The essays in this volume join these women and countless others sharing their lived experiences as a way to create a written form of mentorship as it places nonwhite women's voices at the forefront and center in discussions of what it means to participate as graduate students in higher education.

Frank and honest reflections about what it means to be in graduate school bridge the personal and political in *Degrees of Difference*. The act of writing is an act of intervention, representing authors' desire to participate in activism to change the academy, transforming it into a radical space for women of color and indigenous feminisms. Contributors come from across the academy, including social work, medicine, history, and ethnic studies. These voices provide diverse perspectives on what it means to be a woman of color and indigenous woman in graduate school, moving beyond the black/white binary that historically girds understandings of race in the United States. Essays cover a range of topics and experiences, including but not exclusive to: navigating one's intersectional identity in the classroom, their departments, and the university; recognizing how women of color experience internal and external expectations concerning their ability to "give back"; creating community and balancing one's self-care; building a mentoring network; negotiating the academic job market; and transitioning from graduate student to junior faculty member. This collection is a site for women to enact change, but also to express their frustrations, to share their successes, and to air their truths.

Airing Our Truths

The essays in this volume reflect women of color and indigenous women's positioning as scholar-activists, intervening in recent conversations concerning effective mentoring, professional development, and constructing supportive, nourishing networks. *Degrees of Difference* offers an opportunity for these women as well as their mentors and allies to connect and explore the similarities that nonwhite women experience in graduate school regardless of discipline. Contributors' reflections elucidate the complexities of what it means to negotiate their intersectional identities in departments, fields, and communities that may not account for what it means to enter into higher education as nonwhite and woman-identified. *Degrees of Difference* suggests that a deeper discussion of the graduate school experience is needed to promote professional growth and create a sustained pipeline of women of color and indigenous women from graduate school to the academy. As universities assert a commitment to diversity and inclusivity, this directive must translate into actual support for students and faculty from underrepresented communities.

This collection does not aim to be exhaustive nor does it attempt to tokenize the experiences of women of color and indigenous women by having one woman of a different racial or ethnic background or one woman discussing a particular field. Rather, *Degrees of Difference* aims to facilitate generative conversations about commonalities across experiences, both to create a sense of shared experience and community for nonwhite women scholars and as a guide for those considering graduate and professional programs. Women of color and Native women frequently discuss the ways they experience racial microaggressions, isolation, tokenism, and imposter syndrome. In addition to professional struggles, the narratives touch upon personal issues that exacerbate the stress of graduate school. This volume elucidates key themes from our collective experiences without arguing that all women of color and indigenous women share a common experience of graduate school or the same personal issues.

While the contributions represent multiple disciplines, there are areas that we were unfortunately unable to touch. We solicited contributions from women in STEM, but because of the ways in which women of color and indigenous women in STEM are frequently underrepresented, they could not commit to joining the collection. It is also worth noting that, for scholars in STEM, a publication in an edited collection like this would not count for promotion or tenure in the same ways an essay in this collection is legible for scholars in the humanities and some of the social sciences. However, for those either interested or currently in one of the STEM fields, we do believe that this volume has information pertinent to that experience.

By discussing both the spoken and unspoken norms of graduate school, *Degrees of Difference* complicates the concept of graduate school from a static notion bound to assumptions of white, middle-classness to one that accounts for its impact on individuals' holistic, intersectional identities. This volume bridges academic research on what it means to be successful in graduate school and the lived experiences of those who recently completed or are enrolled in masters or doctoral programs. *Degrees of Difference* addresses the critical time in which we live, where women of color find themselves heavily scrutinized as they carve out a space for themselves in the academy, as seen in the experiences of Shannon Gibney at Minneapolis Community and Technical College in 2013 and Saida Grundy at Boston University in 2015.

Contributors reflect on what it means to negotiate racial and ethnic identity inside and outside of the United States. They underscore the complexities of what it means to experience displacement as a result of their intersecting identities. *Degrees of Difference* captures the ways women of color and Native women negotiate transnational existences as adoptees, indigenous scholars, and persons born outside of the United States. We hear from women discussing what it means to be Asian in North America, negotiating stereotypes concerning the forever foreigner and model minority, as well as assumptions concerning Latinx identity and belonging. We consider the ways indigenous women exist both within and outside of the United States as a result of settler colonialism. We hear the stories of women who left their home countries in the Global South to study in the United States and the specific struggles and needs that come from this experience. Part of this examination includes considering the ways Arab women experience gendered racism as a result of xenophobia concerning the Middle East and how Islamophobia positions Arabs and Arab Americans as persons of color. The United States' War on Terror coupled with anti-Arab sentiment spreading across North America and Europe contributes to the ways in which those who identify as Arab experience the world as persons of color. The myriad of experiences captured in *Degrees of Difference* underscores the complexities of what it means to be a nonwhite woman in predominately white institutions. This volume creates a space for radically plural critiques that combine analytic rigor with accessibility.

The featured narratives reveal the power relationships that exist within higher education as it relates to women of color and indigenous women's negotiation of their position in the academy. These women traverse the visible and invisible boundaries associated with their multiple roles as students, scholars, teachers, activists, and family members. The contributors ruminate on their personal and professional experiences of higher education in order to foster a community of women of color scholars. In addition to sharing these often painful and troubling tales, the women discuss tips for negotiating the complex relationships and responsibilities of graduate school, advice on how to find and form supportive communities, and organizations that provide much needed assistance.

By providing multiple perspectives, the editors of this collection seek to impart a realistic perspective to what it means to be a nonwhite woman in graduate school. We begin our journey through this volume by focusing on the personal—the body that constructs women of color as Other. Our physicality is an integral part of understanding the experiences of women of color. This discussion underscores how women of color's bodies are both hypervisible and invisible. In "Evoking My *Shadow Beast*: A Critical Analysis of Caretaking as a Woman of Color Doctoral Student," Carrie Sampson offers insight regarding the costs of care labor as parents, partners, and children. Weaving critical race scholarship with personal experiences, Sampson offers strategies and recommendations on how to succeed in graduate school. Soha Youssef moves readers to continually reflect on how one's gender and racial identity impacts their graduate school experiences, specifically interactions with students, former cohorts, and faculty. "*Sett bmit ragel 'A Woman as Good as 100 Men'*: An Arab Woman's Narratives on Discrimination in and outside Academia" gives voice to the aggressions of the academy, offering an avenue to discuss the realities of Arab women alongside women of color more broadly. And yet, sometimes survival is rooted in fostering self-assurance and recognizing that one's life does not begin or end with only graduate school. By writing their experiences into the written record, Sampson and Youssef offer opportunities for women to consider how pregnancy and religion become operationalized to further affect women of color in the academy.

While Sampson and Youssef center the ways women experience marginalization within their families and graduate cohorts, the next two essays encourage readers to consider nonwhite women's deep investment in giving back to their peers, programs, and undergraduates even if higher education was never designed for their presence. Focusing on undergraduate training, Delia Fernández's chapter, "You're Going to Need a Team: Community, Mentoring, Self-Care and Other Lessons from the McNair Scholars Program," highlights the role of the Ronald E. McNair Scholars Program in providing her the skills to thrive and succeed in graduate school and the tenure track. Regina Emily Idoate's chapter, "Stats and Stories: The Path of One Native Scholar in the Medical Sciences," focuses on navigating higher education as a Native American woman and forming community with her siblings, who are also in academia. The creation of community helps disperse the feelings of Otherness and the isolation of graduate school.

Part of this community building includes considerations of what it means to engage in self-care practices and forge supportive networks and relationships. In "Disciplinary Peripheries: A Conversation between Canadian Women of Color," Jenny Heijun Wills and Délice Mugabo discuss the realities of what it means when Ethnic Studies lacks legibility in Canadian institutions. Wills and Mugabo reveal the precarious nature of the academy as women of color carve out space for resistance and mentorship under multicultural Canadian discourse. Their conversation underscores the importance of building relationships and connections to avoid isolation in the academy. Similarly addressing the need for community, Nwadiogo I. Ejiogu's "For Those Considering Medical School: A Black Queer Feminist Perspective" offers survival strategies and tips for queer and trans* people of color as they seek to create more spaces in medicine. Relying on strong support networks provides women of color graduate students opportunities not only to develop professionally, but also offer the chance to find solace among one another. These essays elucidate what it means for community to serve as a place of change.

The final two essays move our attention forward to consider how contributors remain poised and externally confident even as they may second-guess whether they truly belong in the academy while encountering assumptions based on their raced and gendered presentations of self. Aeriel A. Ashlee considers the impact of imposter syndrome and racial microaggressions alongside the need for strong mentorship in her essay, "Finding Grace: An Asian American Womxn's Counterstory to Graduate School Racial Microaggressions." Addressing the intersections of gender, race, and professional identities in "How to Help: Learning the Legacy of the Social Work Professional," Arianna Taboada reflects on what it means to be one of the sole Chicana graduate students in a predominately white Social Work program. Taboada elucidates the impact of curriculum that fails to fully address racial/ethnic minorities and immigrant communities in coursework in a profession that aims to support and aid underserved, underrepresented communities.

The essays in this collection offer different perspectives that are often overlooked in conversations concerning what it means to be a nonwhite graduate student. Contributors examine the relationships between gendered transits of power and globalizing capital of education. In doing so, these essays inform the growth of new knowledges that disrupt assumptions of who belongs in the academy. These women are scholar-activists continuing to pave the way for future generations of women of color and indigenous women.

Notes

1. National Center for Education Statistics, "The Condition of Education—Postsecondary Education—Postsecondary Institutions—Characteristics of Postsecondary Faculty—Indicator May (2018)." *Revenues and Expenditures for Public Elementary and Secondary Education: School Year 2001–2002, E.D.* Tab. May 2018. https://nces.ed.gov/programs/coe/indicator_csc.asp.

2. Social Sciences Feminist Network Research Group, "The Burden of Invisible Work in Academia Social Inequalities and Time Use in Five University Departments," *Humboldt Journal of Social Relations* 39 (2017): 236.

3. Katherine L. Vaughns, "Women of Color in Law Teaching: Shared Identities, Different Experiences," *Journal of Legal Education* 53, no. 4 (2003): 496–504.

4. Barbara McCaskill, Julie Abraham, Barbara Becker-Cantarino, Kimberly Blockett, Dana Dragunoiu, Rosemary Feal, Jane Moss, Karen Shimakawa, Gerhard Sonnert, Karen Swann, Kimberly Wallace Sanders, and Monika Zagar, "Women in the Profession, 2000: MLA Committee on the Status of Women in the Profession," *Profession* (2000): 193.

5. Donna K. Ginther and Shalamit Kahn, "Education and Academic Career Outcomes for Women of Color in Science and Engineering," *Seeking Solutions: Maximizing American Talent by Advancing Women of Color in Academia: A Summary of a Conference* (2013): 76.

6. Ibid.

7. This erasure persists as seen in the important study regarding women of color and pay equity in higher education; Jasper McChesney, *Representation and Pay of Women of Color in the Higher Education Workforce* (Research Report). CUPA-HR (May 2018). https://www.cupahr.org/wp-content/uploads/CUPA-HR-Brief-Women-Of-Color.pdf.

8. Patti Duncan, "Hot Commodities, Cheap Labor: Women of Color in the Academy," *Frontiers: A Journal of Women Studies* 35, no. 3 (2014); Minelle Mahtani, "Mapping Race and Gender in the Academy: The Experiences of Women of Colour Faculty and Graduate Students in Britain, the US and Canada," *Journal of Geography in Higher Education* 28, no. 1 (2004).

9. Douglas M. Haynes, "Always the Exception: Women and Women of Color Scientists in Historical Perspective," *Peer Review* 16, no. 2 (Spring 2014): 26. https://www.aacu.org/publications-research/periodicals/always-exception-women-and-women-color-scientists-historical.

10. Sara Ahmed, *The Promise of Happiness* (Chapel Hill: Duke University Press, 2010), 65.

11. Kia Lilly Caldwell and Margaret Hunter, "Creating a Feminist Community on a Woman of Color Campus," *Frontiers: A Journal of Women Studies* 25, no.1 (2004): 25–26.

12. Caroline Sotello Viernes Turner, "Women of Color in Academe: Living with Multiple Marginality," *The Journal of Higher Education* 73, no. 1 (2002); Patti

Duncan, "Outsiders, Interlopers, and Ingrates: The Tenuous Position of Women of Color in Women's Studies," *Women's Studies Quarterly* 30, no. 3/4 (Winter 2002); Lynne Goodstein and La Verne Gyant, "A Minor of Our Own: A Cause for an Academic Program in Women of Color," *Women's Studies Quarterly* 18, no. 1/2 (Summer 1990): 39–45.

13. Maria Ong, Janet M. Smith, and Lily T. Ko, "Counterspaces for Women of Color in STEM Higher Education: Marginal and Central Spaces for Persistence and Success," *Journal of Research in Science Teaching* 55, no. 2 (2018).

14. Martin N. Davidson and Lynn Foster-Johnson, "Mentoring in the Preparation of Graduate Researchers of Color," *Review of Educational Research* 71, no. 4 (Winter 2001); Bushra Aryan and Fernando Guzman, "Women of Color and the PhD: Experiences in Formal Graduate Support Programs," *Journal of Business Quarterly* 1, no. 4 (2010); Ann Withorn, "Dual Citizenship: (An Interview with) Women of Color in Graduate School," *Women's Studies Quarterly* 25, no. 1/2 (Spring/Summer 1997).

15. Mary Romero, "Reflections on 'The Department Is Very Male, Very White, Very Old, and Very Conservative': The Functioning of the Hidden Curriculum in Graduate Sociology Departments," *Social Problems* 64, no. 2 (2017): 213.

16. Mariana Souto-Manning and Nichole Ray, "Beyond Survival in the Ivory Tower: Black and Brown Women's Living Narratives," *Equity & Excellence in Education* 40, no. 4 (2007).

17. Donna J. Nichol and Jennifer A. Yee, "'Reclaiming Our Time': Women of Color Faculty and Radical Self-Care in the Academy," *Feminist Teacher* 27, no. 2–3 (2017).

18. Joretta Joseph, "From One Culture to Another: Years One and Two of Graduate School for African American Women in the STEM Fields," *International Journal of Doctoral Studies* 7 (2012).

19. Halaevalu F. O. Vakalahi, Michelle Sermon, Andrea Richardson, Veronica Dillard, and Aryka Moncrief, "Do You See Me? The Complex Experiences of Women of Color MSW Students," *Intercultural Education* 25, no. 5 (2014).

CHAPTER 1

Evoking My *Shadow Beast*

A Critical Analysis of Caretaking as a Woman of Color Doctoral Student

Carrie Sampson

About a month after bringing our little girl home from the hospital, my husband and I were finally getting adjusted. We decided to leave the house with her to attend a family-friendly event. Trying not to be late, I hurried to get myself ready, dress the baby, and pack the diaper bag. While juggling my crying child in one arm and packing her diaper bag with the other, I hear my husband playing the piano—one of the things he does to relax. Although I enjoy his musical talent, it was one of many moments that hit me—he presumed that I would take care of everything. The conversation that followed went something like this:

ME FRUSTRATED: Why are you playing the piano when there are several things that need to be done before we can leave?

HIM: Oh, well just tell me what to do.

MY THOUGHTS: Why must I tell you what to do? You never have to tell me what to do when it comes to taking care of our child.

MY WORDS: Prepare a bottle of formula just in case. (Even though I was breast-feeding, I did not know how comfortable I would feel nursing in public yet.)

HIM: I don't know how.

ME: What?!? Do you think I knew how to prepare a bottle before having a baby? No, I read the directions. Read the directions!

This incident marked the beginning of several similar situations that reflected the same presumption. For instance, one morning he woke me up to tell me that he was leaving for work early. He had showered, dressed, eaten breakfast, and was ready to go. Annoyed, I sarcastically told him that it must be nice to get yourself ready and leave without being concerned about getting your baby ready or having to get ready *while* taking care of a baby. When it was time to consider daycares, I did the research. When our baby needed to go to the doctor, I made the appointments and took her. When our baby grew out of her clothes, I shopped for new (or used) ones, rotated her closet, and stored her old clothes for a potential future baby. When our baby started eating solids, I found recipes and made her food. When our baby was sick, it was almost always me who stayed home from work or school to take care of her. I did all of these things in addition to day-to-day tasks including changing diapers, breast-feeding for 16 months, and managing the household responsibilities of cleaning, grocery shopping, and finances. After I took care of all of this, I was exhausted and had little time or energy to work on my dissertation.

Speaking Truth

When I first decided to write about taking care of family while in a doctoral program, I expected to address all of the institutional inequities that made this balancing act challenging. Yet, when I really thought about my experience, and after talking to several other women of color in graduate school, I realized that while institutional patriarchy and racism is alive and well in the academy, the intimate and daily inequities that we faced in our own families made finishing equally, and sometimes more challenging.

As the introduction implies, this is a story of caretaking as a graduate student, a counterstory from a critical race feminist framework and one that is grounded in relevant literature.[1] I borrow from Daniel G. Solórzano and Tara J. Yosso's definition of *counterstory* "as a method of telling the stories of those people whose experiences are not often told (i.e., those on the margins of society)."[2] I am a mixed-race (Black and Chicana) feminist woman who was raised in a bicultural family and is now married to a Black man. I am a daughter, sister, and mother of two children whom I gave birth to while in graduate school. While first writing this chapter, I was a doctoral student, part-time university instructor, and aspiring professor. Using a critical race feminist perspective, I am working from the assumption that women of color are oppressed by systems, institutions, and communities dominated by white supremacy and patriarchy, that gender is a social construct rather than biological, and that we must identify racism, patriarchy, and the intersections of these occurrences before we can achieve equity and liberation.

Existing scholarship underscores the need for a deeper understanding of complex experiences among women of color in graduate school. Studies that highlight the underrepresentation of women of color in science, technology, engineering, and math (STEM) fields show considerable trends regarding institutional barriers.[3] Nonetheless, Maria Ong, Carol Wright, Lorelle Espinosa, and Gary Orfield call for more studies "on the influences of family on the experiences and advancement" with particular attention to "the roles played by parents, siblings, extended family, spouses/partners, and/or children" and point out that "many women are in graduate school during the years that are culturally considered peak childbearing years."[4] The complexities of the many roles that women of color in graduate school often contend with make it difficult to understand using traditional research methods. Connecting individual stories to theory and data can help better explain these complex experiences. Thus, similar to Jessica T. DeCuir-Gunby and Dina C. Walker-DeVose's description of counterstorytelling as "a narrative that is grounded in real-life experiences and empirical data and contextualized within a specific social setting,"[5] I ground my story in related-research, theory, and context.

My attraction to social justice work began through a racialized lens, yet over the years, I came to understand the urgency to embrace feminism. I agree with hooks's proclamation that we should prioritize the elimination of patriarchy. She explains, "Unlike other forms of domination, sexism directly shapes and determines relations of power in our private lives, in familiar social spaces, in that most intimate context—home—and in that most intimate sphere of relations—family."[6] This space, hooks says, reflects the tension between "the urge to promote growth and the urge to inhibit growth" offering an opportunity for "feminist critique, resistance, and transformation."[7] Thus, although a macro-level analysis of institutional barriers for women of color in graduate school is certainly necessary, exploring the micro-level of individual and family experiences is also needed.

Research focused on women of color in graduate school or in the academy that goes beyond the walls of the institution is very limited. A few scholars, however, point to factors that contribute to either academic success or lack thereof among women of color. One older, but seminal, piece is Patricia Gándara's "Passing through the Eye of the Needle."[8] Among the 45 successful Chicana/os she studied, all of whom earned a PhD, JD, or MD, she finds one major difference across gender lines. Among all the female participants, "whether by chance or design, the single characteristic that would become most critical was the fact that they were unmarried."[9] She goes on to point out, "At an age when most Chicanas have married and begun to take on new familial responsibilities (Grebler et al., 1970), these women remained unmarried and childless."[10] Another study by Maria Chacón, Elizabeth Cohen, and Sharon Strover echoes a similar sentiment.[11] These authors examine obstacles Chicanas faced in pursuing higher education and find that domestic labor, lack of parental support, and stress are among the top challenges. Focused on women of color in STEM academic fields, one study emphasizes three women's experiences and their inability to find career-life balance while feeling the need to choose between their career and family, struggling to maintain their careers while caring for elders, and even hiding a pregnancy.[12] These few studies provide evidence to suggest that women of color in graduate school across different fields likely experience unique challenges in achieving professional success because of familial obligations. Based on my experiences, I argue that patriarchy and sexism perpetuated by men of color is partly to blame for this inequity.

At times, women of color avoid critiques that might publicly insult men of color. As the writers of "A Black Feminist Statement" acknowledge, "Our situations as black people necessitates that we have solidarity around the fact of race."[13] They further explain, "We struggle together with black men against racism, while we also struggle with black men about sexism."[14] Yet in the desire to maintain an antiracist stance, we too often succumb to silence while men of color exploit, assault, and desecrate us. The well-known story of law professor Anita Hill's sexual harassment allegations aimed at Clarence Thomas during his nomination to the U.S. Supreme Court brought to surface many issues of patriarchy and sexism within the Black community in the 1990s.[15] Among the most recent and similar situations are the multitude of charges against Bill Cosby. Beverly Johnson is one of the many women who joined these allegations. She explained her hesitancy to share her story because she did not want to be disregarded as the "angry Black woman" nor damage the reputation of a highly regarded Black man.[16] Women of color are often forced to choose between our race and our gender in which pledging allegiance to either might mean the betrayal of the other.

In telling this deeply personal counterstory, I "air our dirty laundry." I expose the microaggressions that I faced not only within my university, but also within my family. But should I? By most accounts, I am considered "lucky" to have married a well-accomplished Black man who holds three university degrees, is an involved community member, and is present in our home as a father. My father was also a college-educated Black man, and although he was incarcerated for two years post-college, he remained married to my mother and lived in our home throughout my childhood. The men in my family, especially these two men, supported my decision to go to graduate school and cheered me on throughout my studies. Yet, they are part of a truth I must speak, which exposes the intimate barriers that have made succeeding in graduate school difficult.

My truth goes beyond *my* family. It is a truth that many women of color face. As a Chicana queer woman working on her PhD and raised in Texas near the Mexican border, Gloria Anzaldúa highlights the difficulties of living in spaces full of contradictions, spaces of both belonging and alienation.[17] Anzaldúa explains that our culture pressures women to be married and have children, to be submissive to the men in our families (while also not trusting them), and to take care of all household and child-rearing duties. These expectations remain for those who choose to pursue additional schooling. Women who venture from this path are considered inadequate. Anzaldúa contends that these cultural pressures are particularly heavy for women of color who yearn for a sense of belonging as a result of being excluded, dismissed, and condemned within their own communities as well as the dominant culture.

Moving away from cultural norms means that we must live, as Anzaldúa refers—a "life on the borderlands"—which she describes as "intimate terrorism."[18] She explains, "Alienated from her mother culture, 'alien' in the dominant culture, the woman of color does not feel safe within the inner life of her Self. Petrified, she can't respond, her face caught between *los intersticios*, the spaces between the different worlds she inhabits."[19] We, as women of color pursuing education, often assume several roles, many of which expect us to be submissive—daughters, mothers, partners, sisters, scholars—while being rejected and constantly at risk of being attacked by a dominant culture, particularly within institutions of higher education that do not value us.

As a queer Chicana feminist, Anzaldúa shares her refusal to be confined to these cultural norms. Though her culture is embedded in her, she critiques the homophobia, sexism, and patriarchy that it reproduces.

21

Anzaldúa writes, "Though I'll defend my race and culture when they are attacked by non-*mexicanos, conozco el malestar de mi cultura.* I abhor some of my culture's ways, how it cripples women, *como burras,* our strengths used against us, lowly *burras* bearing humility with dignity. The ability to serve, claim the males, is our highest virtue."[20] In rebellion, Anzaldúa urges us to create a new way of being—"*una cultura mestiza*"—a mixed culture.[21] This term reflects the possibility of establishing a community, a space of liberation that recognizes and embraces all of our identities, no matter how contradictory they might appear. Similarly, by telling my story, I aim to reexamine ways in which women of color might exist more freely in their myriad roles that include caretaking and scholarship, resisting the oppressive expectations to inhibit our freedom and ability to think, act, and write.

My Counterstory

Although I often questioned existing presumptions that placed me in the traditional gender-role within my family, I was still quick to take care of everything. The discussion of my family dynamics provides context to the roles I play in relationships with my parents, siblings, and spouse. These inclinations are deeply embedded within us—a form of what Anzaldúa terms *cultural tyranny.*[22] These messages are spread through patriarchy, internalized, and rarely interrogated. This is especially true for those of us growing up in families that conveyed these ideologies. Sometimes these ideas and myths are hidden in contradictions between traditional gender-roles and aspirational roles—reliable daughter versus successful professional. Regardless, these notions are difficult to identify, challenge, and change.

Family Dynamics

Even though my alcoholic and abusive father was part of the house-hold, my mother worked full-time, cooked, cleaned, and was our primary caretaker. With two brothers, and as the only daughter, my father always expected a lot more from me. His aspirations included an education, a successful career, *and* taking care of the family. As a little girl, he called me Dr. Sampson and always told me that I would do "big things" when I grew up. Indeed, he also insisted that I would be, as he referred to it, "the rock of our family." This expectation was not placed on my broth-ers. Watching my mother who often adopted a subservient role while I internalized these cultural messages, it was not surprising that I assumed this role in both my immediate and extended family.

As often happens with children from communities of color who grew up in poverty and later successfully completed college despite the odds, I became "a rock" for my family.[23] When my father became chronically ill, I relocated to be closer to home. Unlike my brothers, I helped my parents financially, domestically, and in managing their healthcare. When my mother became ill, she moved in with me and my husband so that I could care for her. This also happened to be the same year I decided to pursue a PhD.

Prior to becoming a doctoral student, I worked in multicultural affairs at a university. Although my position focused mostly on promoting diversity, much of my work actually centered on caring for students of color. I supported them in the often difficult journey through their educational experience. As one of the few professionals of color in my department, I was often tokenized and bureaucratically limited. I pursued a PhD in hopes of achieving more autonomy in my work so that I could make a greater contribution to my community through teaching, womyn-toring and doing research that mattered.[24]

With my husband in law school and my parents ill, I made the decision to attend the nearest university. This university and program is less prestigious than many others I could have attended. It also has relatively little support in terms of advising, research, and quality instruction. Yet, by going to school full-time, I assumed that I could successfully navigate the institution in order to make the most of my program and finish my PhD in three years. After a myriad of life moments filled with caring for others, my three-year plan extended to six years.

Questioning and Attempting Motherhood

Many women doctoral students are in their childbearing years. We are forced to make the difficult and unfair decision between the attempt to balance the process of both having and caring for children while in graduate school, waiting until we finish when it might be more physically challenging or even impossible, or simply not having biological children of our own. When I asked for advice, many women faculty also explained that having children during graduate school was best because there was less pressure and more flexibility than if I were to wait until I was in a tenure-track position. These cultural messages suggest that, although we all come from women, society has yet to grant us the adequate respect, time, flexibility, and support to bear children and still maintain success in other roles.

My *Shadow Beast* emerged. Anzaldúa describes the *Shadow Beast* as the "rebel" inside of her, "that part of me that hates constraints of any kind, even those self-imposed. At the least hint of limitations on my time or space by others, it kicks out with both feet. Bolts."[25] I never thought I would resist the idea of having children, but my exhaustion from caring for my family and my rising consciousness about the "cultural tyranny" that subjected me to this role caused me to anticipate motherhood as a constraint rather than a blessing. After months of grappling with this internal struggle and my husband repeatedly insisting he would be a true partner in parenting, I decided that I did not want to regret the opportunity to experience parenthood.

After my coursework and before my dissertation, we started trying for children. Following two miscarriages, one of which happened while completing my comprehensive exams, I got pregnant a third time. My pregnancy consisted of daily vomiting for the first three months, constant fatigue, and other physical, emotional, and mental ups and downs for 41 weeks. On top of that, I was six months pregnant when my father experienced cardiac arrest. He remained hospitalized for the next five months, and I spent the rest of my pregnancy in and out of the hospital, advocating and caring for him. My dissertation work came to a halt, but since graduate assistants (GA) do not qualify for either paid or unpaid leave under the Family and Medical Leave Act, I had to complete my GA duties online.

Similarly, my university offered no official parental leave for graduate assistants. I was expected to negotiate parental leave with my supervisor and hope she would understand. Fortunately, my supervisor was a woman of color with three small children. She was supportive and expected me to take a semester of paid leave. The next year I successfully led the charge for the university to change its policy, which now consists of a minimum of six weeks paid parental leave. While this is a step forward, it is still not sufficient.

The physical and emotional demands of new motherhood were shocking to me. I planned for a beautiful home birth that ended in an emergency caesarean section. My body and spirit were healing from this major surgery and transforming hormonally back to its nonpregnant state. Meanwhile, I was extremely sleep-deprived as I struggled to breast-feed and comfort our colicky newborn. I was an emotional rollercoaster, and one day I literally cried over spilled milk—the two ounces of breast milk that took me 45 minutes to hand pump. It was nearly impossible to focus on my dissertation.

My father died five months after my daughter was born. Even though when he fell ill and his frail appearance undermined the physical threat he once projected, after years of abuse and manipulation, I still found it challenging to resist his unfair demands and expectations that I care for him. While my *Shadow Beast* often managed to keep him from taking advantage of me, this constant negotiation with him and my inner-self was emotionally and physically exhausting. In *The Will to Change*, bell hooks explains, "This is the most painful truth of male domination, that men wield patriarchal power in daily life in ways that are awesomely life-threatening, that women and children cower in fear and various states of powerlessness, believing that the only way out of their suffering, their only hope is for men to die, for the patriarchal father not to come home."[26] Similarly, my father's domination over my family and my countless attempts, both successful and unsuccessful, to resist feelings of powerlessness, led me to assume that his death would allow me to live more freely. When he died, I was both sad and relieved. I was heartbroken to know that I would no longer hear his words of encouragement and laughter. I was distraught over the thought that he would not know my children or witness me becoming the doctor he always knew I would be. Yet, with him being gone, I could finally breathe easier and shift my focus on raising our daughter and finishing my PhD.

Motherhood as a Graduate Student

After our daughter's birth, my spouse took a position at a law firm and was soon working exceptionally long days, including weekends. Even still, I thought I could squeeze in sufficient time to write when he was not working or while my daughter was napping. When that did not happen, I started to doubt my ability to finish my dissertation. I wrestled with feelings of resentment toward my spouse because I began to recognize that he was not what I considered a "true partner." I felt regret about having a child because it took so much of my time and energy. I was sad and fearful about the possibility of not finishing my degree. Realizing I needed help, I enrolled my daughter in a daycare part-time near campus and solicited my mother to babysit her on non-daycare days. To offset childcare expenses,

I applied and received graduate student childcare scholarships offered through my institution.

That summer, I wrote and wrote. I worked on my dissertation proposal and completed dissertation fellowship applications for the following year. After successfully defending my proposal the next semester, I was awarded a two-year dissertation fellowship. Since I did not think it would take two years to finish my dissertation, some of my academic womyn-tors recommended that I use the additional year to have another baby. Through these conversations, I learned that the "fellowship baby" (or having a baby during a paid fellowship designed to support your writing/research goals) was fairly common. Furthermore, at 34 years old, I was getting close to the "high risk" age. Pregnant women over 35 years old are expected to undergo relatively more tests and doctor visits to address the higher risks associated with age. Not wanting to be subject to these requirements and with a desire for my daughter to have a sibling, I decided that it was now or never.

Yet my *Shadow Beast* was in full force as I began to rebel against the gendered role I assumed. By this time, my partner and I had countless conversations, arguments, and debates about managing parenthood. These incidents were often instigated by my feelings of resentment about undertaking considerably more in terms of parenting and household responsibilities. On a deeper level, I felt that my time, my personhood, and my contributions were not adequately respected and valued by my partner. Even though he made more money than I did, we had and could survive on less. Moreover, I think that my flexibility as a graduate student, especially post-coursework, for him meant that I seemingly had more time to manage everything, when reality was far from that. And while, for a moment, I tried to "do it all" including my dissertation work, I resented it, and eventually resisted.

Several scholars note the unfair workload among women, using terms such as the "second shift," "double bind," "double burden," and "dual" or "triple roles."[27] These terms describe women, like my mother, who assume responsibilities both inside and outside of the household (often in the form of paid work). In her analysis of parenting, Amy Richards contends that couples experiencing larger gaps in paid income deal with even more inequality in parenting responsibilities.[28] For graduate students, especially those who are graduate, research, or teaching assistants, our meager pay often results in relatively less financial contribution to our household than our partners. Sometimes this adds to the pressure of feeling obligated to take on more responsibilities. Meanwhile, the "job" of finishing our degrees can easily be overlooked.

Cultural tyranny also confines us regardless of what we contribute. Culture, which is influenced and enforced by institutions, systems, and families, is complex. Anzaldúa explains, "The culture expects women to show greater acceptance and commitment to, the value system than men. The culture and the Church insist that women are subservient to males. If a woman rebels she is a *mujer mala*."[29] She points out the contradictory messages mothers tell their daughters. "Which was it to be—strong or submissive, rebellious or conforming?"[30] While our culture holds high aspirations for us to get "a good education," it also expects us to be, as Anzaldúa noted, full of "humility and selflessness," putting our families first.[31] And for many of us who are first-generation college students, our families might not understand what it takes to get that "good education." The reality is that sometimes we must put ourselves first to finish. In other words, we must consider how to rebel against cultural messages of submission and conforming so that we can make time and space for ourselves to be successful in graduate school.

Being Superwoman or Super Depleted?

Don't get me wrong. I get pumped up when Alicia Keys sings about being a superwoman and "all my women sitting here trying to come home before the sun."[32] But this fictional character is not who I aspire to be in real life. We often idolize the women who seem to "do it all" as role models and then come to expect this of ourselves. I fall victim to this. I am always in awe of successful scholars that are women of color with children. But in talking to them, these women tend to be overwhelmed, exhausted, and struggling to be successful. Moreover, they often compromise self-care in order to take care of their family and fulfill their career goals. What is super about being depleted?

I am part of a social media group of Latina doctoral students that includes over 1,700 current and former students. Frequently, I read posts from women juggling motherhood while finishing their degree. As they explain their dilemmas, they state "I" have kids; never "we" or my "partner/ spouse/husband/baby daddy and I" have kids. When one woman posted asking for tips on how to balance her newborn twins and her dissertation, thirty group members replied, including me. The advice consisted of tips such as prioritizing family, taking a leave of absence, using paid childcare, and doing work in small chunks. A couple of replies indicated that self-care was important but still within the context of putting family first. In another post requesting similar tips, many group members mentioned that their mothers helped them by watching their kids while they wrote. However, none of the replies on either post suggested that these PhD-bound women enlist their partners' support or help. It is as if we had children by ourselves.

Still, one Latina's reply pointed out that we must stop abiding by the patriarchal standards instituted in our graduate programs. I agree with her 100%. Examples of these standards include strict completion timelines, no paid family leave for graduate assistants or part-time instructors, lack of breast-pumping facilities, and unrealistic expectations such as conference attendance without sufficient financial or family-friendly support. These standards often assume we have no life outside of our programs. They fail to acknowledge the incredible familial responsibilities we, especially women of color, are likely to experience. These standards are often discussed at length within our communities and many of us, including me, are fighting to change these oppressive policies at our institutions.

Yet, what is often not discussed is the fact that we must stop abiding by the patriarchal standards internalized and instituted within our own families and communities. These standards place women's roles as mothers and daughters, and in some cases as sisters and aunts, *before* rather than *alongside* our roles as students, scholars, and individuals. Although some women choose to value these traditionally gendered roles more than others, the problem lies in the assumption that accompanies these roles—that we will always be the primary caretaker. Moreover, when we internalize these cultural messages of what a "good" woman is, and idolize the superwoman, we partake in this culture that limits our choices. In other words, we often either feel the need to satisfy these cultural norms by being perfect caretakers while sacrificing our scholarship or refusing caretaking roles in order to be the scholars we envision.

I must admit, I was happy to give birth to a little girl. Among many things, I internalized patriarchy in my thoughts that a daughter, rather than a son, would be more likely to take care of me when I get older. The messages we send and receive are deeply embedded. Even those who want to resist, struggle to consider new ways of thinking.

Co-caring as Self-care

Before getting pregnant a second time, my partner and I grappled to satisfy my *Shadow Beast*. We went through several months of counseling to negotiate our roles as parents and partners. In addition to placing my daughter in daycare, my partner eventually began taking on more household responsibilities with her and within the household. Eventually he changed jobs, which created more space for him to be more present as a parent and partner.

As he stepped in, I had to consciously step back. Letting go was surprisingly challenging. As Richards suggests, women believe that we *must* be the primary caretaker for our children's sake. Behind this notion is "women's own belief that they are better parents than their husbands, or their need to control the parenting, or their fear of social disapproval."[33] I thought my partner could never parent as good as me. For instance, when he took on the role of bathing our daughter, I watched him closely, ready with critiques. Offended when I started spewing those critiques, he offered the responsibility back to me if I was too uncomfortable with the way he was doing it. At first, I added his quickness to return the bathing responsibility to me to the list of his inadequacies as a parent. But then I stopped myself, walked away, and decided to let it go. Since then, this has been his primary responsibility.

He has also been more vocal in asserting his parenting. Recently my daughter injured herself and without a second thought, I ran downstairs and began to take her from my partner's arms. He reminded me that he could also comfort her, and by taking her from him, I was undermining his desire and attempt to co-parent.

When I became pregnant with our second child, after two years of negotiating responsibilities with my partner, I was clearer about my expectations of co-parenting. I knew that with two young children, co-parenting was my best bet to finish my dissertation and prepare for the job market. While pregnant, I completed my dissertation data collection, which consisted of 30 interviews across three states. I also completed two manuscripts for publication and presented my work at a national conference. To do this, I had to step back and rely on my partner to step in.

Our second child, a boy, is now six weeks old. While everyone around us kept saying how great it was that we have a girl *and* a boy, I was less thrilled. The thought of raising a male in such a patriarchal society felt daunting to me. Over time, however, I became more excited about the possibility of raising children, regardless of their gender, in a feminist space where expectations of caring are genderless.

Since our son's birth, parenting is different. A few days after his birth, I realized that I had not changed one diaper because my partner assumed that responsibility. He also became the primary caretaker for our daughter, as I focused on healing and breast-feeding. Of course, my spouse's career change may have impacted our restructured roles. His time is more flexible and our financial contributions are more equal now.

Despite these positive changes, our attempts at true co-parenting and managing household responsibilities are a constant negotiation. Yet, I recognized the necessity of co-parenting if I wanted to complete my dissertation and ensure that I am also practicing self-care. For me, self-care means doing things like making time to connect with my community, exercising, and participating in pleasurable activities regularly. While these may seem easy to do, I have to force myself to take the time to do them without guilt. I also began conversations with my brother about co-caring for our mother. He did not receive these conversations positively at first; it required my persistence and vulnerability. But he is now more amenable to the idea of co-caring.

Through all of these challenges, I not only survived in graduate school, but I thrived. I earned A's in all my courses, passed my comprehensive exams, successfully defended my dissertation proposal, and was awarded a two-year dissertation fellowship. I also took advantage of many opportunities to work on research projects, publish, present at conferences, teach courses, and be active in several university and community organizations, including being a member and the president of my institution's Black Graduate Student Association. I did some of this work to meet the often arbitrary institutional standards required to secure a job in this increasingly difficult academic market, standards that typically are not taught in classes. Other work, such as the protests I helped organize and the research that helped change restrictive policies, was more personally meaningful but often less recognized.

Building a Village

My ability to thrive would never have been possible without support. While my partner pushed me relentlessly to *be* fierce and my mother helped us tremendously in caring for our babies, it was my womyn-tors that taught me *how* to be fierce. I am lucky to have many amazing women in my life, but three special women of color faculty members truly impacted me. They gave me alternative perspectives on caring and guided me through my doctoral journey, showing me that being an academically successful woman of color scholar and caretaker was possible.

These women have not only guided me, but they cared for me. They invited my family into their homes. We share meals together, we laugh together, and we grieve together. They also pushed me to be more honest and critical in my work. They are my Othermothers.[34] These are the women that are there for me when I need a last-minute letter of recommendation or feedback on a proposal, or whom I can send a text to with academic and personal questions. None of these women are in my program or department. My program is dominated by White men and a few White women. As part of my ability to navigate graduate school, I was intentional about finding womyn-tors, specifically women of color. These women have shown me that our caring goes beyond family. One of them invited me to attend the Mujeres Activas en Letras y Cambio Social (MALCS) institute, a conference that she often attended with her children. I decided to join her, bringing my one-year-old daughter, my mother, and my cousin. It was the only time I brought any family to an academic conference. It was a beautiful and empowering space with other women of color and many other children. The first night while we enjoyed mariachi music and ate, the organization's president picked up my daughter and danced with her through the crowd. Together we danced, laughed, cried, ate, and engaged in critical dialogue about our research and work to nourish our bodies, souls, and minds in ways that affirmed our place as women of color scholars and activists. It was these types of spaces that reenergized me in the midst of racism and patriarchy in the academy and in my family, and it is these types of spaces that I continue to seek and cherish as a faculty member. Having Othermothers, being Othermothers, and building sisterhood that is grounded in honesty and love is necessary for our success within these often challenging academic spaces that women of color are forced to endure if we hope to complete graduate school.

Conclusion

Admittedly, I sometimes envied graduate students that did not have responsibilities of taking care of children or parents, or even having to attend to a partner. I imagined them enjoying free time, having theoretical discussions over cocktails with other graduate students, networking at conferences, or traveling around the world during their breaks. Whether these images are true or not, I live in a different world. A world where caring for my family has been difficult and oppressive at times, but also rewarding. A world in which I want to honor my family and my community, but where I must speak truth, breaking the oppressive ties that slow down our progress. By progress, I mean more than just graduation. Progress is our ability to develop and flourish into whatever it is we hope to become in our deepest desires. That might be a full-time parent, a leading scholar, or both. However, as women of color, to do both we must begin practicing true co-caring.

My *Shadow Beast* dominates this space—filled with stories of barriers and rebellion. But like the act of breast-feeding in its ability to nourish and be nourished, caring for my family has made me a better scholar and my scholarship has made me a better partner, mother, and daughter. Practically speaking, I have become amazing at time management, prioritizing, and multitasking. Like our ancestors who carried children in wraps while they gathered food for their families, I am nursing my son as I write this. We have always found creative ways to accomplish our hopes, desires, and needs.

More importantly, the intimate participation in other people's lives forces me to witness and experience so much more. Living the struggles my family experiences—struggles of addiction, poverty, racism, sexism, and criminalization—keeps me grounded in doing scholarship that matters. It gives me epistemological privilege and the desire to do work that does not just sit in academic journals. Instead, I aim to do work for the healing and empowerment of my family, my community. When I look at my children's sweet and innocent faces, I am motivated to do work that will make their world better.

I have five points of advice for prospective or current women of color in graduate school who are caretakers. First, take time to reflect and identify who you want to be and what your goals are as a graduate student and beyond. More importantly, consider what you need to get there. Second, be kind to yourself and be flexible when it comes to meeting your goals while also being very clear about what you expect and need from those around you in terms of support. Third, remember that caretaking responsibilities change over time. Continuously discuss (and perhaps even document) what these responsibilities are, who is responsible for what, and how you have agreed to meet these responsibilities. If necessary, seek an outside perspective (i.e., counseling, coaching, and so forth) to help facilitate these conversations, particularly if deep resentment exists. Fourth, schedule time for yourself and guard this time! This should include something you enjoy doing that brings positivity to your life. I practice yoga three times a week, hike often, and schedule time out with friends (no kids or spouse) at least once a month. Finally, I urge you to develop a community of supporters at all levels whom you can have honest and authentic conversations with about caretaking while in graduate school. While in graduate school, I had a monthly date with a fellow woman of color graduate student. Now, as a faculty member I started an informal monthly book club with other women of color. These spaces, for me, are critical in allowing me to speak my truth, affirm my experiences, and build community. Sharing our stories and perspectives can help us feel less isolated in these experiences. It also helps us recognize the systemic nature of our oppression that can provoke us toward challenging, and hopefully changing, these circumstances.

In his foreword to the first edition of the *Critical Race Feminism Reader*, the late Derrick Bell acknowledged that Black women, unlike Black men, are often successful regardless of their relationship status. He calls on Black people to recognize Black women as our greatest strength and for Black men to discontinue contributing to patriarchy but instead to "work with women toward a more natural and healthy equality between the sexes."[35] Finally, Bell points out that while the erroneous perceptions of Black men might explain the dichotomy of strong women and weak men within the Black community, Black women often have relatively fewer opportunities and deal with more stereotypes. He further notes, "And yet, in a puzzling contradiction, many women of color derive strength from oppression, whereas many minority men use their oppression to justify unjustifiable behavior—often against women of color."[36] If this is the case, and our contribution to our communities as women of color have been essential despite our oppression, can you imagine our potential if our intimate spaces were full of support and equality?

To bring this image to life, we must develop new ways of being— ways that women of color feminists have been urging us to consider for a long time—by living on the margins in a space of resistance, using our outsider within status, and embracing our mestiza consciousness.[37] A commonality within these metaphors is the ability to be creative, to think and act uniquely, and reimagine our world in liberating ways. As women of color, our oppression and intersectional experiences allow us to see non-oppressive possibilities that are empowering. Sadly, our backs are sometimes too tired and frail to be bridges between oppressed and op-pressive communities.[38] We need to create new spaces, spaces of co-caring and self-care so that we not only survive but thrive in graduate school in ways that allow us to progress far beyond these walls.

Notes

1. Adrien Katherine Wing, *Critical Race Feminism: A Reader* (New York: New York University Press, 2003).

2. Daniel G. Solórzano and Tara J. Yosso, "Critical Race Methodology: Counter-Storytelling as an Analytical Framework for Education Research," *Qualitative Inquiry* 8, no. 1 (2002): 32.

3. Pauline Chinn, "Multiple Worlds/Mismatched Meanings: Barriers to Minority Women Engineers," *Journal of Research in Science Teaching* 36, no. 6 (1999): 621–636; Maria Ong, Carol Wright, Lorelle Espinosa, and Gary Orfield, "Inside the Double Bind: A Synthesis of Empirical Research on Undergraduate and Graduate Women of Color in Science, Technology, Engineering, and Mathematics," *Harvard Educational Review* 81, no. 2 (2011): 172–209.

4. Ong et al., 199.

5. Jessica T. DeCuir-Gunby and Dina C. Walker-DeVose, "Expanding the Counter-story: The Potential for Critical Race Mixed Methods Studies in Education," *Handbook of Critical Race Theory in Education*, ed. Marvin Lynn and Adrian Dixson (New York: Routledge, 2013), 252, 248–259.

6. bell hooks, *Talking Back: Thinking Feminist, Thinking Black* (Boston: South End Press, 1989), 21.

7. Ibid.

8. Patricia Gándara's "Passing through the Eye of the Needle: High-Achieving Chicanas," *Hispanic Journal of Behavioral Sciences* 4, no. 2 (1982): 167–179.

9. Ibid., 177.

10. Ibid.; Leo Grebler, Joan W. Moore, Ralph C. Guzman, *The Mexican American People* (New York: The Free Press, 1970).

11. Maria Chacón, Elizabeth Cohen, and Sharon Strover, "Chicanas and Chicanos: Barriers to Progress in Higher Education," *Latino College Students*, ed. Michael A. Olivas (New York: Teachers College Press, 1986): 296–324.

12. Rachel Kachchaf, Lily Ko, Apriel Hodari, and Maria Ong, "Career-Life Balance for Women of Color: Experiences in Science and Engineering Academia," *Journal of Diversity in Higher Education* 8, no. 3 (2015): 175–191.

13. The Combahee River Collective, "Black Feminist Statement," *The Second Wave: A Reader in Feminist Theory, 1977*, ed. Linda Nicholson (New York: Routledge, 1997), 65.

14. Ibid.

15. Evelyn Simien, "Gender Differences in Attitudes toward Black Feminism among African Americans," *Political Science Quarterly* 119, no. 2 (2004): 315–338.

16. Beverly Johnson, "Bill Cosby Drugged Me. This Is My Story," *Vanity Fair*, December, 2014.

17. Gloria Anzaldúa, *Borderlands/La Frontera: The New Mestiza* (San Francisco: Spinsters/Aunt Lute, 1987).

18. Ibid., 42.

19. Ibid., 43.

20. Ibid.

21. Ibid.

22. Ibid., 38.

23. Tara Yosso, *Critical Race Counterstories Along the Chicana/Chicano Educational Pipeline* (New York: Routledge, 2006).

24. Anita T. Revilla, "What Happens in Vegas Does Not Stay in Vegas: Youth Leadership in the Immigrant Rights Movement in Las Vegas, 2006," *AZTLAN—A Journal of Chicano Studies* 37, no. 1 (2012): 87–115. In an act of resistance to the patriarchal nature of the word *mentor* that includes *men* as a main part of the word used for all genders, *womyn-toring* is a term that means women who mentor and yet replaces the *men* in both the words *women* and *mentor* while combining these two words.

25. Anzaldúa, *Borderlands*, 38.

26. bell hooks, *The Will to Change: Men, Masculinity, and Love* (New York: Atria Books, 2004), xv.

27. Arlie Russell Hochschild and Anne Machung, *The Second Shift* (New York: Penguin Books, 2003); Mari Castañeda and Kirsten Lynn Isgro, *Mothers in Academia* (New York: Columbia University Press, 2013); Angela Y. Davis, *Women, Race & Class* (New York: Vintage Books, 1983); Anthony J. Onwuegbuzie, Roslinda Rosli, Jacqueline M. Ingram, and Rebecca K. Frels, "A Critical Dialectical Pluralistic Examination of the Lived Experience of Select Women Doctoral Students," *The Qualitative Report* 19, no. 3 (2014): 1–35.

28. Amy Richards, *Opting In: Having a Child without Losing Yourself* (New York: Farrar, Straus and Giroux, 2008).

29. Anzaldúa, *Borderlands*, 39.

30. Ibid.

31. Ibid.

32. Alicia Keys, Linda Perry, and Steve Mostyn, *Superwomen*, Alicia Keys, 2008, Oven Studios.

33. Richards, *Opting In*, 171.

34. Patricia Hill Collins, *Black Feminist Thought: Knowledge, Consciousness, and the Politics of Empowerment* (New York: Routledge, 2002).

35. Derrick Bell, "Foreword to the First Edition," *Critical Race Feminism: A Reader*, ed. Adrien Katherine Wing (New York: New York University Press, 2003), xix.

36. Ibid.

37. Anzaldúa, *Borderlands*; bell hooks, *Yearning: Race, Gender, and Cultural Politics* (Boston: South End Press, 1990); Hill Collins, *Black Feminist Thought*.

38. Cherríe Moraga and Gloria Anzaldúa, eds., *This Bridge Called My Back: Writings by Radical Women of Color* (New York: Kitchen Table, Women of Color Press, 1983).

CHAPTER 2

Sett bmit ragel "A Woman as Good as 100 Men"

An Arab Woman's Narratives on Discrimination in and outside Academia

Soha Youssef

More than 15 years ago, Victor Villanueva reminded the field of Rhetoric and Composition that the ambiguity of racism is considered one of the reasons behind its persistence. He contends, "Racism continues to be among the most compelling problems we face. Part of the reason why this is so is because we're still unclear about what we're dealing with, so we must thereby be unclear about how to deal with it."[1] Sadly, Villanueva's statement still holds true. What further complicates his statement is that not only are those racist actions subtle, they also occur in academic spaces that are commonly expected to liberate its members from externally inflicted oppression. Often and despite those members' faith in the academy, microaggressions occur. Microaggressions are subtle verbal or nonverbal acts that may or may not be intended to inflict harm; however, the consequences of those acts may be damaging or insulting to those who have to tolerate such acts. The term *microaggressions* was coined and introduced more than three decades ago by the psychiatrist Chester M. Pierce, who contended that "it is the insidious, hard to identify, subtle racist injuries that we must pay attention to if we are to understand or combat racism."[2] An expansion of the term was later introduced by psychologist Derald Wing Sue and his colleagues who researched racial microaggressions and defined the term as "commonplace verbal or behavioral indignities, whether intended or unintended, which communicate hostile, derogatory, or negative racial slights and insults."[3] Though stories about microaggressions in academia can cause a sense of discomfort to both discriminating and discriminated against parties, that sense of discomfort is needed, since "unwelcome stories are crucial" as a decolonial practice.[4] Stories about microaggressions in academia must be shared, in the words of Sara Ahmed, to "give the killjoy back her voice."[5] Embodying a feminist killjoy, I speak up against microaggressions and share uncomfortable truths as a refusal to subside to or be silenced by agents of power in academia. Because of the subtle nature of microaggressions, well-intentioned microaggressors may not be aware of the adverse impact of their words or actions. And silence, in such scenarios, only perpetuates more microaggressions. If academia is to be decolonized of hegemonic, subtle microaggressions, then it is the voices of minorities that should create channels for those unwelcome stories to be heard.

Graduate students, particularly those who belong to a minority group, typically perceive academia as a safe haven where they can express their otherwise silenced perspectives. But when discrimination in academic spaces takes the shape of microaggressions, it is quite possible that minority students will either fail to recognize such microaggressions, experience a state of shock that slows their reactions down, or fear the consequences of voicing their reactions in a system where power dynamics play a major role. In other words, with the typical hierarchical nature of academic institutions, minority students may be hesitant to report incidents of microaggressions. While one may argue that inviting graduate students of color to share their unwelcome stories is problematic, since that places the onus on those who were discriminated against in the first place, what I perceive as truly troublesome is when these graduate students abstain from sharing moments of microaggressions with the world, particularly with agents of authority in academia such as faculty and individuals in administration.

Discomforting, unwelcome stories, like the ones I am about to share, can reunite bodies and minds of the storytellers. This reunion can liberate minority students from "toiling away in the service of a discourse that disadvantages almost every one of us."[6] In speaking up against discrimination and racism in graduate school—even if it does not offer an instant, easy fix for the problem—I intend to create a space where individuals participating in those systems of oppression are more aware of their well-intentioned microaggressions and where Arab women like myself are less afraid to disrupt existing power dynamics and become the killjoys of the academy by joining in the conversation and sharing their uncomfortable truths.

I will first map the cultural systems of oppression some Arab women tend to face before entering graduate school in the United States. Like any culture, the Arab culture functions on a continuum that stretches from far-right conservatism to far-left liberalism. Though the Arab subculture of conservatism bares resemblance to any other conservative subculture, the cultural mapping I present later will set the context for audiences, while simultaneously allowing me to highlight the existing tension between women's education and the patriarchal system. I will then describe the prototypical gender identity of Arab women and how it shaped my up-bringing in a traditional household in Egypt. My goal is to contextualize the four vignettes that highlight my experiences with both interpersonal and systematic microaggressions in U.S. graduate school, as I completed two master's degrees and my doctorate. What I was shocked to discover about U.S. graduate school is that it is not a panacea for the inequality and discrimination I experienced in Egypt.

I employ personal narratives as a rhetorical trope to express my au-thentic, lived experience. For me, like it is for Debra Journet, narratives are "conventionalized ways of representing disciplinary knowledge."[7] My use of narratives to express my experiences in the academy is my way of dismantling and disrupting the common tendency in the discipline to perceive "objective" and "impersonal accounts" to be an accurate repre-sentation of truth.[8] The integration of narratives embodies the feminist killjoy who is learning to find her voice that has been trained to be silent for so long. Finally, I propose a call to the academy to cultivate spaces for Arab women to gain the courage to share their own experiences of racial microaggressions. A growing awareness of these racial microaggressions can consequently maintain a healthy pipeline of Arab female graduate students. In sharing my experiences with microaggressions, I join voices in this collection, such as Carrie Sampson and Aeriel A. Ashlee, to col-lectively speak up and speak out against problematics in the academy that might be too subtle to recognize, yet too consequential if left unattended.

I want to take a moment to note that I do not speak for all Arab women and men. In fact, throughout this paper, I use the term *Arab women* loosely to denote Egyptian women specifically. This term also accounts for how other women from the rest of the Arab world and their Western counterparts may identify with my experiences. My twenty-seven-year upbringing in Egypt can attest only to my own stories with gender and racial discrimination. These narratives, however, are not meant to represent immutable truth of all Arab women's experiences, as I do not believe such truth exists. In fact, although I identify as a Muslim Egyptian woman of color, the experiences I share in the four vignettes in this essay do not by any means reflect the experiences of all Egyptian women. It is not my intention to make pathological generalizations about Egyptian culture. I hereby caution the readers from making broad assumptions about Egyptian culture, but instead perceive the narratives as a representation of my own unique lived experiences that are informed by the intersectionality of my identity. My goal is for these vignettes to start and encourage much needed conversations regarding the experiences of some—not all—Arab women in and outside graduate school.

The Value of Education in the Lives of Arab Women

Almost every young Arab woman is familiar with the common saying, "El sett malhash gher bet-ha wi goz-ha," which translates to "A woman is destined to stay at home and have a husband." This saying is typically used by Arab parents, especially very traditional, conservative ones. It is used to silence a woman whenever she considers starting a conversation about a potential job promotion or a desire to pursue a graduate degree. The persistence of this old saying does not, for the most part, dissuade women or weaken their conviction in perceiving education as a source of empowerment. However, the saying's continual circulation in society is quite telling, as it reflects deeply imbedded beliefs and traditions.

In a traditional Arab society, the societal pressure on women to fish for husbands teaches women from a young age to seek strength from without rather than within. Lahib Jaddo, an Iraqi American associate professor in architecture, shares my sentiments about the societal expectations of women to belong to a man. Jaddo comments, "A woman in that part of the world start[s] her life by marriage, by belonging to a man, and having his children. Her identity [is] supposed to come from the extension of people around her and not from any achievement of her own."[9] But those societal expectations of women are better understood within the context of the patriarchal contract. Jennifer C. Olmsted explains that the patriarchal contract in the Arab world is directly grounded in women's financial dependency on men. Marriage and child bearing ensue from the power of the patriarchal contract and become "nearly compulsory."[10] Moreover, patriarchy is present in social, political, and religious contexts. In addition to male privilege, patriarchy grants privileges to elders over juniors even if the former are not blood-related to the latter. The patriarchal contract, however, breaks when women have "access to the labor market."[11] It is worth noting, though, that the way the patriarchal contract operates in the Arab world is not at all that distinct or unique from how it operates in the rest of the world.

Gender socialization maintains the patriarchal contract as Arab boys and men are socialized to believe from a young age that they are the intellectually and physically abler sex. This may occur through selective reading and skewed hermeneutics of specific verses from the Quran—especially when interpreted out of context. Although Arabs are not exclusively Muslim, Islam is the dominant religion, affecting Muslims and non-Muslims alike. Such gendered understandings of superiority are also embedded in other cultural norms similar to Western and Christian investments in supporting male privilege. To this end, Valentine M. Moghadam contends that traditionalist views of women's subordinate status are not exclusive to Muslim conservatives.[12] In fact, both Muslim and Christian conservatives hold very similar beliefs when it comes to women's perceived subordination in society. In other words, such patriarchal conservatism is not unique, by any means, to the Arab world or Islam.

Patriarchal systems shift in the Middle East and elsewhere with the rise of educated and employed women who often form women's rights organizations and get involved in professional associations. These women are catalysts for families taking an egalitarian rather than a patriarchal form. This notion of challenging the existing patriarchal system through economic changes and women's activism speaks to Halim Barakat's thoughts on male dominance in the Arab society. Barakat sees a gradual solution for such dominance in the rise of "competing socioeconomic units, the employment of women, and the migration of children to the city [for] education and work."[13] Therefore, education, especially for women, is the means to liberate ourselves from male dominance that manifests itself in old sayings like, "El sett malhash gher bet-ha wi goz-ha."

Even if my brown skin and black curly hair were not considered a privilege in Egypt—a country that still places a high value on whiteness, one of many ramifications of years of British and French colonization—I consider myself privileged due to my education and socioeconomic status. Both my late father and mother were first-generation college graduates, who understood the value of education. However, their advanced educational background did not have a strong impact on their parenting style. They abided by Egyptian social norms. I grew up in a traditional, patriarchal household, where my older, firstborn brother had distinctively more freedoms and fewer responsibilities than my sister or me. However, when it came to education, going to college was nonnegotiable for any of us. Having familial support and financial resources are privileges some other Arab women may not have access to, which can make their journeys more difficult than mine. In addition to these two privileges, my far from conservative religious background most likely made my move to the United States for graduate education easier than others.

Gender Identity of Arab Women

In Egypt, when a woman displays signs of bravery, chivalry, independence, or intelligence, she is immediately considered *sett bmit ragel*, which translates to "a woman as good as 100 men." This hyperbole has been so carelessly and thoughtlessly thrown around that it evolved into a frequent saying used equally by men and women, young and old. One wonders why such positive qualities can be associated only with masculinity, why women do not realize the implication of ourselves using such self-deprecating words, or why a hyperbole needs to equate a woman to one hundred men in order to achieve its effect. When I ponder Arab women's collective situation in the Middle East, I cannot help but reflect on the deeply engraved pejorative that has been associated with us and scarred our gender identity since a very young age. Because language has the power to filter our perceptions of the world, using male-oriented rhetoric is consequential.[14] In other words, if we are saturated in a rhetoric that perceives independence and intelligence as male attributes, then our own perceptions and observations of our gender identity will be tainted by that rhetoric. Eventually, the male-oriented rhetoric shapes and becomes our reality. Therefore, being surrounded by sexist and perpetually disparaging rhetoric, such as "sett bmit ragel," frequently results in women internalizing those statements and adopting similar rhetoric when referring to ourselves.

Because I was raised in a household that reinforced my self-perception as a "sett bmit ragel," I embodied that reality. Though I grew up to believe I am as good as 100 men with all the independence the statement *superficially* implies, I always felt the confinement of my female body. Such confinement was grounded in the predominant Arab culture regarding women's bodies as temptations or a source of "social disorder (*fitna*)."[15] I

41

buried my body under layers of garment. Because donning the hijab has increasingly become more a cultural norm than a religious obligation for Muslim women, I chose to assimilate. In Egypt, I donned the hijab as a sign of modesty. However, soon after I moved to the United States, the hijab paired with my brown skin managed to attract only more attention. Because that excessive attention conflicted with modesty—the main purpose of hijab, I decided to take it off. My decision came as a reaction to the stares I consistently received on campus—a space I naively assumed to be free of prejudice. And, I do not believe my experience to be random or idiosyncratic. For instance, Yusr Mahmud and Viren Swami examine the effect the hijab has on men's perceptions of women's attractiveness and intelligence. In their study, 98 British male undergraduate students were shown full-face photographs of five Caucasian and five South Asian women. Each of those women had two pictures taken of her: one with her hair displayed and the other with a hijab. Mahmud and Swami found that women who were pictured wearing the hijab were rated significantly lower on both attractiveness and intelligence than women not wearing the hijab.[16] I speculate that those stares I received on campus may have stemmed from similar negative perceptions of the hijab. For me, in addition to the emotional reasons for taking the hijab off, there were rational reasons. I was worried that subconscious prejudice by faculty, staff, or students may stand in my way to academic achievement. However, erasing the superficial Islamic symbol I once represented was a precaution that merely protected me from daily, on-campus stares, but failed to protect me from the Islamophobia that inhabits American academia.

I arrived in the United States in July 2009, thinking of America as a country where personal and equal freedoms are experienced by all as a result of the separation of church and state. I assumed racism was in the past and would never happen to me, especially as most of my daily interactions are with intellectual, educated, cultured folks. I was naive and oblivious to the fact that some Americans' perceptions of my identity as an Arab woman, who is also of color, would be based on misconceptions, stereotypes, judgments, and racial discrimination. What was especially surprising to me is that there are more similarities than meets the eye between the Arab and Western cultures when it comes to sexism. Sexism that operates within the patriarchal contract and manifests itself in silencing women's voices and controlling their bodies is quite comparable between the two cultures. Though those similarities can in some cases be subtler than others, they present themselves in comparable forms both inside and outside academia. Those forms can take the shape of the silencing of women, the pejorative rhetoric that surrounds the representation of women, the perceptions of and control over women's bodies, and discriminations against women in the job market. The four vignettes that follow particularly depict such moments of gender and racial discrimination I experienced in the U.S. academy.

First Vignette: Silence in Graduate School

Shortly after I arrived in the United States, I started my first master's degree in Linguistics and Teaching English as a Second Language (TESL) at a prestigious university in the South. Like typical graduate students who try to squeeze in some social events in our busy schedules, a few students from the program organized a small potluck. Almost half of the invitees were Americans, and the other half were international students from different countries: Bangladesh, Russia, Taiwan, and Egypt. The son of one of my mentors, who was then a PhD student in the Composition program (he dropped out later), also attended. In fact, his girlfriend at the time was the host. With the conversation turning to politics, and after having a little too much to drink, he became drunkenly obnoxious. In so many words, and in the presence of the entire group, he commented that Arabs are terrorists. I froze. I never expected such a racist, stereotypical comment to come from an educated colleague—and worst of all—the son of an esteemed faculty member. What added to the complexity of the situation is that that specific mentor has never been anything but nice and helpful to me throughout my work with her and even after my graduation. In fact, she was happy to write me one of the recommendation letters for my PhD applications. But that night, there was a power dynamic that silenced me and prevented me from responding to her son's racist remark. Questions raced in my mind about my rights—or rather my lack of rights—as an Arab woman of color insulted by a white man. I wondered what the appropriate reaction would be to such public microaggression, a reaction that would not hurt my career or ruin my relationship with that faculty member. Further complicating my reaction is the culture of silence I was raised with in Egypt, which encouraged women's submissive behavior to men.[17] The gendered and raced intersectionality of my identity as not only a woman of color but also an international student must have informed the silencing I experienced that evening by a white man, whom I recognized held power over me—and probably he recognized his power too—due to that intersectionality.

However, I hate to project my lack of wit in that specific situation with the faculty member's son on my culture. My story rather sheds light upon a bigger issue—the struggle Arab women may face in American graduate school because of both the silence we have been enculturated to practice throughout our lives and our lack of power in a foreign culture where Islamophobia is present.[18] The latter should not be underestimated. Similarly, Zeina Zaatari, a Muslim Arab woman who grew up in Lebanon and moved to the United States in 1995 for graduate school, reflects on her experiences being silenced in the United States. Zaatari highlights incidents when discussions of the Middle East or the Arab world were silenced in the American classrooms or when her choices of political research topics were turned down for being "controversial and divisive." She states:

> Silencing comes from a neocolonial, imperial, and paternal attitude on behalf of various members of society. Arabs and Arab Americans and Muslims and Muslim Americans are discriminated against, seen as lesser humans by the dominant society, thus denying us the right to even claim victimization, discrimination, or love and care. . . . As community members and activists, we have come not to expect an administration (be it a government or a university) to protect our rights and make us feel safe even when we are attacked on a daily basis.[19]

Though Zaatari is silenced in graduate school in a different way than I, the nature of our silencing is similar. She, too, "expected to find more enlightened people" in graduate school, "yet most were acting in dangerous patronizing ignorance laden with power."[20] She considers silencing to be "the strongest form of racism" she experiences in the United States.[21] Whether silenced within the walls of the classroom or at a graduate student gathering, we experience silencing from the top down that may also go unnoticed. Because of the subtlety of these silences, I identify them as microaggressions. Joanna Kadi explains, "Systems of oppression . . . function most effectively when victims don't talk. Silence isolates, keeps us focusing inward rather than outward, makes perpetrators' work easier, confuses and overwhelms."[22] In both Zaatari's case and mine, there are power dynamics at play. We both are challenged and silenced by a system that holds more power than we are capable of as international, female, graduate students. This is why our voices are needed to break the silence in graduate school.

Second Vignette: Brownness in Graduate School

White American men are not the sole oppressors of Arab women in higher education graduate school. A few years later, and during my second master's degree program in Composition and Rhetoric at a small university in the Midwest, I was once again made to feel less. This time the experience occurred in one of my graduate-level classes. Again, I was in a position of weakness as the sole foreign student of color and as one of three women of color in the classroom.

Despite the diverse backgrounds of my class members, almost half of us shared the experience of being novice first-year composition (FYC) teachers. As any typical first-year cohort, we just started teaching as our assistantship duty. Most professors were curious about our experiences and willing to provide us well-intended advice whether it was regarding teaching, classroom management skills, or professionalism. A discussion started about the dress code expected from FYC instructors. The professor—a white woman, probably in her fifties—provided us with the typical advice that teaching assistants have to dress professionally on our teaching days, as our appearances influence students' perceptions of us. Because that professor held an authoritative position in the Women's Studies program at the time, I thought she would be the best candidate to respond to a nagging question concerning the professionalism of women of color in the academy and the common perception that we need to overdress. Her response to the entire class came without hesitation. She confirmed that for women of color, like me, to gain our students' respect, we had to overdress in order to overcompensate for our skin color. For me, and probably for the other two women of color in the classroom, our professor's response meant extra work for us. We had to dress more formally than our white peers. Her response implied a lack that needs to be compensated for and reinforced my assumptions that as a woman of color, my credentials were not enough. Assuming a position of power in academia, that professor consciously chose the side of the microaggressor. Rather than empowering me to revolt against the existing institutional microaggression that perceives my brown skin as lacking, she encouraged me to acquiesce to the microaggressor's wishes, hence, she was a microaggressor herself. My expectations of equality in academia were evidently too high, too naive, too utopian.

I realized I was presumed incompetent in a graduate school that claims to promote and support diversity.[23] What disturbed me about my professor's advice is that it came from a figure of authority in academia, whose knowledge must be informed by her experience in the academy. Her honest, well-intended advice is not only problematic, but the implications of her advice have particular consequences for racial minorities. That moment prompted my hyperawareness of assumptions of professionalism uniquely affecting instructors of color. But what I consider to be more disconcerting is the racial hyperawareness I developed about my body. I became more aware of my brownness and what it means to be a brown woman in academia. It appalls me to learn that women's dark skin color is perceived as a factor that can weaken our credibility in the classroom to the extent that requires compensation through embellishments and accessories. It intimidates me to learn that my qualifications and years of hard work are still not enough. My qualifications will never be enough as long as nonwhiteness is perceived as a deficiency.

Third Vignette: Dismissed Ethos in Graduate School

This experience with microaggressions was more horizontal than vertical. Horizontal microaggressions come from individuals who inhabit academic spaces that are hierarchically adjacent, such as colleagues and classmates. They are the subtlest because of the covert nature of the power dynamics at play. Contrastingly, vertical microaggressions are more noticeable because of the overt power dynamics involved. In this vignette, I unveil an incident of horizontal microaggressions in academia that can easily pass unnoticed.

When I pursued my master's degree in Composition, I developed a wonderful relationship with one of my faculty mentors. He recognized the hard work I put toward my teaching and assisted me with means for professional development. Not only did he provide academic advice, he later served as a reference on my PhD applications. We also collaborated on research and presented together at conferences. During my work alongside him, I was never made to feel subordinate as an international young Arab female student. Because of his authoritative position in the Composition program, he made sure graduate assistants received the training and mentored teaching necessary during our first year in the program before we were assigned teaching positions in our second year. During that fall semester, there was no real competition when it came to securing a teaching position, as the number of graduate assistants was conveniently equal to the number of openings. Nonetheless, when it was time for spring assistantship assignments, only one position opened. This created quite a bit of competition among the three of us who showed interest: two white Americans and myself. It was quite an intimidating experience, but I gave it all I had because I generally enjoy challenging situations and, more importantly, I wanted to prove to myself that discrimination does not exist in academia. I updated and revised my C.V. and teaching philosophy statement and tailored my cover letter. All my efforts did not go to waste. I was selected for the teaching position. However, the news was not well-received by the graduate students I competed against, particularly by the white woman with much less teaching experience than I had. Nepotism was her sole reasoning for my accomplishment. "Of course, you're his favorite. He must have a crush on you," she reacted. I surmise that her bitterness caused her to dismiss my hard work, qualifications, and past teaching experiences in a single statement.

I remain shocked when considering that this comment came from an-other woman, from whom I expected support based on the shared gender discrimination and microaggression we both are likely to experience as women in academia. Her statement also reminded me of my struggles as an Arab woman in academia—struggles whose lack of recognition by white women tend to infuriate women of color. In the introduction of this collection, Kimberly and Denise share their experience with a white female colleague who failed to recognize her own privilege and the fact that women of color navigate the academy differently than their white counterparts. Though the remarks of the white women in the two stories might be different, they reflect an ignorance about the labor involved in navigating the academy as women of color. My colleague's comment re-inforced the "pre-existing societal stereotypes, biases and discriminations that negatively impact [our] progress and [our] image . . . in the male-dominated, patriarchal, and sexist structure of academe."[24] Yet, what is more problematic is the subtlety of the microaggression. One may argue that her comment is her way of coping with a moment of low self-esteem, or a mere joke, or a subtle questioning of my qualifications. However, the indefiniteness of the motivation or intention for microaggressions does not make that instance any easier on, or less hurtful for, the individual experiencing it.

Fourth Vignette: Non-Americans on the American Job Market

With a master's degree in Linguistics and TESL and another in Composition and Rhetoric, I started applying for teaching jobs at community colleges. However, early on in the job-hunting process, I became discouraged after I noticed language on the very last page of a digital application form for a midwestern community college informing applicants that the school does not sponsor applicants who do not hold a green card. I was, indeed, frustrated and disappointed to learn about the unavailability of sponsorship after spending a significant amount of time completing the required documents and forms. Usually, non-American graduate students who are interested in pursuing a career in the United States apply for Optional Practical Training, which I did.[25] I was legally authorized to work in the United States, and all I needed was a university that would be willing to sponsor me. I understand that sponsorship of immigrants entails financial and legal obligations that not all academic institutions are able to undertake. However, my criticism here is not about some institutions' inability to sponsor immigrants but about their lack of transparency. More transparency and clear language on the job posting would have been appreciated, especially because one reason I was attracted to the position in the first place was the advertisement's clear interest in applicants of color. On one hand, that institution claimed to be an Equal Employment Opportunity employer that promises its potential employees freedom from discrimination based on race, religion, disability, or national origin. On the other hand, the hiring practices of that institution were opaque in a way that discriminates against only one group of applicants: international graduate students—a group whose visa status is particularly time sensitive, adding to our vulnerability on the job market. Given the financial and legal burdens of institutional sponsoring of international graduate students, the least that academic institutions could do is to be cognizant of international graduate students' statuses and to, accordingly, practice true transparency and openness with the language used to reflect their sponsorship practices.

With the job market in sight, as a doctoral student I often discussed issues in academia—such as the increasing workload, challenges of conducting research with a heavy teaching load, and the situation of the academic job market—with my cohort and colleagues who are or have been on the job market. Such discussions kept us engaged and well informed about changes in the field. One of those discussions I had with my partner, who held a fulltime position as a writing instructor at a reputable community college in the Midwest at the time. I expressed to him my worries about my future as an Arab woman on the job market. Being a white American man, my partner is often able to help me see things from a different perspective. Without diminishing my qualifications, he referenced tokenism, which he encouraged me to see in a positive light, arguing that it can facilitate my future job hunt—especially in the current deplorable job market. Despite his goodwill and well-intentioned advice, he was unaware of the destructive consequences of tokenism for people of color, so I found it an opportune moment to have that discussion. And he listened. That moment, though, made me realize that white folks might not necessarily be aware of the struggles people of color go through in academia. Though my partner did not have any malicious intentions, he could be perceived as a microaggressor by those who do not know him personally. It is true that his lack of intention did not make my experience any less valid, but that moment made me realize the ways familiarity with the microaggressor and the latter's willingness to listen and learn can—instead of creating tension that never gets to be addressed—open a channel of conversation and create learning opportunities about microaggression.

Tokens become highly visible, as everything they do or say is closely monitored. They are usually regarded as representatives of their under-represented demographic group. Thus, their failures only reinforce an existing stereotype, and their successes are regarded as exceptions of those stereotypes. Tokenism often results in feelings of isolation and loneliness, as tokenized persons are often marginalized on their predominantly white college campuses and communities. Another consequence of tokenism is "attributional ambiguity," which is the inability to trust evaluations or to determine whether the feedback that tokens get is valid or merely attributed to racism, sexism, and biases.[26] I may be perceived as *sett bmit ragel* by the Arab society, but I hate to be perceived as a token in U.S. academia. In short, in both the Arab society and the U.S. academy, my accomplishments are diminished and affiliated with defying gender expectations, and gender and racial norms, respectively.

Looking Back and Moving Forward

I write these vignettes and reflect on the microaggressions I face in academia with the hope that my stories will encourage other oppressed, silenced, and discriminated against Arab women to construct their own narratives. Those stories can collectively help deconstruct existing systems of oppression against women of color in the American academy. Intelligent and independent Arab women who make it to U.S. graduate school may indeed be labeled in their countries of origin as *sett bmit ragel* for their achievements. I propose that Arab women need to appropriate pejoratives, such as *sett bmit ragel*, and utilize their inherent power as a method to speak up, speak out, and dismantle microaggressions experienced in academia.

I utilized the power of *sett bmit ragel* in order to reflect on incidents of interpersonal and systematic microaggressions I experience in graduate school. While reflecting on those microaggressions, I perceive a heightened level of threat and experience a deeper level of pain when microaggressions are vertical than when they are horizontal. When microaggressions come from figures of authority in academia, potential motivations, such as misinformation or unawareness, are dismissed. The authority of those figures intensifies the impact and implications of their microaggressions regardless of intention. Stories like mine are important and needed, and a close and careful listening to those stories is imperative if academia is to be a safe haven indeed for minorities or if graduate school is to provide a healthy pipeline for minorities like me.

Notes

1. Victor Villanueva, "On the Rhetoric and Precedents of Racism," *College Composition and Communication* 50, no. 4 (1999): 648.

2. Julie Minikel-Lacocque, "Racism, College, and the Power of Words: Racial Microaggressions Reconsidered," *American Educational Research Journal* 50, no. 3 (2013): 435.

3. Derald Wing Sue, Christina M. Capodilupo, Gina C. Torino, Jennifer M. Bucceri, Aisha M. B. Holder, Kevin L. Nadal, and Marta Esquilin, "Racial Microaggressions in Everyday Life: Implications for Clinical Practice," *American Psychologist* 62 (2007): 271–286.

4. David Wallace, "Unwelcome Stories, Identity Matters, and Strategies for Engaging in Cross-Boundary Discourses," *College English* 76, no. 6 (2014): 547.

5. Sara Ahmed, "Feminist Killjoys (and Other Willful Subjects)," *The Scholar and Feminist Online* 8, no. 3 (2010): 1–8, http://sfonline.barnard.edu/polyphonic /ahmed_01.htm.

6. Malea Powell, "Stories Take Place: A Performance in One Act," *CCC* 64, no. 2 (2012): 401.

7. Debra Journet, "Narrative Turns in Writing Studies Research," in *Writing Studies Research in Practice: Methods and Methodologies*, ed. Lee Nickoson and Mary P. Sheridan (Carbondale: Southern Illinois University Press, 2012), 13.

8. Ibid., 19.

9. Aretha Faye Marbley, Aliza Wong, Sheryl L. Santos-Hatchett, Comfort Pratt, and Lahib Jaddo, "Women Faculty of Color: Voices, Gender, and the Expression of Our Multiple Identities within Academia," *Advancing Women in Leadership* 31 (2011): 170.

10. Jennifer C. Olmsted, "Gender, Aging, and the Evolving Arab Patriarchal Contract," *Feminist Economics* 11, no. 2 (2005): 56.

11. Ibid.

12. Valentine M. Moghadam, "Patriarchy in Transition: Women and the Changing Family in the Middle East," *Journal of Comparative Family Studies* 35, no. 2 (2004): 137, 157.

13. Halim Isber Barakat, *The Arab World: Society, Culture, and State* (Berkeley: University of California Press, 1993), 97–102.

14. Kenneth Burke, "Terministic Screens," *Language as Symbolic Action: Essays on Life, Literature, and Method* (Berkeley: The University of California Press, 1966), 45–46.

15. Barakat, *The Arab World*, 97–102.

16. Yusr Mahmud and Viren Swami, "The Influence of the *hijab* (Islamic head-cover) on Perceptions of Attractiveness and Intelligence," *Body Image* (2010): 90–93.

17. Barakat, *The Arab World*, 102.

18. It is widely known that in the United States as well as in other Western countries, Arabs and Muslims are conflated and experience similar rates of xenophobia as a result of Islamophobia.

19. Zeina Zaatari, "In the Belly of the Beast: Struggling for Nonviolent Belonging," *MIT Electronic Journal of Middle East Studies* 5 (2005): 76.

20. Ibid., 80.

21. Ibid.

22. Joanna Kadi, *Thinking Class: Sketches from a Cultural Worker* (Boston: South End Press, 1996), 11.

23. Gabriella Gutierrez y Muhs et al., *Presumed Incompetent: The Intersections of Race and Class for Women in Academia* (Boulder: University of Colorado Press, 2012).

24. Marbley et al., "Women Faculty of Color," 167.

25. Optional Practical Training (OPT) is an application that students with non-U.S. citizenship can apply for from the U.S. Citizenship and Immigration services in order to be granted a 12–17–month period (depending on their major) during which they are eligible to work or receive training in the United States.

26. Yolanda Niemann, "Lessons from the Experiences of Women of Color Working in Academia," *Presumed Incompetent: The Intersections of Race and Class for Women in Academia*, ed. Gabriella Gutiérrez y Muhs, Yolanda Flores Niemann, Angela P. Harris, and Carmen G. González (Boulder: University of Colorado Press, 2012), 473.

CHAPTER 3

You're Going to Need a Team

Community, Mentoring, Self-Care, and Other Lessons from the McNair Scholars Program

Delia Fernández

I thank the McNair Scholars first in my dissertation acknowledgments. Quite literally, I would not have been in a PhD program if were not for the Ronald E. McNair Scholars program—a federally funded initiative to increase the number of first-generation, low-income, and underrepresented populations in academia.[1] Simply put, the program changed my life. The McNair staff and my cohort members became a team of support I did not know I needed to make a serious life change. Before I started the program, I had no desire to leave my hometown of Grand Rapids, Michigan. Not many people I knew ever left. I was going to be a 6th–12th grade social studies teacher. However, one professor saw that I had the potential to apply to graduate school and complete a PhD. He told me about McNair. Before that intervention, as a first-generation Latina college student at Grand Valley State University (GVSU), a midsize state institution in Michigan, I had not the slightest idea that getting a doctorate degree was something I, the daughter of teenage parents, the granddaughter of immigrants and migrants, could do. The McNair Scholars program transformed everything I thought about what people like me were capable of accomplishing and how they accomplished it. My participation in the program gave me the tools I needed to do something unthinkable—something my family and friends would not understand and something that would make me doubt myself constantly.

My path to graduate school began when David Stark, a Latino professor in the history department at GVSU, asked me about my plans after graduation during the spring of 2009. He asked me if I had any desire to go to graduate school and my first thought was that I could not afford it. I was only at a four-year college because of a scholarship, I explained. He then gently informed me that there were PhD programs that would waive tuition and pay me a small, but usually sufficient, stipend. Most importantly, however, he told me he thought I possessed the ability to apply and finish a PhD program. A year before I was set to graduate, I changed my life plan and started McNair. That one-on-one conversation and, specifically, vote of confidence opened up academia as a possibility for me.

The McNair Scholars Program has been helping students like me since 1986. The program was named to honor Ronald E. McNair, one of the fallen astronauts of the famed Challenger space shuttle explosion and someone who also felt underprepared for undergraduate and graduate school. This program is a part of a federal initiative, "designed to identify and provide series for individuals from disadvantaged backgrounds," and it offers support to students from low-income families, first-generation college students, and people who are underrepresented in their fields of study.[2] Quite frankly, McNair makes doctorate degrees available to people who would have been shut out of that opportunity otherwise.

I was one of the 5,000 students who participated in a McNair Program in 2009 and my life has changed dramatically because of it. The following fall I applied to history graduate programs and selected Ohio State University (OSU) to attend. I entered graduate school in the fall of 2010, received my master's degree in 2012, and earned my history doctorate with a concentration in U.S. Latino history in 2015. Currently, I am an assistant professor at Michigan State University in the history department and hold an affiliation with the Chicano/Latino Studies Program. Just six years after being accepted into the McNair Scholars Program, I joined the 0.3% of all Latinos in the United States that hold a PhD.[3]

While I moved through my graduate program quickly, it was very clear to me why I needed the preparation McNair offered. Academia is an institution built for elite, white men. My McNair program highlighted that I would need to navigate this terrain once I was a graduate student. This became more evident as I began my graduate program. I saw firsthand that the presence of poor and working-class women of color at universities disrupts the very foundation of higher education in this country. On a daily basis throughout all of those phases, I was reminded that academia is not a space designed for people of color and certainly not for women of color. For example, when I was a graduate student, my white peers made no secret that they thought I got into graduate school because of "affirmative action." To them, there could be no other possible reason I could be there. Now I am a professor, and white undergraduate students have publicly questioned my authority and expertise. These moments reinforce the ideas that I was not supposed to be in graduate school nor was I supposed to become a professor.

I still consider myself to be extremely fortunate to have the opportunities I had in McNair, getting into graduate school, and getting a tenure-track job, but the feelings I have about academia are much more complicated than being happy or not. I embrace my feminist killjoy. Indeed, I am one of the "lucky ones" who landed a secure position in a tough job market that is only getting more and more tough. But I make no claims that academia has been the perfect option for me nor do I claim that it is the perfect option for other women of color. The process to get to this stage was long, arduous, and filled with anxiety, self-doubt, and stress. I could not have done it without teams of support in my family, friends, and colleagues—many of whom were also women of color. All of these feelings have not completely gone away, but I am thankful that McNair prepared me for this.

There are parts about academia that I love and that make the sacrifices worthwhile in many ways. As a professor of Latino history and Latino studies, I have intellectual freedom and a purpose that I can describe only as greater than myself. I research a community of Latinos that I came from and serve as a conduit for their voices on a larger stage. My position as a Latina professor challenges common stereotypes about who can be a professor and what Latinas are capable of doing—even if students question my authority. More importantly, I am able to understand deeply the problems of racism, sexism, and classism that plague our society and contribute to solving them through my work, if even in a small part. Every day I am humbled and honored to be a part of a team of women of color who are changing the world with their determination, creativity, and passion. Lastly, I would be remiss if I did not mention the excitement that I possess when thinking about getting tenure—the closest thing to ultimate job security a child of working-class parents can imagine. Growing up, there was always the fear of what would happen to our family if my parents lost their jobs. While many people think of tenure as a protection for academic freedom, which it is, as a first-generation college student it also means stability in a way that I could only dream of. Years of preparation, beginning with McNair, brought me to this moment where I can recognize the pitfalls of academia, but also spend my time cultivating the areas that I enjoy.

This essay discusses the importance of various forms of support for women of color graduate students. To that end, I detail the comprehensive McNair Scholars program I participated in as an undergraduate at GVSU—my first encounter with an extensive, support, and guidance program for underrepresented people in academia. I then discuss the ways that lessons learned in McNair led me to find other forms of support in graduate school and on the tenure track. Those lessons can be summarized as learning how and why building community is necessary, finding the right mentor, and prioritizing self-care. I conclude with suggestions for staff, administrators, undergraduate students, and graduate students. This chapter should serve as a resource for women of color who face a challenging time in their life as they pursue a graduate degree.

Transitions in life call for support. In many ways, graduate school is essentially a series of stressful transitions. For example, during the first couple of years, graduate students generally just take classes. During that time, they get used to supporting their intellectual growth, familiarizing themselves with new surroundings, and forming new relationships, all while also managing the relationships they held before coming to graduate school. After finishing course work, planning, taking, and succeeding in candidacy exams—a test on all the content one has learned that generally certifies them as an expert in their field—is another phase and thus, a transition. Generally, passing this test usually allows graduate students to begin writing their dissertations, which is also a different part of the journey to a PhD. The period when graduate students start applying to jobs can be another transition and often an incredibly stressful one. During all of these phases, graduate students will likely have to fight to keep themselves balanced. They should surround themselves with a positive, supportive community, thoughtful guidance, and taking care of themselves—all of which can be keys to their success.

This chapter builds upon the many studies and essays concerning women of color's well-being in academia.[4] Living balanced and whole lives as academics of color has long been a concern. Scholarship on this topic deals with a range of issues that women of color as racial and gender minorities face in academia. The theoretical and practical writing on this topic have long influenced the strategies I learned and employed while surviving graduate school. Doctoral programs and life on the tenure track are competitive spaces in which to exist. Less than 2% of the general population has chosen this route.[5] In taking on this challenge, the best advice for women of color will often come from other women of color who have trekked this path.

I wrote this piece with various audiences and purposes in mind. It is my hope that undergraduate women of color with McNair Scholars at their university might seek out this program. For those women at institutions that do not have this program, I hope that this chapter can give them a framework for understanding what type of support and resources one might find useful in preparing for graduate school. For staff members at institutions of higher education, with or without McNair programs, I hope some of the examples of programming and organizations I offer can serve as a model for the creation and sustaining of programs with similar goals. Lastly, for those with influence at institutions of higher education, I intend for this work to act as a promotion of the McNair Scholars program, and to that end, I encourage proactive decision making that keeps McNair on college campuses and creates programs that address racial and gendered inequalities for those students who want to attend graduate school.

The McNair Scholars Program

Each McNair Scholars Program follows a national framework, but they also have the freedom to customize aspects of their programs. Generally, McNair ensures that its participants have access to GRE prep, seminars in research and writing, a research project under the guidance of a mentor, and other preparation as the institution determines.[6] Usually, McNair programs also try to address the most pressing issues that scholars of color face. Scholarship identifies these as isolation, financial challenges, and trouble identifying sources of support.[7] Programs vary by institutions, usually depending on available resources. Research into the various McNair Programs across the country reveals that some programs with access to resources in STEM offer more comprehensive programming in that field for students, for example.[8] Another program received considerable support from university librarians who offered their mentoring services.[9] Tailoring the program to student needs and university resources is one of the unique yet attractive aspects of this federal program. Regardless of the differences, the program as a whole is a powerful mechanism for increasing the odds of being accepted into graduate school and being prepared to complete it.

An Overview of GVSU McNair Scholars

Grand Valley State University received their first federal grant to host the program in 2001. Dolli Lutes served as the associate director of McNair from 2002 to 2011 and then as director from 2011 to 2017 until her retirement. By the time I entered the McNair Scholars program at Grand Valley in 2009, Lutes had made numerous revisions to the program in an effort to make it more effective and more relevant as academia continued to evolve. This meant that McNair at GVSU entailed a comprehensive plan to prepare us for graduate school, but also was particularly specialized because of the program's leadership. It is important to note that while not all McNair Scholars will have the exact same experience as I had, many of them will recognize the broad underpinnings of the program.

As a first-generation college student, I could not have imagined how helpful our rigorous twelve-week program would be in the summer of 2009. Equipped with a stipend, free summer housing on campus, GRE prep courses, a university writing course, Toastmaster's International memberships, weekly yoga classes, a small research budget, and direct contact with a mentor, my cohort embarked on a journey to learn how to be graduate students. In the sections that follow, I discuss the overarching academic structure of the program and then I reflect on the lessons I took from McNair to my graduate program.

Prepping for the GRE was one of the main focuses of our time together. While a growing number of programs are no longer using the GRE as part of their application process, many traditional disciplines still use this standardized test as an essential part of their application. To prepare us to take this test, we took at least three practice tests throughout our summer: one at the beginning, middle, and end. This was a vulnerable task. As students who had limited familiarity with standardized tests, which were often biased against us, the first practice test was anxiety inducing.[10] This was an important benchmarking tool, but at the same time, many of us feared what that benchmarking might mean. The thought that we might not be academically prepared for graduate school as indicated in the GRE only furthered our individual and collective *imposter syndrome*—that is we doubted ourselves despite all of our accomplishments.[11] A large part of being in this program, however, was acknowledging that we did not know everything about graduate school. For that reason, we needed to trust that our director had our best interests at heart.

After that first test, with our scores in mind, we headed straight into weekly GRE classes for writing, reading, and math. Each of the instructors—GVSU faculty members or individuals who specialized in standardized exam prep—met our anxiety with patience and understanding. These weekly classes consisted of working through problem sets out of GRE prep manuals. Over the course of the summer, many of us saw our scores steadily improve. This was just one part of our preparation, however.

As a requirement for graduation, Grand Valley students needed to complete a junior level writing course. In a display of institutional support, GVSU allowed McNair students to receive that credit through taking a specialized writing course that concentrated on writing for graduate school. We wrote our curriculum vitae, cover letters, personal statements, and other essays as needed for our applications.[12] This biweekly summer course ensured that our applications had been vetted individually through at least one professor, in addition to our mentors and program director.

The McNair Program also included a course titled, "Transition to McNair and Graduate School." While reading Kaplan's *Graduate School Admissions Advisor*, we discussed topics including: how to identify graduate programs that were a good fit for us, what was important for personal statements, and how to find fellowships.[13] During these sessions, former McNair Scholars and professors at our institution came in to discuss their personal experiences with this process. These firsthand conversations complemented what we read in the secondary materials.

Program director Lutes also required GVSU McNair Scholars to take part in Toastmasters International. This program is intended to develop leadership and communication skills.[14] Comprised of weekly one-hour meetings, we practiced our cadence, tone, and delivery of speeches of varying lengths. While undoubtedly this program was included to help us prepare for what would have been our first conference presentations, the effects went far beyond that. In this yearlong program, I learned the speaking skills I needed to speak confidently in my graduate courses, with professors, and in conference presentations. Eventually, I applied those same skills for job interviews.

The last and most important component of our program centered on our research projects. With a faculty mentor, in twelve weeks we carried out research, drafted a manuscript, and revised it for publication in Grand Valley's *McNair Scholars Journal*.[15] We also created five, ten, and fifteen-minute research presentations. The latter was presented at a national McNair Scholars conference at the end of our twelve-week program. The intention behind this exercise was that we not only learn valuable research skills in our discipline but that we had a polished writing sample to submit with our grad school applications and experience presenting at conferences.

During my time as a McNair Scholar, I could not have imagined that all of the different parts of our program would be helpful for not just graduate school but for the rest of my career. In the following, I discuss three themes (cohort and community; mentoring; and self-care) that I learned as a McNair Scholar and how I carried those into graduate school.

Cohort and Community

The McNair Scholars Program at Grand Valley planned to mimic the graduate school environment as much as possible. Like many graduate students, our first interactions with this program came via an introduction to being a part of a cohort—the group of people who are admitted into a program during a certain year. While other mentoring programs I was a part of included group participation, this was my first opportunity for consistent contact with a group of people with whom we would share a significant amount of time together. My cohort experience taught me that I enjoyed being part of a group with the same goals with people from somewhat similar backgrounds. In addition, I found that I was most successful when I did this. Being part of a group of people with the same goals in mind can bring up healthy motivation and competition, but it can also bring about feelings of self-doubt as people compare themselves to others. Potential graduate students should be aware that all of these types of feelings are normal for everyone.

During my McNair summer, the course we took together meant we spent daily time with one another. Many of the McNair Scholars also took advantage of opportunities to be with one another in social settings outside of our classes. These trips to dinner and other unstructured time allowed for some of us to create bonds with one another and served as a space for airing out many of our worries about grad school. This turned out to be a very encouraging space for one another.

The other side of being part of a cohort, however, is that feelings of insecurity might also come from being around other motivated people.

At first, I felt very underprepared in comparison to some of my cohort members. I came to the idea of graduate school at the end of the fourth of five years of my undergraduate career. Some of my colleagues knew they were going to apply to graduate school since they started college. For the first couple of weeks, I wondered if McNair and graduate school were really for me. Other cohort members' certainty about getting a PhD intimidated me, but it was also through this cohort that I found support to express these ideas. Our program director made sure conversations about our concerns for graduate school were frequent and frank. I learned that even if people decided to go to graduate school early on, they still worried about being good enough. Those feelings were commonplace and an everyday part of the journey to a PhD.

Upon entering graduate school, I looked to replicate some of the types of relationships I learned I needed in McNair. I also recognized that I come from a large Latino family and a very connected community of extended family and friends. During my journey through undergrad, my community affirmed my quest for education and praised me for my confidence and determination. As a graduate student, I was determined to seek out and cultivate my own supportive spaces. Forming a community for myself at that stage was an essential part of my success. This was not always an easy task, but it was a more than worthwhile.

Many graduate students will look to their cohort as a central part of their community. It is often the first network of people with whom students come into contact. The reality for many women of color, especially for those in the sciences or "traditional" disciplines, is that they may look around only to find that they are one of the few if not the only one person of color in their cohort and/or the only woman. For students who went to predominately white institutions for undergrad, this might not bring about new feelings of culture shock. For others who were used to diverse spaces, this sudden transition can be alarming. Unlike McNair, there is a large likelihood that not everyone in a graduate program will be first-generation, low-income, or underrepresented. If graduate students cannot relate to anyone in their program, they should be aware that this could bring feelings of isolation.

To avoid seclusion, I urge incoming graduate students to work toward forming a community as soon as they get to campus, but also to be aware that there are a couple of issues that might arise in that process. Many people have positive experiences with their cohort members and others may experience a range of racial microaggressions in these interactions.

These are the "brief, everyday exchanges that send denigrating messages to people of color because they belong to a racial minority group."[16]

When I started graduate school, I found many pleasant, agreeable people in my cohort and in the cohorts before and after mine, but I learned hard lessons about allyship and building supportive networks. In many ways, I was unable to relate to members of my cohort who were not first-generation college students, including those who may be the second or third generation of their families to become professors. In some cases, I found my colleagues to be skeptical about why I was in the program. One person, in particular, referenced affirmative action as the reason why people of color were in graduate school. When I looked to the friends I made in my classes for support, they did not say anything in my defense. Needless to say, sharing a communal office with people who felt like that was uncomfortable to say the least. I often found other places to do work, like at a coffee shop, for example, because of this.

I was also naive to believe that everyone who looked like me was going to be my ally. It was a heavy disappointment when I learned that someone, whom I assumed would be my friend because he was also a person of color, was not supportive of me. When that same colleague said offensive remarks about immigrants, I challenged him. I had hoped a man of color in the office would back me up, but instead he avoided taking sides. After being let down in those situations, I was cautious to continue making new friends, but it did not stop me from still trying to build relationships with new people, albeit slowly.

Through my first year of graduate school, I learned that those people who would be my friends and allies came from various backgrounds. Ideologies and political stances set people apart because, as graduate students quickly learn, the personal is always political—especially at these types of institutions. Who one is might be intimately tied with what they are studying, making it impossible to separate the two. Graduate students might also have a vested interest in their topic, even if it does not directly relate to them. My intellectual support system included people from a variety of backgrounds both like and unlike my own (race, generation in college, gender), but most importantly, they were people who supported my work and me, and I did the same for them. As a Latina who studied Latinos in the 20th century, when people affirmed the validity of the topic I studied, it also affirmed my legitimacy as a scholar and my belonging in graduate school.

I encourage women of color to also look outside of their departments for their community. The most meaningful connections with my peers happened in this way. People in my field understood the particularities about our graduate school experience in regard to the academic challenges that were posed to us. I found, however, that people from other disciplines made graduate school a rich and worthwhile experience for many reasons. First, graduate students might find, if they have not already, that they do not always want to talk about their research and work. Many conversations with people inside one's department, no matter how hard one tries, often circle back to department politics or other topics within one's fields. Second, when graduate students do want to vent about what is happening in their department, someone from outside will be extremely helpful. Often it will feel like less of a risk to discuss issues openly than it would be with someone in their department. Third, when graduate students want to talk about their work in a substantive way, friends from outside of their discipline can offer different lenses and provide much needed insights they might not find in their department. Likewise, they should expect to provide this type of support to their colleagues as well.

Making these networks might require some work depending on the institution. I was fortunate to find the Graduate Association of Latino/ Latin Americans at Ohio State University when I arrived on campus. Made up of students across disciplines and fields, we organized around our identity as Latinos and Latin Americans at OSU. As a group, we took up philanthropic causes like mentoring K-12 students, fund-raising for local food pantries, or lending our voices to local issues like immigration reform and police brutality. In addition, we tried to provide academic support to one another. Study tables, writing days, and presentation practice were very helpful, for example. Most importantly, we scheduled social activities to balance out our demanding work schedules. Whenever possible we held game nights, happy hours, potlucks, and other affordable activities on a graduate student stipend. All of these activities helped to shape our Latino community.

We also built relationships with other groups for students of color. For example, shared events with the Black Graduate Student Caucus or the Graduate Pan Asian Caucus helped us form networks of solidarity. These relationships transformed Ohio State's campus into a place where we felt comfortable. Not every university will have these organizations, but I would encourage graduate students to form networks based upon whatever identities or affinities they have so that they may also feel supported and set up support for incoming students.

I also suggest that women of color cultivate their own spaces on campus. Dr. Gisell Jeter-Bennett, a fellow history graduate student at the time, and others pioneered Colorful Women in the Academy at OSU. This organization included social outings, volunteering, and also "Write on Girl"—a weekly meeting of women of color wherein we wrote and worked on other projects. The work it took for this was not arduous, but it made a substantial impact on our quality of lives and our collective productivity working toward our academic goals. The organization's administration created a listserv, reserved space at a local coffee shop, and every week, as schedules permitted, women of color worked side by side. Even if not much conversation occurred among us, personally, it was refreshing to have a space where I was not the "other." Women of color in the Office of Diversity and Inclusion (ODI) at Ohio State also created a Women of Color Retreat for undergraduates, graduate students, faculty, and staff, which ODI helped to fund. This three-day event allowed women of color to reaffirm their value and worth on a predominately white campus that often rendered us invisible.

Finally, I suggest making connections with people outside of academia during graduate school. This is surely not an easy task given the heavy workload assigned to graduate students. It can be rewarding and enrich a graduate student's life, however. For women of color, especially first-generation college students, spending time in the ivory tower can be a dissociating experience. So much of our background and experiences are not a part of life in academia. Having regular reminders that we have existed and thrived outside of the politics of universities can be a humanizing experience. Many of my friends in graduate school did this by participating in faith-based institutions, volunteering, pursuing healthy lifestyles, and engaging in other interests that graduate school simply did not meet. In the midst of the emotional stress graduate school can bring, these relationships can make a difference in graduate students' quality of life.

Mentoring

The mentoring I had in McNair drastically changed my college experience. Up until that point in my undergraduate career, I had not identified a mentor and had limited experiences with peer mentoring. While I signed up for various programs that helped underrepresented students at my institution, I never put time into forming a relationship with a professor. My understanding of college prior to McNair rested on the ideas of going to class, getting good grades, winning scholarships, and graduating. I had no idea that social capital in the form of making strong connections with mentors would be the most important aspect of getting a degree. It was through mentoring that I discovered that much of the information I needed to be successful in my career would not come from a course or a book (though this one is working to change that). In fact, most of the helpful suggestions for graduate school came directly from someone who had gone through it themselves.

McNair taught me how to identify a possible mentor. I learned that there are a variety of ways that a mentor and mentee "fit" together. In having us choose a mentor, McNair aimed to mimic the advisor-advisee relationship that many of us would enter into in graduate school. Dr. David Stark, the professor who introduced me to the McNair, agreed to be my mentor. While in some cases having similar project ideas can be extremely helpful, it does not need to be the case and in many situations it might not be possible. I chose to research gender roles in the Mexican Revolution even though his work centered on race and slavery in Puerto Rico. Despite this difference, his responsibilities included guiding me through the process of researching and writing and answering questions I had about history graduate school programs. He also helped me find primary and secondary sources to complete my project and supported the development of my writing skills. I realized that at no point in my education had I ever received thorough training in writing for an academic purpose. His instruction over six weeks by no means taught me the entirety of this type of writing, but it did introduce me to the foundational concepts of this genre. His willingness to help and patience supported my intellectual growth more than any course.

From my time with Dr. Stark, I learned that I work best with mentors who take hands-on approaches. For example, I discovered that I am a better writer when a mentor gives me direct and substantive feedback. As a student who was used to earning high grades, the type of work I needed to do on my writing came as a shock to me. One can imagine my dismay when he returned a draft to me for the first time and I saw that it was covered in red ink. While I wondered briefly if that meant I was not prepared for this type of work, he assured me that I was. Editing was a part of writing. Though I had a lot to learn, I came to understand that this was a normal part of the process. I see now that those were opportunities for me to grow and learn as a scholar. With this approach, I try to reframe the shame and embarrassment I felt for not being the best writer to a chance for me to become one and a challenge for me to work toward.

Finding out what works for graduate students as individuals and as scholars is an important task. Not everyone is receptive to hands-on mentoring and it is not always the best for each phase of a scholar's development. That summer I also learned that I needed to be given the freedom to direct my own intellectual development. But, telling my advisor that I was going to shift the geographical area of my research from Latin America to Latinos in the United States was a daunting challenge for me even if it may have been an innocuous request. I was a first-generation college student and daughter of Latino parents. Questioning authority was a practice that seldom occurred and needed to happen with great caution if it did at all. I learned the very beginning of what it meant to take an active role in my own academic trajectory and speak up for myself when I needed more or less direction from my mentors throughout my graduate career. To accomplish this, I had to acknowledge a growing confidence I had in myself. When I began in McNair, I did not know much about what I was getting into and needed to trust my mentors.

As I entered graduate school, I took more courses, attended conferences, and gained more knowledge about academia. I learned to trust myself through this process. I still took my mentors' advice into consideration, but I was the one who made decisions about how I wanted to execute my project and what I wanted it to contribute. Admittedly, the process of being assertive was hard and still something that I work on today, but it was in McNair that I learned that I possessed the ability to be my own advocate.

McNair showed us that not all the mentoring we needed would come from one person. While we met weekly with our assigned mentors, we also saw our program director, Dolli Lutes, at least once a week. In many ways, our assigned mentors offered academic guidance regarding graduate school—teaching us the norms in our discipline, and how to engage with literature, among other important skills. Our meetings with Dolli, however, focused on our emotional well-being. She checked in with us about how we felt about the research process and what, if any, anxieties we had about graduate school. A first-generation college student from a low-income family, Dolli knew our worries before we said them aloud. Sitting across from her, I divulged how nervous I was at the prospect of leaving my tight-knit Latino family behind to pursue this degree and my concerns about whether I could be ready for graduate school, when it was never a possibility until that summer. I disclosed my worries about changing the plan I had for my life without knowing if it would work. She consoled me and asked me questions to further explore what I really wanted for my life and how graduate school fit in. All I knew then was that I wanted to have an impact on society. Also, I knew I loved to learn. She helped me to come to the conclusion that graduate school would be a good place for me.

The mentoring given while an undergraduate continued when I entered graduate school. Within a week of starting graduate school, I received the best advice about graduate student success at the Office of Diversity and Inclusion's (ODI) welcome reception. Cyndi Freeman, the senior director of Graduate Recruitment and Diversity Initiatives at Ohio State, told the incoming scholars of color that we needed three types of people to get through graduate school: a mentor, an advisor, and a cultural translator. While they could be three different people, they could also be just one, she explained.

A mentor helps personally and professionally guide graduate students to the next level. In many cases, a mentor can be identified by finding someone who lives a life the mentee wants to live. I suggest genuinely getting to know them and learning from their experiences. Their guidance could open up information that might not be available elsewhere.

An advisor supports the academic portion of graduate school experiences. This person makes sure that graduate students finish their degrees in a timely manner; guides their intellectual development and scholarly production; and should serve as an advocate for the graduate student at their institution.

A cultural translator provides a bridge to understanding the nuances of academic life that are especially foreign to first-generation students. For example, a cultural translator might help a graduate student phrase an email request in a manner that would be well received by a department chair. In so many words, they teach graduate students how to decode academia and how to speak and act in away academics understand and expect.

Some people find that their academic advisor plays the other two roles as well, while others will need to find a team of people to fill all of these roles. This person or people will likely help with issues outside of graduate school. They are the first people in a graduate student's network, and they may then extend the graduate student access to their networks. In turn, this can give them important connections for their intellectual and professional future.

I was very deliberate about finding women of color mentors. I had excellent guidance from a Latino man on my journey to graduate school during McNair, but for the next phase, I wanted to work closely with someone who understood the particular challenges I faced as a woman of color. I was very fortunate to find a generous, helpful, and rigorous advisor who played all the above-mentioned roles for me. I also formed relationships with other women of color faculty whom I encountered during graduate school. These women taught me a range of lessons including how to respond to the microaggressions I faced within my department, how to interact with faculty at conferences, and how to manage my relationships with family and friends back home, among other topics. These relationships can make a difference in the quality of life women of color have during and after graduate school.

It is important to mention that while I thought women of color would be the only mentors I would ever want or need, I found mentors in unusual spaces occasionally. Outside of my advisor, a white male professor became a strong advocate for me inside my department. After taking a couple of courses with him, I eventually felt comfortable enough to reveal to him that I dealt with imposter syndrome. This mentor admitted that, as a first-generation college student and son of immigrants himself, he felt this way during graduate school. In fact, he told me that this was a normal feeling. That helped me to see that I was not deficient as a scholar or as a person. Perhaps the rigorous task of getting a PhD at an elite university brought out those feelings in everyone.

The Office of Diversity and Inclusion also facilitated the mentoring process for graduate students of color through their workshops and retreats. During my time at Ohio State, ODI hosted a weekend workshop for underrepresented graduate students to discuss the specific issues we faced. We also received advice from faculty of color. Over the course of three days, graduate students attended workshops with faculty panelists that ranged from topics such as work-life balance, time management, advisor-advisee relations, what to expect on the tenure track, and more. This not only served as another way to learn valuable information, it gave us as graduate students the opportunities to get to know each other. We strengthened our bonds with one another there. Most importantly, we formed relationships with faculty who were outside of our discipline.

A second retreat, a writing workshop, was available only to PhD candidates. For a weekend, graduate students wrote and received formal feedback from faculty members. ODI staff paired graduate students with faculty members in a related field and tried to make sure those pairings were not advisees with advisors. This was an opportunity for students to form relationships with other faculty members and thus grow their network. Graduate students would have an initial meeting with their assigned mentor to check in about writing goals and concerns. Over the next two days, they would get feedback from their assigned mentor. In turn, faculty members could use the unstructured time to write and work on their own projects. These retreats were mutually beneficial and added an opportunity for PhD candidates to motivate each other to finish their writing goals.

Finding the right fit with a mentor is an important part of one's development in graduate school and it may take time. Should graduate students find that their advisor cannot play all three roles (advisor, mentor, and cultural translator), they should take initiative to find others who can fill them. If they find that they do not have a good relationship with their advisor, they can always find another one. Listening to a trusted mentor to navigate that process will make it easier. Mentoring is an integral part of how we support and produce other women of color scholars. When I told my advisor that I could not come up with a way that I would ever be able to repay her for what she has done for me, she replied that the way I could do that was to mentor other women of color.

Self-Care

As a Latina, I grew up with ideas that women took care of everyone else around them. Self-care seemed to be the antithesis of who I was supposed to be. A part of becoming a healthy woman of color scholar rested on accepting the idea that taking care of myself first, in many cases, was absolutely necessary for me to live a whole life and be successful in both personal and professional endeavors. I learned that I could only effectively support others if I was in a balanced and stable place emotionally, physically, and mentally.

Imposter syndrome, microaggressions, or guilt and sadness related to being away from family and friends are all very real aspects about being in graduate school. To reiterate, one of the most practical exercises organized by the McNair Scholars director was inviting graduate students of color to talk about these issues with us. Knowing the challenges that occur alongside graduate school preempted the shock and confusion that I watched other people endure when we started graduate school. More importantly, I learned coping mechanisms as part of my McNair experience. Through an introduction to counseling and yoga, Dolli Lutes gave us two tools that many of us utilized in graduate school.

Our McNair cohort joked that a meeting with Dolli often made even the strongest students tear up in her office. With her master's degree in Social Work and background in counseling, Dolli's innocuous weekly meetings were more than just opportunities to check-in. Dolli knew how to ask questions that made us face our insecurities head on. For example, we brainstormed ways that I could maintain contact with them while I was gone when I told her, through tears, that I worried about leaving my family. She pointed out my accomplishments thus far and my determination to keep challenging myself when I was concerned that I was not academically prepared for graduate school. With the stigma against openly discussing mental health in many communities of color, she gently opened many of our eyes to the value of one-on-one counseling as a means to taking care of ourselves.

Beyond the subtle attempts, she more overtly introduced the concept of mental and physical well-being through our required weekly yoga sessions. For many of us, this was a foreign concept and we resisted at first. As a task-oriented person with a strong working-class background, practicing mindfulness did not seem as if it would breed productivity. However, the twelve weeks of practicing yoga helped manage my anxiety, leading me to feel better overall and thus produce higher quality work. Not everyone continued with yoga, but we learned the value of self-care in our lives—in whatever form we chose.

From my preparation in McNair, I learned that self-care meant not letting graduate school control all aspects of my life. I tried a couple of different avenues to maintain that balance. Maintaining my physical well-being was a major aspect of this process. All-nighters, cheap fast food, and going out all the time were the norm in undergrad, but graduate school would require much more focus and care to keep up with the steady demand on one's time and mind. For stress relief, I took up rowing, boxing, spinning, yoga, and running at different points. Friends did the same or trained for half marathons and fitness competitions, among other organized activities. Group outings to the recreational center on campus complemented the many individual ways my group of friends approached our physical fitness. It also became a regular part of our routine, which helped foment the bonds we had with one another. Wellness goals gave us a measurable way to see our personal progress outside of graduate school. While in part this was to keep one's physical health intact, it was also to maintain one's mental health. If possible, graduate students should take advantage of waived block tuition and take one-credit exercise classes or other extracurricular activities like dance or art. This can ensure that graduate students have a healthy outlet for stress.

The most helpful part of my self-care regimen came in the form of individual and group counseling. I am thankful that Ohio State invested in its counseling services so that they were far-reaching. I saw an individual counselor at various stages in my graduate career. Having an unbiased person listen to fears and offer reassurance that these doubts are normal and surmountable can give peace of mind. Additionally, I participated in a counseling group for graduate students who were writing their dissertations. Drawing from graduate students from departments across the university, the sessions served as places where we could divulge our greatest fears about the job market. After the Great Recession of 2008, the number of academic jobs shrank. Knowing this, we worried we would never get jobs after putting this much work into our degrees. Though those conversations about fears could get overwhelming, we collectively brainstormed ideas about what we could and would do should the job market not go our way. Group counseling also served as a place to celebrate when we did, in fact, get our jobs. The celebration of each of these small milestones in our last year turned out to be a great source of support. These types of spaces can also be cultivated for people of color, specifically, and for people at varying stages of their PhD programs.

It is absolutely imperative that graduate students cultivate their own regimens of self-care and look for institutional support whenever possible. I was fortunate to attend a large, research university with ample funds to support their graduate students, but it was not the university who came up with the ideas of how we should be supported. Instead, it was graduate students themselves who asked for these services and planned them. If graduate students find themselves at a university that does not have support, I implore them to request these services and support from their administration. This is part of an ethical commitment universities should make to fully support the next generation of scholars.

Conclusion

McNair did not just change my life—it changed the life of my family and friends, too. My contemplation of going to graduate school opened up conversations with my siblings about pursuing advanced degrees. Within a year of starting my program, both my older brother and sister started graduate programs and before I finished my degree, my younger brother, also a McNair scholar, started one as well. All of this was completely unplanned given that none of us knew much about college until we were in it as first-generation students, but suddenly we became a built-in support team for one another. For a long time, our holiday gatherings entailed all four of us reading and working on our research in our parents' living room. Within months from now, however, all of my siblings will hold advanced degrees. Of my once-teenaged parents' four children, we hold three doctorates and one master's degree in fine arts.

It did not stop with just my family. At every opportunity, the four of us share the lessons we have learned and have watched friends and extended family members also pursue graduate degrees. While overwhelming to think about, I recognize that because I am a professor and my siblings hold master's degrees and doctorates, the educational experiences of the next generation of my family will be profoundly different than ours. For any women of color considering graduate school, my hope is that they recognize the challenges, evaluate what they are for themselves, and consider the impact they will have on their community in making the best decision that is right for them.

For staff and administrators at universities, I hope that they can see the value in investing time, money, and resources in women of color and preparation programs. I benefited greatly along with other women of color from having access to programs, workshops, and other resources that my university provided. Ensuring that we have mentors in faculty that look like us, programs that address our specific challenges as women of color, and funding for the solutions we offer to those challenges can make higher education a possibility for us. Many of the programs and initiatives that I participated in can be replicated with the proper financial support and leadership. If a university does not have a McNair Scholars Program, I encourage administrators to look into how they can begin one or replicate the programming discussed here. There will likely be more universities without McNair Programs as time goes on. Funding for it and other federal programs for underrepresented students is under constant threat of being eliminated.[17] When possible, administrators should fight to keep the federal government invested in this programming.

For those undergraduate readers considering graduate school, hopefully this essay has provided them with what resources they should seek. If their university has McNair, they should inquire about the application to the program sooner rather than later. If they do not have a program, the first step might include forming a relationship with a professor in a field in which they are interested. They can do this by taking classes in their major and informing their professors that they intend on going to graduate school. They can also check the office of student services to see if they have any GRE prep courses available. Undergraduate students should not be afraid to look across the university for research opportunities to build their skillset. Identifying other women of color who also have a goal of going to graduate school will be extremely helpful. Together, the women can form a community of people who can support each other through the application process. Most importantly, I highly suggest undergraduate women of color practice self-care regularly. Building healthy habits at the undergraduate level will only make the transition to graduate school easier.

For graduate students who have just arrived at their new institutions, please take time to identify an advisor, a mentor, and a cultural translator. Having these roles filled can save time and anxiety as graduate students try to situate themselves at a large, new university. They should seek out communities that can support them and that they would like to support in turn. If they are not there, graduate students can build them. They can also remind each other why it is they chose this path when their workload is heavy. I recommend fighting to maintain a life outside of graduate school. Work is like air—it will fill the space it is given. Finding recreational activities and alternative spaces to exist in can sustain graduate students emotionally throughout their journeys. Most importantly, women of color students should make their mental and physical health a priority. The stress of graduate school can take a toll on people in a number of ways. Seeing a therapist and a doctor regularly, even if it seems like there is not a lot of time for these appointments, can ensure that they will make it to the end of their degree with their mind, body, and spirit intact. I hope that when those graduate women of color are finished with their degrees and start their careers, they will be the professor that changes the life of an undergraduate woman of color. They will be the person who sees potential in someone who cannot see it in themselves. As women of color have done for generations, it is important to continue to pass along all they have learned to the next generation. This will ensure that women of color always have a place in academia.

Notes

1. Scott Willison and Emily Gibson, "Graduate School Learning Curves: McNair Scholars' Postbaccalaureate Transitions," *Equity & Excellence in Education* 44, no. 2 (2012): 53–168.

2. Gabrielle Vanessa Helene Johnson, "Time with College Graduates, Family Member Academic Level, and Time Spent in Federal Trio Programs as Predictive Factors of Higher GPA in Post-Secondary Education among Ethnic Minority College Students," Oklahoma State University, Doctoral Thesis, 2015, 19.

3. Nathan E. Bell, "Data Sources: Graduate Degree Attainment of the U.S. Population," *Council of Graduate Schools* (July 2009): 1. http://cgsnet.org/ckfinder /userfiles/files/DataSources_2009_07.pdf.

4. Mari Castañeda and Kirsten Lynn Isgro, *Mothers in Academia* (New York: Columbia University Press, 2013); Debra R. Comer and Susan Stites-Doe, "Antecedents and Consequences of Faculty Women's Academic–Parental Role Balancing," *Journal of Family and Economic Issues* 27, no. 3 (September 2006): 495–512; Gabriella Gutiérrez y Muhs, Yolanda Flores Niemann, Carmen G. González, and Angela P. Harris, *Presumed Incompetent: The Intersections of Race and Class for Women in Academia* (Boulder: University of Colorado Press, 2012); Emily Lenning, Sara Brightman, and Susan Caringella, eds., *A Guide to Surviving a Career in Academia: Navigating the Rites of Passage* (London: Routledge, 2011); Aretha Faye Marbley, Aliza Wong, Sheryl L. Santos-Hatchett, and Comfort Pratt, "Women Faculty of Color: Voices, Gender, and the Expression of Our Multiple Identities within Academia," *Advancing Women in Leadership* 31 (2011): 166; Ellen C. Mayock and Dominica Radulescum, *Feminist Activism in Academia* (Jefferson, N.C.: McFarland and Co., 2010); Lilliana Patricia Saldana, Felicia Castro-Villarreal, and Erica Sosa, "'Testimonios' of Latina Junior Faculty: Bridging Academia, Family, and Community Lives in the Academy," *Educational Foundations* 27, no. 1–2 (2013): 31; Eunkyong Lee Yook, *Culture Shock for Asians in U.S. Academia* (Lanham, Md.: Lexington Books, 2013).

5. U.S. Census Bureau, "Educational Attainment: Five Key Data Releases from the U.S. Census Bureau," U.S. Department of Census. https://www.census.gov /newsroom/cspan/educ/educ_attain_slides.pdf.

6. Willison and Gibson, "Graduate School Learning Curves," 156.

7. Johnson, "Time with College Graduates," 6.

8. Samesha R. Barnes, "McNair Scholars Program Prepares Students for the PhD Program in Materials Research," *MRS Bulletin*, 2015, 40 (6): 470–472.

9. Allison J. Scripa, Edward F. Lener, Cherly B. Gittens, and Connie Stovall, "The McNair Scholars Program at Virginia Tech: A Unique Model of Librarian Mentoring," *Virginia Libraries* 58, no. 3 (2012).

10. For more information on bias in standardized testing at various educational levels, see Ramazan Basturk, *"The Relationship of Graduate Record Examination Aptitude Test Scores and Graduate School Performance of International Students at the United States Universities,"* 1–15. *Proceedings of Annual Conference of the Mid-Western Educational Research Association, Chicago, 1999*; Committee on Maximizing the Potential of Women in Academic Science and Engineering (U.S.), and Committee on Science, Engineering, and Public Policy (U.S.), eds. *Beyond Bias and Barriers: Fulfilling the Potential of Women in Academic Science and Engineering* (Washington, DC: National Academies Press, 2007); Donna Y. Ford and Janet E. Helms, "Overview and Introduction: Testing and Assessing African Americans: 'Unbiased' Tests Are Still Unfair," *The Journal of Negro Education* 81, no. 3 (2012): 186; Phillip Harris, Bruce M. Smith, and Joan Harris, *The Myths of Standardized Tests* (Lanham, Md.: Rowman & Littlefield Publishers, 2011); Mary Hirschfeld, Robert L. Moore, and Eleanor Brown, "Exploring the Gender Gap on the GRE Subject Test in Economics," *The Journal of Economic Education* 26, no. 1 (January 1, 1995): 3–15; Adam J. Kruse, "Cultural Bias in Testing: A Review of Literature and Implications for Music Education," *Update: Applications of Research in Music Education* 35, no. 1 (October 1, 2016): 23–31; Mark J. Landau, Jeff Greenberg, and Zachary K. Rothschild, "Motivated Cultural Worldview Adherence and Culturally Loaded Test Performance," *Personality & Social Psychology Bulletin* 35, no. 4 (April 1, 2009): 442.

11. The term refers to the idea that we were imposters and feared being found out as not good enough.

12. A curriculum vitae is similar to a resume, but it is specifically for academia. It is a summation of one's educational experiences and academic production.

13. Kaplan and *Newsweek, Graduate School Admissions Advisor* (New York: Simon and Schuster, 2001).

14. Toastmasters International, "Where Leaders Are Made." *Toastmasters International.* http://www.toastmasters.org/.

15. This is a non–peer-reviewed journal published at Grand Valley State University for the purposes of McNair only.

16. Pilar Hernández, Mirna Carranza, and Rhea Almeida, "Mental Health Professionals' Adaptive Responses to Racial Microaggressions: An Exploratory Study," *Professional Psychology: Research and Practice* 41, no. 3 (2010): 202–209.

17. C-Span, "McNair Program Cuts," *C-SPAN.org.* https://www.c-span.org/video/?c4671411/mcnair-program-cuts.

CHAPTER 4

Stats and Stories

The Path of One Native Scholar in the Medical Sciences

Regina Emily Idoate

Stories help us teach and learn lessons. They serve as a conduit for passing on wisdom, guidance, and understanding from one generation to the next. Narratives, in particular, can actively involve storytellers and storylisteners in analysis and inquiry. Every semester, I ask students to share their stories with me. I usually start by asking where they are from. Some respond with one word—the name of a city, a state, or even a country. Very few mention their families or their cultural ties. I ask them to journal about where they came from to consider family history, their values, the languages they speak, the traditions they carry, and the environments that they came from.

Recognizing peoples' backgrounds and identities can help establish meaningful learning landscapes. I invite students to share lived experiences that represent the breadth of our diversity through journaling and open dialogue. In discussing our differences, we can create environments that respect diversity. My pedagogical practices are informed by my lived experiences of meaning making. For example, I could never make meaning of ballet. In fact, I am a ballet dropout. At six years old, I attended ballet class for one day and professedly quit, telling my parents that I didn't like the teacher telling me what to do. What I meant was that I didn't understand why I should follow the teacher. I didn't have a relationship with the teacher, and I couldn't see why I should dance the way a stranger told me to when I felt the music move me in another way. But, when my grandmother told me what to do, whether it be how to dance, what to wear, how to speak, or what to eat, I listened and learned, even if it wasn't how I felt like doing it, because she was my grandma. I was taught to value the knowledge and wisdom that my relatives shared with me. I could trust that my family had my best interest in mind.

Honoring Relationships

Building relationships with places and people is critical to teaching and learning. I have been guided by family and mentors to develop a sense of knowing what is the next right step for me and the more I learn about my family, my people, my history, and myself, the more I come to know my own roles and responsibilities in life. In my youth, I would not have been able to tell you that I wanted to be a professor when I grew up. My dad worked in construction, and he stressed the importance of an education, telling my siblings and I that we could do anything, and he didn't want us to have to "dig ditches." My mom, a registered nurse, worked in healthcare and emphasized what she did want us to have: passion, compassion, and a sense of pride. Both of my parents enjoyed their careers and taught me to do the same.

Where I come from is important to me. My great grandparents were born in "Indian territory," and much of my family is from what we know today as Rogers County, Oklahoma. I, however, grew up in Southern California. Will Rogers was closely related to my paternal great-grandmother, and he brought my dad's side of my family out West. My mom's side of the family, we know little about. She has told me that her grandmother died in her early forties, and although we know she is Cherokee, we know little more. What I do know is that I come from a long line of strong, intelligent, respectable Cherokee women including my great-grandmother, a teacher; my grandmother, an artist; and my mom, a nurse. Their skills and knowledge and wisdom that have been passed down to me are undeniably embodied in my life as an academic with research focused on medical humanities and teaching in the field of tribal public health.

Mentoring the Next Generation

Knowing where I come from helps me know who I am. Knowing who I am helps me know my purpose. And, knowing my purpose helps me know where I belong. My husband has a Basque saying, "Izan ziralako gara, garelakoz izango dira" / "Because of whom they were, we are. And, because of who we are, they will be." This idea aligns with other Indigenous perspectives, like that of Wilma Mankiller (first woman to serve as Chief of Cherokee Nation and leading advocate for Cherokee health) who explained that "leaders are encouraged to remember seven generations in the past and consider seven generations in the future when making decisions that affect the people" in the present.[1] Vine Deloria Jr., a leading Native American scholar and member of the Standing Rock Sioux Tribe, also explained that Native people are expected to hold the lives, memories, and hopes of their relatives close by teaching, learning, and protecting the generations that came before us, their own, and those to come.[2]

My parents passed on their ways to my siblings and me by teaching and protecting us. I am the middle child in my family. All three of my parents' children turned out to be academics, although all in different fields and with different life paths. My siblings and I all traveled a long distance from home and spent time living far apart during graduate school—in California, Arizona, Florida, Pennsylvania, and Nebraska. Graduate school can be alienating. It does not work family time into the academic calendar, and there seems to be an unwritten rule that anyone who takes a break is a slacker and less deserving of respect. But, family is very important to me. So, I was strategic about making every effort I could to go home. I scheduled conferences near home, created opportunities to apply my studies and experience to work projects at home, capitalized on break time, and got a Southwest credit card to use points to fly home more often. My brother, sister, and I also created work together and attended some of the same conferences to craft opportunities to reunite with purpose. Each year, we try to attend the Native American and Indigenous Studies Association conference (NAISA) together. This gives us time to reconnect, recharge, and return home in a sense. This also gives us time together to think creatively and mentor one another. Being home, both in relation to place and people, is not only restorative but also encouraging because it reminds me of where I am from and who I am and that drives my purpose.

My siblings forged the way and made earning a doctorate degree seem possible for me. My brother is an ecologist/herpetologist, professor of biology. My sister is a creative writer/poet, professor of English. Both earned terminal degrees before me and both have had tenure-track positions. I consult with them when making choices about school, work, and life. Their insight and humor are a constant support. My brother incurred massive debt during his doctoral studies, and he always said that I shouldn't pay for graduate school, steering me to get a job on campus (a graduate assistantship or teaching assistantship) to not only fund my graduate studies but also get me plugged into the campus community and developing marketable skills. I listened to him. And, when I was accepted to more than one school, I chose the one that offered me a graduate assistantship and tuition waiver. My brother also taught me to choose a school that had good teachers. Before he decided where to study, he went to the library, found the research that inspired him, identified the authors of those works and learned their institutional affiliations. He chose which universities to apply for by which professors would be mentoring him. I followed his lead in this and identified my mentors before I ever arrived to start my doctoral studies. I chose to work with a few professors who were recommended by friends, and they all helped me develop my program of study, find research opportunities, and jump through the hoops of academia. But, I found one mentor, in particular, who seemed to be able to support me in ways that the others could not. Dr. Michele Desmarais is a poet and scholar of Métis (Canada), Dakota (Spirit Lake Nation), and European descent who serves as a professor of Religious Studies and Native American Studies. I could trust that Dr. Desmarais would understand me not only because of where she is from but also because of her demonstrated purpose in my field of study.

Having a good mentor is critical. I have had many good mentors and they all have helped me in their own unique ways. I have done nothing alone. My mentors helped me plan my studies, pick my classes, identify constructive work opportunities, write a convincing résumé, apply for grants, manage grants, conduct good research, publish my work, and negotiate job offers. Dr. Desmarais stands out because no matter what I need help with, she is there to offer wisdom and bring me back to my heart with a clear mind.

I didn't have an Indigenous mentor until I completed my bachelor's degree and two graduate programs. Finding the right mentors may take some time and effort, but it is worth the investment. The process of finding the right mentor can be a bit grueling. I spent a lot of time surfing the internet to read through bios and research articles, view photos, and sift through contact information for scores of potential mentors before I found Dr. Desmarais. I recognize that I was incredibly blessed to find a teacher, mentor, and friend all in one. I don't think it is common for graduate students to have such a remarkable connection with and support from their mentors. The structure and administration of the Western Academy encourages faculty to avoid friendships with students. Indigenous perspectives do not honor these hierarchical understandings of position but rather, promote intergenerational and intersectoral relationships, appreciating the ways that we are all related. Dr. Desmarais treated me as an equal, with respect and dignity. She is loyal and stands by my side through all of the highs and lows of academia. Having completed my degree and landed a tenure-track position, I can say that my brother was right. Graduating without debt and with teaching and research skills was worth the effort of doing my homework on the institution, program, resources, faculty, and mentors. I highly recommend that all students considering graduate school reflect on the people and places that may potentially influence their work, studies, and life and be proactive in finding a good match.

In my doctoral studies, I pursued a PhD in public health at a medical center. Although I enjoyed the medical sciences, I needed to balance that with the humanities and social sciences. So, I sought out classes and mentors and lessons that my college could not provide me with. I took it upon myself to find unique and inspiring courses and professors. I looked to neighboring institutions and online programs to find Native American Studies and Teacher Education and Religious Studies classes that completed my education and inspired my own unique work.

Dr. Desmarais was not a faculty member at the institution from which I received my doctoral degree. But, she was able to serve on my committee. She patiently and generously met me for coffee every week for years to listen to me massage ideas until a solid research proposal finally evolved for my dissertation topic. She was never too busy to hear me or make connections and create opportunities for me to have *Aha! Moments*. She allowed my spirit and culture to factor into the research process and she defended it when other colleagues questioned Indigenous research methods. Having a professor that resonated with me on such a profound, almost genetic, level gave me confidence and determination. Her sustained, passionate commitment to my work helped me develop into the student, the professor, and the Native scholar that I am. I can't even imagine doing what I did without her. She guided me with such grace and the experience and the love and knowledge of a Native elder, sharing wisdom and knowledge and stories and laughter and meals. Within Native American communities, there is an abiding tradition of respect for elders and this is what I feel for Dr. Desmarais. Through stories, modeling, and engaged dialogue,

Dr. Desmarais taught me how to respectfully navigate my way through the world of Western academia. Beyond that, she gave me a family and a home in a state where I had no family and no sense of place. She treated me like her relation and welcomed me into her circle, showing me the importance and depth of a student-teacher relationship.

I ended up not only earning a PhD in Preventive and Societal Medicine but also a graduate minor in Native American Studies and a graduate certificate in Maternal and Child Health Epidemiology. Fellow classmates, advisers, and professors taught me the rules of the system, the loopholes, and the possibilities to modify programs of study. They empowered me to develop a multidisciplinary committee for a unique and individually designed program of an interdisciplinary nature within the medical sciences. This allowed me to study Public Health with specific focus on Native American health and wellness. Having the choice to work with Indigenous research methods and understand wellness through a Native lens allowed me the ability to feel good about my ways of knowing, being, and doing. And, when these ways came under question, having a mentor that backed me up at every turn was invaluable. I encourage all students to ask questions, ask permission, seek alternative possibilities, and find mentors who can support them in doing things in the ways that make them proud.

Celebrating

When I graduated with my PhD, the Native American Studies program held a graduation ceremony where I was honored with a stole, a blanket, a buffalo bone necklace, and an eagle feather. The eagle feather was the greatest honor, one that only doctoral graduates are gifted. The buffalo bone necklace was made by hand and placed around my neck by a member of one of my teacher's *tiospaye* (Lakota word for spiritual family). I was wrapped in a Pendleton blanket, *Raven and the Box of Knowledge*, that acknowledged all that I had learned and protected me as I began my journey in the workforce. The stole, a Western way of honoring students and identifying members of a specific group, had the logo for the Native American Studies program and showcased sacred Indigenous colors associated with the region (red, yellow, black, and white). In the graduation ceremony at the medical center, I chose to wear my Native American Studies stole. Stoles representing various fields of study (e.g., Occupational Therapy; Nursing) were a common piece that many fellow graduates were wearing. While in line, preparing to walk out and be seated on the stage, the staff supervising the graduation event objected to my stole, telling me, "you can't wear that." I attempted to explain the significance of the piece, but the supervisor proceeded to say, "put that away." No one else was asked to put away their stoles. Struggling to understand, I asked why she objected. After not receiving a reasoned response, I chose to disregard the staff member's requests. When she circled back around and realized that I was still wearing my stole, she said, "you need to go give that to your family." After being told four separate times that my regalia was unacceptable, I reluctantly took the stole off and tucked it away in my pocket under my gown. I felt fear, rejection, and anxiety throughout the entire graduation ceremony, at a time when I should have been feeling joy and pride. I was tormented by all of the reasons that I could think of to keep the stole tucked away and hidden or to take the stole out and wear it with pride. I was afraid of any repercussions and even considered the chance that they may revoke my PhD. When they called my name, trembling, I pulled my stole out of my pocket and placed it on in such a frantic hurry that one side hung blank, back-side-front.

My official graduation photos came to me with one half of my Native American Studies stole brilliant in color and design and the other, back-side-front, blank and pasty white. It is a picture that tells a thousand words. It is a picture that I hope no other student takes. I have shared my story and these images with the Dean of Graduate Studies and Vice Chancellor of Student Affairs to ensure that future students are not treated in the same manner. I now serve on the advisory and executive committees intended to support underrepresented minority students and I am working with the Senior Vice Chancellor for Academic Affairs to develop a policy that allows Native students to wear stoles, feathers, or regalia of cultural significance at graduation ceremonies. The common Native students' right to wear feathers, moccasins, beads, or any religious or culturally significant regalia, is something that we all need to be aware of and fighting to protect. Native American resilience is embodied when people come together and rally in resistance to assimilation and colonization. There are times that being a part of an academic institution calls us to acknowledge our history of genocide and loss of life, land, and culture. Representing our heritage, our families, and our community is important, even in an academic environment! In 2005, only 1% of the total American Indian/Alaskan Native (AI/AN) population earned a doctorate degree and this statistic has not changed in any significant way in this decade.[3] Wearing stoles and regalia is a demonstration of pride in who we are.

Being in a faculty position gives me a voice and platform to help establish policies and practices that protect and support future generations. Protecting students from experiencing graduation like I did is just one example of the many ways that I get to use my voice in support of Native people, land, and culture. Other examples include planting an Indigenous garden on campus, mentoring Native students in health science research, speaking up when curriculum is culturally insensitive or denying participation in proposals that disrespect Native ways of being. The Senior Vice Chancellor for Academic Affairs says that we need to question those who are using their voice to silence us or object to us because they have no more power to say "yes" than they do to say "no." We can't let fear of being judged, rejected, or disliked stop us from acknowledging the rights and power that come from being who we are and owning our purpose.

More than Ticking a Box

In a way, my graduation photo, that image, depicts the two worlds I walk in. Often times, it seems that the academy confuses matters even more, expecting Native students and faculty to play by the pasty-white rules but walk the stage with attractive colorful designs. On a regular basis, I am invited to speak on panels, present at various conferences, represent Native voices at political events, teach about Native American culture, help community-based fund-raising efforts, facilitate intercultural work trainings, lead underrepresented minority professional organizations, review journal articles, contribute to grant proposals, serve on strategic planning teams, and participate on diversity advisory boards and committee after committee after committee to represent the underrepresented. This is an honor. But, it is also baffling to me that the same university that denied me the right to wear a Native stole asks me to participate in these activities, sometimes solely because I am a Native American woman. The same university that would not allow me to wear Native regalia invited me to be a role model in a poster series for Native American leaders.

The difference between being a role model and being a "token" can get convoluted when people don't understand the reason why minorities are chosen to serve in these roles and when we are not recognized for all of the work we do. The "cultural taxation" from engagement in diversity-related service as a minority faculty may benefit my institution but is often "invisible labor" that is taken for granted and not acknowledged in the retention, promotion, and tenure process.[4] The National Institutes of Health (NIH) grants specifically encourage "individuals from diverse backgrounds, including underrepresented racial and ethnic groups" and "women," to apply for NIH support. As an administrator said the other day, "when you note that you are Native American, your application bubbles to the top." More often than not, without seeking out additional opportunities to teach or conduct research or speak to a crowd or attend an event, or join another committee, these opportunities come my way. I am sure that at times these opportunities surface because I am a woman and I am a faculty member enrolled in a federally recognized tribe. I would prefer to believe that it is because I have a strong work ethic and skills and insight and knowledge that makes me a valuable academic. I took it as a compliment when my Dean told me that when he hired me he had no idea that I was Native American. I have colleagues who are enrolled in federally recognized tribes who do not disclose their identity because they want to be known for their work in their field rather than their affiliation with a minority population.

Still, I always tick the box *American Indian/Alaskan Native* to represent my people. NIH grant proposals, school questionnaires, federal government papers, financial aid documents, Indian preference forms, profile inquiries, and random surveys all ask for this kind of demographic information. Although I am proud to represent our Native American population, I don't want to be used as a "token Indian" or give lip service to inclusion. Inviting Native peoples to "participate" without actually making space to honor their perspectives and decolonizing ideas and constructive input is something that I speak up against.

Academics with no genuine interest or respect for my people, my perspective, my principles, or my input have invited me to contribute toward grant proposals, film productions, and curriculum development as an attempt to demonstrate to funders, reviewers, and administrators a certain level of "cultural competence" or relationship with the targeted Native American community. I have been asked for consultation on a number of matters for which an Indigenous perspective was ultimately not respected. I have also sat in numerous meetings, presentations, and trainings where I was heard and I did contribute significantly, but I was never acknowledged. I harness these experiences as fuel to encourage me to remember to be respectful as I continue promoting Indigenous ways of being, knowing, and doing.

In my second year as a faculty member in a tenure-track line, I was invited to participate in the Chancellor's Native American cabinet meeting where the community was consulted on academic matters. In that meeting, I voiced interest in hiring more Native American faculty at the University, citing that in 2005, American Indians/Alaskan Natives accounted for the lowest percent (.5) of assistant professors in degree-granting institutions, compared to their White (78.6%), Asian (10.2%), Black (6.8%), and Hispanic (3.9%) peers.[5] The president of our Inter Tribal Student Council, a biology major, said that she had never taken any science courses that were taught by Native faculty or women faculty and specifically requested more diversity in STEM faculty on campus. At this same time, one of the STEM-related departments was contacted and asked about their interest in taking advantage of a recent notification that a few diversity tenure-track positions had become available for potential hires. In response to the inquiry, I learned that that particular department recently received their diversity goals for faculty and "0%" was listed as the goal for Native Americans, with the explanation that "because there are so few, it rounds to zero!" I may never understand what that means or how a number of human beings can round to zero, but I am certain of one thing, there is much more need than is acknowledged and my goal is much greater than 0%.

To address this, I contributed to a NIH grant proposal for funding to support Native American students in STEM fields. We were awarded the grant, and I now work with a number of colleagues across campuses to develop science education and research opportunities for Native American students. The long-term goals of this project, Youth Enjoy Science (YES), are to promote student interest in the sciences, foster a more science-literate public, and ultimately to increase the number of Native Americans entering health and science careers with a particular emphasis in engaging high school and undergraduate students in long-term research projects with the support of mentors. This program reaches beyond the classroom to include parents, community members, and elders in developing culturally relevant resources and a sense of excitement about participating in science and how it relates to life, culture, and tradition. I believe in the YES project and appreciate the community-based participatory approaches employed by our team of investigators. I make it a point to track student progress to be sure that we have not only stories but also the statistics to support future endeavors.

I also have worked with colleagues who were more interested in *studying* Native American peoples than *serving* Native American peoples. And, I have worked with colleagues that were more interested in focusing on the victimization of Native American peoples, rather than the power and strength and ability within our communities. In these situations, I am reminded of what Mankiller says, "cows run away from the storm while the buffalo charges toward it—and gets through it quicker. Whenever I'm confronted with a tough challenge, I do not prolong the torment, I become the buffalo." I am often contacted by principal investigators wanting to conduct research specific to Native populations. They meet with me to share their ideas, their agenda, and their specific aims, often without any consideration for the community that they are proposing to work with, or "on." I usually respond to these investigators by describing Indigenous research methods, decolonizing methods, or the principles of community-based participatory research as formative to such work. If nothing else, I consider our meeting a teachable moment.

Sometimes, this looks like resistance. There was one occasion when an investigator agreed with my methodology and worked with me for weeks on a community-based participatory research proposal. Just hours before submitting the proposal, after we had agreed on the ethical principles foundational to the project, after we had worked tirelessly for weeks to craft a strong proposal, after we had received letters of support from community members, that investigator altered the methodological approach and the specific aims in a way that compromised the community and my own personal research ethics. In the end, I could not support the revised version of the proposal and that investigator would not retract the last-minute changes made. And, I could not retract my values. I did not allow that grant proposal to be submitted. My voice was heard at the expense of the project. Although I may have lost precious research time to the weeks of work I dedicated to developing this project, I am grateful for this opportunity to take a stand and resist colonialism, Western paradigms, and disrespect for Indigenous worldviews. The struggle to balance personal and professional obligations in situations like this creates opportunities to spread a message that there is a certain level of respect required to work with Indigenous communities. I have witnessed people develop programs and proposals that, in an attempt to showcase cultural "competency," include Native languages, pictures of bison, or statistics about people who tick that same demographic box that I do. But, if they don't know the stories behind the numbers, the culture behind the language, the meaning of the images they are referencing in relation to the community and the people and the places of interest, then their attempts to be culture-based are, in reality, culture-blasphemy.

Being a tenure-track faculty member comes with responsibilities. I recognize that Native American academics have a responsibility to know Native American history and to be aware of and speak up against potentially harmful proposals in the name of research. It is our responsibility to pay attention to the details and work to promote care and respect for the communities that we serve. We also have the chore of reintroducing the concept of research to Native communities, to help Indigenous people see the good ways of research and develop a deeper understanding of science and its associated benefits. Some of our Native community is not receptive to or interested in research or the long-term vision of scholarly efforts because of many reasons, one of which is our history of abuse in the name of research. In fact, at times, I have observed how some consider grants as a quick fix that funds jobs rather than research and work toward long-term solutions and progress. Creating space to understand scholarly work and support Native scholars, in particular, is an important part of establishing our sovereignty. I pray for this kind of shift. I pray that more and more Native people will become expert scientists and researchers who support Indigenous ways of being and knowing and doing. It is our responsibility to work hard, share our stories, and track our progress for future generations. It is also our responsibility to pray.

Don't Forget to Pray!

Recently, I was approached by textile artists, Camille Voorhees and Victoria Hoyt, looking to cocurate an exhibition weaving intersectional feminisms in our local community. Their project, *Woven: Grounding Feminist Thoughts and Practices in Omaha*, included Open Floor events and Skill Shares. Voorhees and Hoyt invited Brittan Strong and I to cocurate an exhibit with a group of Native women who advocate for Native American education, health, and wellness in our community. Our art was created to respond to the question, *"What does it mean to be an Urban Indian Woman who advocates for Native health and wellness? What is your story?"* The works included poetry, paintings, performances, sculptures, dolls, shawls, moccasins, and more. The night of the opening, each of the artists presented her work individually. And, before the presentations began, I introduced the project—without prayer. I know better. Prayer is part of my DNA. I prayed while creating my art piece, I smudged the studio before anyone arrived and I prayed in private before the show, asking the Creator to be with us and work through us and bless the evening and all that came from it. But, I regretfully didn't acknowledge the Creator or respect my elders with prayer at the opening of the show. An elder approached me after the presentations and commented on how beautiful the show was and then asked, "But, where was the prayer? What about protocol?" I had no good answer. That evening, I couldn't sleep. I replayed the events in my head over and over. I asked myself why I didn't make the space for prayer, "where was the prayer?" The following day, I sent out an apology to all presenting artists for not starting the program with prayer. It truly pained my heart to know that we didn't all come together in that way before presenting.

When I ask myself, "*Why*, if I had prayed privately, I wouldn't pray in public?" The only answer I could come up with was that it was an academic event. But, I know better than that. That night, my worlds collided and instead of remembering tribal protocol, I remembered academic protocol and how the Western paradigm separates church and state, promotes inclusivity, argues against imposing personal beliefs on others, and suggests that prayer is a private, personal, individual activity. Academia can mislead us into forgetting our values. We become so aware of what is appropriate in academic culture, that we can forget our own worldviews and, at times, what is important in our own culture. I learned from that experience, that I need to stand up for who I am as tribal member not solely a faculty member. Some Indigenous scholars have argued that Indigenous knowledge and the reality of Indigenous women is inconsequential to Western paradigms.[6] I am not alone in asserting that my Indigenous values and worldview and my ways of being, knowing, and doing deserve respect, regardless of where I am or what role I am playing; artists and advocates,[7] researchers and educators,[8] and numerous community leaders have promoted similar ideas. I draw upon the knowledges, beliefs, behaviors, experiences, and realities of those who have traveled this path before me and demonstrate their influence in the framework for my work in teaching, research, and service.

I have learned that I can honor my values and worldview through the ways I do research and the ways that I teach. This is one of the reasons why I chose to work in academia. Before I finished my dissertation, I saw a job posting from an institution close to home serving Native Americans. I applied to ABD (all but done with my dissertation) and was hired as faculty in the College of Education. I was thrilled by the potential to become part of a vibrant campus community, to be surrounded by peoples and places so rich in culture, and to be able to plug into opportunities to learn and grow. I found, however, that even at a Native American–serving institution, Native faculty were few and far between. Before I arrived, there was only one full-time Native faculty member. That faculty member and I emphasized the need for more Native teachers, both in higher education and in secondary and elementary education programs. Recognizing the significant impact that Native mentors can have on individual students, the other Native faculty member and I worked together to write a grant proposal to support training more Native educators. We were awarded funding by the Department of Education's Indian Education Division. Unfortunately, because I was a very new faculty member and we were new to grant management and protocol, I allowed an administrator at the institution to take the role of Principal Investigator and control the funds. In effect, they controlled the whole project. We had limited power in seeing our proposed work through. Our hands were tied on purchasing resources, implementing programming, disseminating resources, providing student support services, and so forth.

While we fought to develop and maintain the grant projects, facilities showed up at our offices with a tape measure and began assessing our space. In that way, we were informed by campus facilities that the space (which was home to Native faculty and staff and students, the place where we all worked together, ate together, laughed together, gathered together, and held meetings) was going to be redistributed to other administration offices. Soon thereafter, we learned that not only had we been displaced but so had our funds. State auditors, subsequently, disclosed that administrators at the institution had embezzled hundreds of thousands of dollars that should have been serving students and faculty. I learned from that experience the importance of working hard to stabilize power relations and to take responsibility for keeping vigil and protecting the projects and people that I work with.

Teaching and Learning

Native people are natural learners who have studied and modeled, explored and observed, analyzed and hypothesized through lived experiences since the beginning. In this way, we developed and translated knowledge, wisdom, skills, and understanding into agriculture, architecture, mathematics, biology, language, and arts. We continue to do this. Below, I share examples of ways that I do this, promoting and employing Indigenous pedagogical approaches in a Western academia setting. The following

Seven Point Indigenous Framework for Native American Education is a modification from the Eight-way framework of Aboriginal Pedagogy:[9]

1. **CIRCLE-BASED:** I employ circle-based education to honor the many connections in the complex cycle of learning and allow intersecting processes to continuously develop and advance. For example, each class has its own circle of community and in the circle, there is no hierarchy. Instructors and students share the same level of regard and respect for one another. This includes interactions among educators and students, acknowledging students' interests, motivations, and points of view and encouraging student responsibility and autonomy. For example, I ask students for their input/feedback on the syllabus at the beginning of the semester and we work, together, as a class to integrate collective ideas into the original draft of the syllabus to modify the plan for the semester. A circle-based approach allows flexibility in the syllabus, assignment requirements, instructions, deadlines, and course topics to organically evolve and be adjusted to meet the class circle's needs. Together with students, I have created new rubrics, revised assignments, added and deleted class themes, and modified activities to better suit the circle.

I also try to create the platform for all voices in the room to be heard when engaging in open dialogue; I often ask students to form a circle and pass a talking stick or a rock around to share their unique responses to a prompt or question. Circle-based lessons do not have a determinate end; they can carry on from one activity to the next, one topic to the next, or even one semester to the next. The focus is much more on the process than any final product.

2. **STORY-BASED:** I employ story-based education to involve storytellers and story-listeners in active introspection as well as concept development and analysis. This approach to teaching makes use of personal narratives in sharing wisdom and transmitting knowledge and information. Stories invite people to share experiences and distinct points of view, learn from one another, and build relationships. They also convey messages and allow listeners and readers space to respond by solving problems, reasoning, and thinking critically and creatively.

Story-based approaches can involve everyone in the circle in open dialogue and/or reflection. As an example, I often share my personal stories, show films and short videos, and assign readings and poetry in an effort to make real-life connections to course topics. I also like to use Rose McGee's story circles teaching methods to encourage students to share their own stories.[10] I invite students to share stories in every medium, through journal writing, in open dialogue, and through the creation of art works/performances of all mediums.

3. **COMMUNITY-BASED:** Community-based education engages community members and scholars in the learning process together. In this approach, life experiences and values connected to real-world local contexts are made meaningful in relation to class topics. To employ this approach, I often teach service learning courses. In other courses, students complete fieldwork assignments that involve community-based learning through attendance at and participation in conferences, lectures, seminars, events, and activities. This allows for connections to be made between course subject areas in relation to local people, institutions, organizations, policies, history and cultural heritage.

One example of community-based education is evidenced in a summer service-learning class, *Traditional Ecological Knowledge: Native Horticulture*, which my brother and I taught. This class involved Native elders, fellow biologists, public schools' Native Indigenous Centered Education program students and teachers, university students, and master gardeners in establishing and maintaining campus-based indigenous gardens in schools across our metro area. In addition, we collaborated to create community-based culturally relevant curriculum and lesson plans associated with the campus-based gardens.

4. **PLACE-BASED:** I employ place-based education to help students contextualize information by connecting class content to the local environment. Traditional Indigenous ways of teaching and learning are instilled with a rich sense of place because people originally learned in relationship with their environment—the land, the water, the sky—and within the context of their culture, their communities, and their families as they explored, examined, observed, analyzed, imitated, and interacted with life. Creating opportunities for students to associate material covered in the classroom with places in the real world can bring learning to life. For example, when Native American Studies students were learning about Indian boarding schools, they took field trips to a boarding school within our region, Genoa Indian School. We walked the grounds from the railroad tracks to the school building and down the halls of the school. We sat in the desks that have remained, and we looked into the same mirrors where boarding school students saw their image. This was a very heavy and powerful experience, one that can only come from a sense of place.

Students have also visited with our campus' Indigenous garden that connects stories to corn, beans, and squash or medicine plants from tribes in all directions. When I teach Interventions in Health Promotion, students work with local organizations to understand and apply what they are learning in class in places outside of class.

5. **ART-BASED**: Arts-based education uses all of the senses to create symbolic meaning at the microlevel of context. I employ the arts in all forms when I teach. Students are introduced to symbols and images through various private art work (e.g., books, films, poems, beadwork, shawls, sculpture, paintings, drawings, pottery, dolls, and so forth) and public works of art (e.g., gardens, museums, installations, galleries, and so forth). Artistic skills, aesthetic processes, and experiences are developed and engaged to foster creativity, innovation, and learning in nonartistic disciplines and domains. For example, in a Native American Health & Wellness course, students worked with community members to create stuffed animal dolls (Buckskin Buddies) with symbols representing personal health and wellness stories. These artworks were analyzed for emergent themes and exhibited publicly along with related literature, speaking to the health disparities among our Native population.

6. **CONTEMPLATIVE-BASED:** Contemplative-based education honors the role of silence and mindfulness in learning. Educators are not required to lecture, to be the only voice in the room, to leave no space for contemplation, to have all of the answers. I require contemplative silent-technology free time at the start of each class to engage in centering practices and use silence to digest information, reflect in action and on action, and promote meta-cognition. In all of my classes, students are given five to ten minutes each class session to engage in contemplative practices such as silent meditation, journaling, drawing, deep listening, visualization, and so forth. I allow time to pause, to reflect, to listen, to notice. I invite students to approach learning in mindful and contemplative ways.

7. **PLAY-BASED**: Play-based education stems from a unique learning environment in which students feel safe and are encouraged to take risks, share their thoughts, and engage in physical and fun activities. Students involved in play activities are more engaged and, as a result, understand and retain the skills and knowledge they develop from a lesson. Play can involve hands-on kinesthetic learning and use all of the senses to explore, examine, and understand the world. I like to have fun while we learn.

Learning can involve playing games, laughing, engaging in hands-on activities, and taking risks. Play is my favorite way to start a semester. I usually circle around the room and ask each student to share two truths and a lie and involve the class in noticing details and cues to uncover the lie. I also play games to review for exams. The students bond in teams and learn from one another in a positive fun environment.

These approaches to teaching are not common. They are also not always acceptable and definitely not expected in higher education. But, if I am going to do what I do, I am going to do it in a way that resonates with me. When preparing for a visit with high school students in the Native Indigenous Centered Education program, some of my students asked "What do we need to know? What do we need to do?" and the president of Inter Tribal Student Council, who happened to be in my class, responded, "Just be honest. That's all they want." This rings just as true to me as I prepare syllabi, activities and lesson plans, research projects, grant proposals, and more. If I can "just be honest" in teaching, researching, and learning, I do what resonates with me, who I am, where I come from, where I am going, and how I see myself belonging to and supporting a community of Native American scholars and families.

Concluding Thoughts

Native scholars walk a path that is not very perceptible, pruned, protected, or populous. Approximately 2% of the U.S. population is American Indian/Alaska Native (AI/AN). According to the 2010 census, while 28% of the general American population hold a college degree, only 13% of AI/ANs have a college degree, with only 9% reporting to have a bachelor's degree completed.[11] An even lower percentage of AI/ANs (5%) have earned a graduate degree, compared to their White (11%) or Asian (21%) peers.[12] Individuals who have earned a PhD make up approximately 2% of the U.S. population. In 2006, of the total 56,067 doctoral degrees conferred, 230 were awarded to AI/AN students (.04%).[13] These statistics testify to the fact that becoming a Native American faculty member, serving in a tenure-track position, is a rare honor.

I hope that my stories encourage future generations of teachers and learners, reminding us that academic achievement is not accomplished alone. This essay critically analyzes forces that both stifle and support Native academics and encourages teachers and learners to engage in constructive discourse that questions the institutional processes that are destabilizing our learning communities. It is my hope that in sharing our voices, we will transform the dismal quantitative data and statistical reports into powerful stories that illustrate significant qualitative realities of Native academics. I hope that in sharing stories along my academic journey, I am able to demonstrate how Indigenous paradigms and Western paradigms have influenced my path as a student, an employee, a faculty member, and a family member.

Notes

1. Wilma Mankiller and Michael Wallis, *Mankiller: A Chief and Her People: An Autobiography by the Principal Chief of the Cherokee Nation* (New York: St. Martin's Press, 1993).

2. Vine Deloria Jr. and Daniel R. Wildcat, *Power and Place: Indian Education in America* (Golden, Colo.: Fulcrum Publishing, 2001).

3. Catherine Freeman and Mary Ann Fox, "Status and Trends in the Education of American Indians and Alaska Natives. NCES 2005-108." *National Center for Education Statistics* (2005).

4. June Williams, "The Invisible Labor of Minority Professors," *The Chronicle of Higher Education,* http://www.chronicle.com/article/The-Invisible-Labor-of/234098 (2015).

5. Freeman and Fox, "Status and Trends."

6. Karen Martin and Booran Mirraboopa, "Ways of Knowing, Being and Doing: A Theoretical Framework and Methods for Indigenous and Indigenist Research, *Journal of Australian Studies* 27, no. 76 (2003): 203–214.

7. Bill Kelley Jr., "Reimagining Ceremonies: A Conversation with Postcommodity," *Afterall: A Journal of Art, Context and Enquiry* 39 (2015): 26–35; Cristobal Martínez, Randy Kemp, and Lisa Tolentino, "Radio Healer," CHI'10 Extended Abstracts on Human Factors in Computing Systems, 3113–3116. ACM, 2010.

8. Linda Tuhiwai Smith, *Decolonizing Methodologies: Research and Indigenous Peoples* (London: Zed Books Ltd., 2013); Bagele Chilisa, *Indigenous Research Methodologies* (London: Sage Publications, 2011); Margaret Kovach, *Indigenous Methodologies: Characteristics, Conversations, and Contexts* (Toronto: University of Toronto Press, 2011).

9. Tyson Yunkaporta, Aboriginal Pedagogies at the Cultural Interface. Unpublished doctoral thesis, James Cook University, Australia (2009).

10. Rose McGee and Ann Fasco, *Story Circle Stories: Featuring Stories of Convening in Circle from 32 Diverse Voices and Visual Artists* (St Paul, Minn.: Belfry Books, 2014).

11. U.S. Census Bureau (2010). American Indian and Alaska Native Heritage Month: November 2011, https://www.census.gov/newsroom/releases/archives/facts_for_features_special_editions/cb11-ff22.html.

12. Freeman and Fox, "Status and Trends."

13. Ibid.

CHAPTER 5

Disciplinary Peripheries

A Conversation between Canadian Women of Color

Jenny Heijun Wills and Délice Mugabo

The last time I saw you, like every time I see you, I felt immediately sustained.

You see, when I am around you it's as if all of the pieces fall back into place, everything shifts just a little bit to the side, and there is this comfort that I don't take for granted because I know it's not an everyday kind of comfort. I think it's this mutual knowledge—a kind of no-need-to-say-it knowledge that we share. It pulls me to you. I imagine it pulls a lot of people to you. You hold on to me for a long time when we say hello, even the very first time we said hello, and I'm always a little bit surprised. I'm surprised because it is so different from the other casual embraces that are slightly more than a handshake but still less than the double-cheek kiss I know we are both familiar with. But you hold on to me for a long time and in those moments, when I start to draw back but you're still there, I think about the no-need-to-say-it knowledge passing between us that tells you to continue. Because I need it. I think a lot of us need it.

We need this kind of communication with women of color doing race work in and beyond academia in Canada because so often we exist in spaces that make us feel alone and distrustful. Academia has left me with the words *don't touch me* on the tip of my tongue. In the Anglo-Canadian universities at which I have attended and worked, I was the only graduate student of color and now faculty member of color in my departments. This mirrors the discomfort I felt growing up a Korean adoptee, the only family member and community member of color as well. There is no one with whom to share any no-need-to-say-it knowledge, and it is too much work to explain all of the back pieces to concerned allies and supportive colleagues. So, when you hold on to me, I feel resolved, secured by your embrace that despite all of the things that separate us, we are together.

That night that I last saw you, I was also unsettled. I wrote to you after about my discomfort over a comment made by a woman witnessing our long embrace. I didn't know her, and you didn't know her, but she was so enthralled by the image of you holding me, of me holding you, that she outrageously exclaimed a desire to take our photograph. What did she want to capture in that moment? What did she see? Was it the liberal fantasy of an Asian woman from the Midwest and a Black woman from Québec brought together as the embodiment of a successful Canadian multicultural moment in Toronto? I'm not sure. But I do know that she didn't see two scholars working—holding on to each other because it is in these reunions that we garner enough courage and energy to sustain us in our day-to-day lives in white, patriarchal academic institutions. She didn't see herself and that her fetishistic gaze was unwelcome.

What you said to me the next day when I brought it up has stayed with me. You commented on her nerve, on her gall to interrupt us in that way. You said you have often seen white people—and women in particular—immerse themselves in the private moments of women of color in a way that tells us that they are always watching us and that they feel entitled to evaluate whether our relationships are appropriate or not. This serves as an important reminder of the institutional and personal blockades that continuously interfere in the work that we are doing, the ways we are separated off into our respective corners, made to feel uncomfortable or weak for needing these kinds of relationships. It also operates as a motivator. It makes me all the more determined to hold on with all my might.

Where We're Coming From

Our contribution is unconventional for a number of reasons. As coauthors we have some very important mutual beliefs about the experiences of women of color in graduate school, but we also come from different racial communities, disciplinary trainings, and geographic and cultural locations. Our research overlaps only insofar as we are both interested in race work and the real, material antecedents to and consequences of this work. But we share a common concern over the relative lack of institutionalized Ethnic Studies programming in Canada—either as an interracial, interdisciplinary collaborative space or as the more focused organization of cultural programming, like Black Studies or Asian North American Studies—and its effect on students of color. Thus, in the following pages, we outline the context in which we are working in Canada, particularly in contrast to the ways that Ethnic Studies operates in the United States. We think about what it means specifically to be women graduate students of color who, because of the lack of institutionalized critical Ethnic Studies in Canada, have to work within non-collaborative disciplines that mirror the tokenistic multiculturalist idealism that characterizes approaches to race relations in this country and is used to dismiss our analysis in the first place. The historical difference in the ways that Ethnic Studies and students' responses in Canada and the United States played out are striking and the effects on graduate students, and particularly women graduate students of color, are notable.

There are two takeaways here: first, that recent scholarly efforts to converse with our American peers via an imagined continentalist Ethnic Studies does not fully attend to the fact that we work and teach within educational systems in Canada that are strikingly different than those in the United States. The second point is that WOC trained in graduate schools in Canada must take on the extra work of finding relationships outside of our institutions in order to care for ourselves and experience a kind of community perhaps more readily available to our sisters in the United States who operate within established critical Ethnic Studies programs. Yet, as contributors to this volume demonstrate, we also recognize that there are commonalities across North America of women of color seeking community outside of their institutions. This takes the form of extracurricular mentoring that does not end at graduate school, and it brings with it a series of blessings and benefits; but that, as the anecdote above reminds, needs to take place in unmonitored spaces where white scholars and "allies" are not policing the work that we do and the relationships we are building. Our voices are sometimes individual, sometimes combined, which reflects the ways that we have had to carve out spaces of political agency at times on our own and at times as a collective. We are not interchangeable but are complements to one another, writing and representing the no-need-to-say-it knowledge that binds us.

On History

First, some familiar background. In 1968, the powerful coalition of students of color from various communities known as the Third World Liberation Front galvanized important curriculum and ideological changes at American West Coast institutes of higher education—most notably San Francisco State College and the University of California, Berkeley—enacting the now-mythical origins story of Ethnic Studies in the United States. Organizing sit-ins, strikes, and protests, students (and some faculty) called for more racially equitable admissions policies, the hiring and retention of faculty of color, the diversification of curriculum beyond the Eurocentric lens currently deployed, independent control over race-related programs, and financial and academic assistance for students of color. As Karen Umemoto summarizes, they "fought for the right to determine their own futures. They believed that they could shape the course of history and define a 'new consciousness.'"[1] As tensions rose, protestors were arrested, suspended, and suffered brutality by both police and other members of campus communities. But in the end, departments and programs of Ethnic Studies were established as early as 1969 and, in many cases, continue to be maintained nearly fifty years later.

Simultaneously, in eastern Canada (and more specifically, the culturally and politically unique province of Québec), racism on campus first spurred student sit-ins at Montréal's Sir George Williams College (now Concordia University) and later culminated in a protest that resulted in riot squad police officers violently arresting nearly one hundred people and close to two million dollars in property damages.[2] In Spring 1968, six black students levied a complaint against a biology instructor, accusing him of assigning failing grades to all of the black students regardless of merit. Dissatisfied with the process through which administration attempted to address their charges, students organized various campaigns, including a peaceful sit-in on February 11, 1969. When the Royal Canadian Mounted Police were summoned by the university, violence erupted. Protestors served prison sentences as long as two years and the biology instructor was reinstated and the charges of racism against him were dropped. And while, as Samah Affan points out, the incidents at Sir George Williams resulted in notable social organization and spurred collaboration and activism within Montréal, they also note that many student unions and politicians either distanced themselves from the protestors or exploited the situation to further anti-Black ideologies.[3] Two years later, the college adopted University Regulations on Rights and Responsibilities and established an ombuds office (a neutral entity meant to lead conflict resolution) to represent students' interests.

We bring up these simultaneous expressions of students' frustrations over on-campus race relations, two of many, not to suggest that they are parallel situations—in fact the Sir George Williams protest is more akin to the armed standoff at Cornell University also in 1969—but rather to highlight the different outcomes of these events.[4] In the United States, the Third World Liberation Front resulted in institutional and curricular changes, whereas in Canada, the Sir George Williams College protests prompted policy change on how better to "deal" with race issues. Mostly, we are struck by this juxtaposition because now, over forty years later, we see the institutionalization of Ethnic Studies departments, which is of course different from area studies, across the United States and their relative absence in Canada—beyond a few research institutes, graduate programs, and minor options. Of course, we recognize that Ethnic Studies is not available across the United States, certainly not always as comparative and interethnic departments, but also that in some locations some ethnic groups are represented while others are not. However, the stark absence of this programming in Canada, the very unavailability of these fields, profoundly affects students, faculties, and communities outside of academia.

In 2015, the Critical Ethnic Studies Association held their annual meeting in Toronto, Ontario, at York University. As it was the third iteration of this conference—the first two being in Riverside, California in 2011 and Chicago, Illinois, in 2013—the choice to meet outside of the United States was appreciated, and the conference goals complemented the elected location. The mandate of the meeting was to "challenge colonial gender binaries; examine genealogies of anti-Black racism and colonial racial formations; and think about resistance and oppression transnationally, in ways that challenge western hegemony and the travels of racist and colonial methods."[5] Toronto offered an opportunity to dispel myths of Canada's race progressiveness. The conference brought together critical race scholars, and over the course of four days we discussed a number of meaningful topics. There was that no-need-to-say-it knowledge circulating, the safety of knowing that it was space where white supremacist elements of society and the academy could be challenged and likely subverted. People talked about the prison system, intersectionality, Palestine, issues pertaining to being mixed-race, decolonization, and education. We all talked together. We all shared the same vocabulary and at least understood one another's perspectives. But at some point it became clear that even though we shared the same terms, were at the same conference, collaborate and write together, publish in the same journals, and teach the same books, we were teaching and thinking about race and academia in differently organized ways—yet no one was talking about it.

The absence of Ethnic Studies as an interracial, interdisciplinary, and official on-campus collaboration alters the meaning of studying and teaching about race and ethnicity, not in the least because students have to piece together programs of studies in interdisciplinary ways that are sometimes incongruent with the degrees they seek. It also means that students might miss out on special events related to Race Studies that might be hosted by departments other than their own. The absence of an institutional space limits us to self-driven interactions between discrete individuals working at different, traditionally disciplinary departments in which teaching about ethnicity is enfolded within larger, race-neutral curriculum expectations. It becomes increasingly difficult for us to organize, create movements, and challenge the status quo when we are segregated by discipline and even faculty. Efforts to encourage the hiring of more faculty of color also are met with obstacles.[6] As Johnnella Butler notes, "When campuses refuse to establish procedures that require discipline-based departments to coordinate and conduct hires in areas that overlap with interdisciplinary departments, duplication then occurs in hiring and the long-established, familiar discipline-based departmental program is favored to teach courses on or reflective of 'race' . . . [As a result,] the content of Ethnic Studies thus remains marginal."[7] Perhaps this is no surprise as this model mirrors the very framework of Canada's well-documented policy of Official Multiculturalism. In other words, we're seeing nonprioritized spaces carved out for what Will Kymlicka has controversially called "group-differentiated rights" but with the understanding that united harmony favoring the comfort of the dominant groups is fundamental.

What we are saying is not new to those of us who work or study here, nor is it much of a surprise given the ways that policies like "official multiculturalism" are supported by federal funds and governmental offices. It is far from original to point out how official multiculturalism silences race-interested discourses by positing them as deviance in the face of cultural harmony. Multiculturalism also runs the risk of putting people of color on a pedestal in a classically tokenistic fashion as signifier for "diversity" that is incorporated within larger disciplinary and/or national-area institutionalized fields. But in its inception, as imagined by the Canadian Multiculturalism Policy of 1971, official multiculturalism was both a deliberate attempt to embrace the mosaic model of cultural diversity in contrast to the American melting pot—and an effort to formulate harmony between French and English Canada. Indeed, official multiculturalism mostly attends to the particular interests of a bilingual, bicultural state.[8] And while official multiculturalism *appears* to encourage people to celebrate racial and ethnic difference, there is a limit to these expressions as they are supported only insofar as they uphold the unity of the Canadian state. It is no wonder that this approach is most often embodied in tokenistic ways: folk festivals and cultural fairs.[9] Canadian multiculturalism is also an alibi that, for many Canadians, imagines racial tension as an American problem, and perhaps for this reason, institutionalized race-centered education here seems a nonpriority and policies like affirmative action for the most part seem unnecessary. This is in many ways compounded in Québec, and other parts of French Canada, where something akin to French Republican ideologies about difference disqualifies de facto both race and claims of racism. How much, then, is official multiculturalism paralleled in the non-institutionalization of Ethnic Studies in Canadian universities and colleges? Individuals are invited to represent or address race and ethnicity, but are segregated, dissociated, and tokenized within the disciplinary-based, race-neutral framework of the academy.

So, what has been the result of this failure to institutionalize Canadian Ethnic Studies? If we are doing race work in different contexts from our American peers, and if the establishment of a unique iteration of Canadian Ethnic Studies appears so daunting a task, how are we to become involved in these conversations? In the last couple of decades there has been a move to combine conversations about ethnicity by way of North American continentalism. Countless books and articles assume compatibility of American and Canadian ethnic experiences and representations, or at the very least use continentalism as a way of including Canadian examples in their largely American-centered studies. In the odd instance when scholars actually articulate the reasons behind this merging, they often focus on things like proximity, shared history, and to some degree ideological similarity, as Eleanor Ty and Don Goellnicht do in the introduction to their collection on Asian North American literature. They explain that, "one common element that runs through articulations of Asian American and Asian Canadian subjectivity over the years is the sense of 'otherness.'"[10] In another book, Ty acknowledges the important distinctions between Canadian and American perspectives but notes that "Asian appearance continues to play a large role in determining how others read our identities" and that those markers "shape, in ways both tangible and intangible, relations between Asian North Americans and non-Asians."[11] In other words, despite somewhat different experiences of immigration, economic development, and cultural expression, Asian Canadians and Asian Americans can be brought together and understood as Asian North Americans mainly because of their shared experiences of marginalization. We see similar gestures in other contexts. Robert Stepto famously understands black identity in a North American context in order to account for prerevolution-era historical experiences and for intracontinental migration both pre- and post-abolition.

Perhaps this move to envision ethnic North American, in lieu of solely American, identities is an attempt to include Canadians in ongoing Americentric conversations, to broaden political reach, to make visible Canadian perspectives by comparing and contrasting with our most proximate counterpart, or to remind that Canada is not the idealized, progressive space it often is mythologized to be. And while we agree with much of the work that has been done to highlight the similarities in Canadian and American experiences of race relations, we are struck by the ways that the contexts in which we teach about ethnic North American studies in our respective nations is less comparable. How can we understand this shift to continental Ethnic Studies, or cross-border Ethnic Studies, given the fact that the United States has a long and important history of institutionalized, collaborative, and interdisciplinary Ethnic Studies whereas, relatively speaking, Canada does not? It seems at least for now that this solution does not fully address the complexities of our differences nor the particular needs of faculty and students of color doing race work in Canada.

ONE RECOURSE: ON MENTORSHIP (DM)

Survival references our living in the context of what we have overcome. Survival is life after disaster, life in honor of our ancestors, despite the genocidal forces worked against them specifically so we would not exist. . . . Survival is a promise. It is not a promise that any university or nonprofit organization can make to me. It is a promise that I make with my currently breathing body to the ancestors who move through it. It is a promise I make in honor of the deaths that make this clarity not only possible, but unavoidable. Survival is a promise.[12]—Alexis Pauline Gumbs

When I reflect on the experiences of Black women and many women of color in academia doing race-critical scholarship, I often go back to the writings of Alexis Pauline Gumbs. As a queer Black feminist writer, poet, artist, teacher, and scholar she has decided to pursue her work outside of academia primarily among elderly queer Black women in the U.S. South, but also across various groups connecting transnational feminist theories with the needs of their communities. To the question of whether Ethnic Studies can change from within universities, Gumbs's approach illustrates how this is not a question of being in or out of academia but about expanding the geographies of this broad work called Ethnic Studies. Where knowledge is produced and disseminated is always in a movement that overflows rigid boundaries.

Gumbs's academic approach has long been part of Black people's practice in Québec primarily because Ethnic Studies in French-language universities is antagonistic to "doing race work," as you just put it, Jenny. Actually, the kind of Critical Ethnic Studies that this book is talking about, or the kind of Black Studies that students at Concordia University have been organizing for,[13] must not be confused with the various Ethnic Studies or Ethnic Relations programs offered at Université de Montréal, Université Laval, or UQAM for instance. In order to understand the difference and why Ethnic Studies cannot be idealized particularly in the context of Québec, I begin with a brief overview of how language politics and anti-Blackness are central to the legacies of colonialism and slavery in the province. From there, I expand on my own experience as a graduate student and the strategies that Black students and Black communities have developed in Montréal to add their brick to the intellectual structure of Black radical thought.

The French language has long been held as the cultural trait that most distinguishes Québec from the rest of Canada. That the French language in Québec requires "protection" is a false idea that continues to be propagated while Indigenous communities struggle to actually revive their own languages; so many young Black women, men, and children of Haitian origin do not master Creole fully, and large numbers of young Black continental Africans do not speak their mother tongues. Far from being a threatened language, French is a language of power and domination in Québec.

One of the key strategies in the erasure of anti-Blackness in Québec is to use language and ethnicity, rather than racial identity, in public discourses and related state-based practices. Ethnicity is the lens through which Québec officially documents, governs, and regulates Black communities. I would contend that ethnicity has been a generative category

for the Québec nation-building project because it allows the French Québecois to emphasize their francophone and Catholic origins as a cultural
marker of distinction from dominant Anglo-Saxon norms. In other words,
ethnicity, and the associated categories of language and religion, situate
French-Québecois national claims as straightforward claims for justice
against the historically dominant Anglo-Saxon population in Québec
and Canada. Given this, speaking in terms of race in Québec undermines
the entire basis of Québecois national aspirations, since it risks situating
people of color as the oppressed population and white, French-Québecois
people as the dominant population. In other words, Blackness as a refusal
of ethnicization troubles the ethnic basis of French Québecois distinction,
for it positions the latter within whiteness and therefore within a broader
historical trajectory of European imperialism and slavery. Québec nationalism, in this case, must evict "race," and especially Blackness, from the
body politic. "Ethnicity" steps into the void constituted by this eviction,
effecting how both white people and Black people are (mis)recognized in
public discourses and state practices.

Undeniably, Blackness in Québec, as in the rest of Canada, troubles
and contests how the nation defines itself. It is an "absented presence"
that forces one to reexamine the two slave-holding white settler societies.[14]
The ways in which white Québec society encounters Black presence as a
surprise or explains it as a contemporary phenomenon elides the history
of Black life in the country since slavery.[15] What Research Chairs and
white academics who work in Ethnic Studies in Québec (it is a field that
is confoundingly and overwhelmingly white in its composition) have
yet to contend with is that Blackness exceeds the space of Québec, and
therefore cannot be contained or eliminated.

Ethnic Studies in French-language universities in Québec does not
have a radical history but an assimilationist one. These programs were not
instituted as an answer to Black activists from the Sir George Williams
Affair, but rather emerged from a collaboration between white academia
and the Québec Ministry of Education and the Québec Ministry of Cultural Relation and Immigration. Since the 19th century, immigration in
Québec had been considered as a machination that would drown out
the French-Canadian population but starting in the 1960s the province
decided to take control over its "immigrant" population and use its political and economic contribution to advance the nation-building project.
Research groups, and later on undergraduate and graduate programs in
ethnic studies, served to construct a particular kind of knowledge about

the different "ethno-cultural communities" that compose Québec. These groups and programs evaluate their political orientations and integration into society, as well as pay particular attention on how much and how soon children in these communities absorb into Québec society. Language laws are specific to Québec and the one that has impacted people of color the most is Bill 101, a legislation that makes it mandatory for children of color to have their schooling in French. Anti-Black violence in Québec academia must therefore be situated in a context where education is a key battleground for assimilationist projects promoted by the state and white Québecois scholars.

The premise of Ethnic Studies in Québec is that this is a society with a "fragile majority," but as a liberal western nation, it still has to make room for pluralism.[16] Ethnic Studies as it exists today in Québec takes immigration as its starting point, whereas a *Critical* Ethnic Studies and Black Studies starts no later than with colonization and slavery. Black political consciousness of Québec's involvement in historical violence in the French Atlantic remains active. Historically, neither language nor geographical location spared Black people from the violence they experienced. Still, to state such a position in French-language universities in Québec can be very costly for Black students and Black professors alike.

During my undergraduate years, I realized how anti-Blackness is produced in Québec as part of its nation-building project.[17] My experiences with anti-Black racism in the French-language university system in Québec led me to put an end to my studies. I eventually decided to pursue my graduate education only when I found the program and the professor that could best support my research at a local English-language university. My story is quite similar to that of many Black students, whether from high school or university, who abruptly end their educational trajectory due to anti-Black racism in the Québec education system. Many, if not most, Black postsecondary students who seek to pursue a research topic related to Black life end up having to migrate from the French to the English-language public university system or leave the province to study elsewhere.

In Québec, university students are permitted to write their exams or submit their papers in French even when they attend an English-language institution. That possibility has at times factored in the decisions of French-speaking Black students who migrate to the English-language university system. That said, universities are more than spaces of learning; they are also spaces where important societal ideas are produced. I left my previous institution because as a space that exists to produce ideas about Québec's "distinct nationhood" and associated myths about Québec's innocence in the history of slavery and continued settler colonialism, it was impossible to develop and nourish a language to research and study counter-histories and modes of relating to Québec. Put more simply, I left the French-speaking university because students, faculty, and administrators alike each had their own ways of telling me that I was trespassing on their institution. One of my professors once declared to the class that postcolonial theorists were all "racists." Another professor warned me that he would fail me if my final paper applied theories of feminists of color.

As Black students at French-language universities in Québec, we are therefore in a double bind. We are consistently reminded that we are out-of-place and prohibited from engaging with ideas and scholars who allow us to reflect on the anti-Black racism we experience. Since anti-Blackness is global, we cannot escape it. When French-speaking Black students leave Québec's French-language universities it is not because we idealize other universities as being magical places devoid of anti-Blackness. English-language universities offer us a certain access to race-critical, decolonial, and radical Black theories and approaches. Unfortunately, the very anti-Blackness driving French-speaking Black students and scholars to the English-language university system ensures that there continues to be an almost-complete lack of race-critical work about Québec in French.

Finding and creating spaces, within or outside those universities, serves not only to break isolation, but most importantly it literally gives us room to breathe and think creatively. Writing about her experience as a student in the 1960s on a predominantly white campus, at a time when there was no Black Studies program, Patricia Hill Collins explains how important it was to have spaces of disobedience. Part of her strategy in graduate school was to juxtapose her scholarship and her practice by teaching at a community school. She writes, "I gave myself the Black studies education that I couldn't get in school and I shared it with others as I got it. . . . I read many books that are now considered classics in Black studies, but because there was no Black studies at that time, I didn't know they were classics."[18] Hill Collins's experience resonates with many Black students in Québec today as they too have had to create a space for their own intellectual survival. When I think about the common experience of young Black scholars in this province, I start with the fact that so many of us have never had a Black teacher or professor. All of the Black scholars whose work I have come to study were first introduced to me via my activism or online community. Practically none of them have been translated to French.

During the summer of 2014, a small group of us founded the Black Intellectuals' Reading Group in Montréal to gather Black students and others who were eager to read and engage with the work of radical Black scholars. We assign a reading every month and meet to discuss, challenge, and learn from one another. Participants engage the work of some of the most important radical Black scholars of this era, namely Joy James, Katherine McKittrick, Tiffany King, Frank Wilderson, and Fred Moten, as well as canonic figures such as Sylvia Wynter. Among those who come are Black undergraduate and graduate students, as well as a few nonblack faculty. We insist on providing ourselves with the Black studies education that none of the five universities in the city offer. The Reading Group has become a space that allows for mentorship, community-building, emotional support, cultural nurturing, strategic planning, and organizing.

The notion of a Black person's right to bodily safety and to mobility, still radical today, has been an important practice of the reading group since its inception. Rachel Zellars, cofounder of the group and a scholar of slavery and education in Québec, writes about how important it has been to instill in her three children the idea that they have a right to be safe in their bodies and to be wherever they are.[19] Our monthly meetings take place mainly at Concordia University, ensuring that university campuses in the city are not solely places that stifle and punish race-critical thinking and Black intellectual life. The classroom in which we meet monthly temporarily takes the shape of our creative engagement. When we transport our meetings outside of those walls, we bring our intellectual engagement, thereby imprinting new possibilities in the space itself.

Universities in Canada are invested in the national multicultural myth of this place, where racism is nonexistent. Intellectual spaces that would provide the means to elaborate and research a reality that is contrary to that myth are difficult to institutionalize within that framing. The circulation of Black ideas across borders has always been a source of anxiety for white settler, slave-holding societies. The powerful example that the Haitian Revolution set for slave rebellions throughout the Americas in the 19th century has been well documented. Vilna Bashi Treitler has pointed out that in Canada and the United Kingdom, policies toward Black immigrants have been more restrictive due to apprehensions about Black people igniting "social unrest."[20] It is no coincidence then that radical Black intellectuals represent a potential breech of civility—a disruption in how this country imagines itself—that universities in Canada, and particularly French-language universities, must contain.

Nonetheless, students and scholars of color have continued to find creative ways to learn from one another across time and space. In Québec, bilingual scholar-activists often translate to French important race-critical articles for students who cannot read English, while through social media others circulate summaries and commentaries in French of talks given by American and British scholars of color. This type of intellectual activism seeks to break the isolation of French-speaking Black people in Québec and to provide possibilities to participate in the intellectual discussions and exchanges that are happening in the rest of the Black Atlantic. Other Black students and scholars among those who are bilingual continue to manifest their discontent through choosing to pursue their academic careers and research in the rest of Canada, the United States, or the United Kingdom. There is such intensity to forms of anti-Blackness in Québec that it often means that prominent members of the Black community must leave their families and communities in order to research and write about their histories and generate ideas that will bring about the visions they have for futures.

Speaking at a panel on "Discourses of Race: The United States, Canada, and Transnational Anti-Blackness" in February 2015, art history professor Charmaine Nelson explained that one notable reason why there is so little known about the history of slavery in Québec is because there is no institutional space on campuses, such as Black Studies programs, through which students could receive the proper training and knowledge to conduct such difficult archival research. Radical Black feminist activists in Montréal have been working to fill the void that Nelson and others have highlighted. The Third Eye Collective is a Montréal-based group led by Black women, mainly graduate students, whose work focuses on sexual and gender violence against Black women. The Collective places critical race feminism, transformative justice, and critical trans politics at the center of our organizing. Since the founding of the group, an important part of our work has been to trace and reconstitute Black feminist history in Québec. Two of the primary research projects that we currently have underway include: a) building an understanding of the violence against and punishment of enslaved Black women in Québec; and b) documenting the impact Black feminist intellectuals (e.g., Louise Langdon-Little in the 1920s and Mariame Kaba in the 1990s) on Montréal. Mentoring Black female students in Black feminism has been critical to the intellectual work of the Collective. Core members continue to identify significant gaps in the official Black history of Montréal and Québec and collaborate with students as they do archival and ethnographic research and develop Black feminist historical analyses of their findings.

The Black Intellectuals' Reading Group and the Third Eye Collective teach us that Black students, scholars, and communities have the capacity to develop their own intellectual spaces that mitigate against the persistent anti-Blackness characterizing our society. We can certainly "do" intellectual work without a Black Studies or Ethnic Studies program. The desperate need for the two activist-intellectual groups introduced in this section speaks to the fact that universities in Québec are deeply embedded in a politics of anti-Blackness. As such, these two groups manifest the radical and transformative possibilities of race-critical activist scholarship.

On a personal note, the Black intellectual community that I found and created in Montréal continues to shape my scholar-activism. It has taught me not only the importance, but also the central role that ideas play in understanding our history and imagining our future. Because of my trajectory in the Québec education system, creating spaces of community learning and research outside of institutions has become an important part of my activism. Being an active member of the Black Intellectuals Reading Group and the Third Eye Collective, studying the work of radical Black thinkers as well as researching and archiving the history of Black communities in Québec has motivated and propelled my graduate research. Finding grammar to name my experience and that of other Black girls and women across the (French) Black Atlantic has been central to my activism and has grounded my academic work.

Another Solution: On Autocritical Approaches (JW)

I felt the loneliness of being the only student of color in my graduate cohort(s) immediately. It was not just during my PhD class, which was so small that I was one of only three. It was also in my MA and during my undergraduate studies. In undergraduate classes, difference and isolation were easier to accept because, as an English literature major, none (except a handful) of texts had any ethnic representation in the first place. Darkness as silenced and separated was naturalized through the very works we were studying. In graduate school, however, as course work leaned more toward contemporary literatures, more toward interesting writers of color, a different discomfort appeared. I was either expected to be a leader in seminar discussions on race-based issues or, alternatively, would need to sit passively while (mostly) white women voiced their supportive-albeit-liberal multiculturalist views. Within my particular discipline and at the universities that I attended, neither the work nor my colleagues reflected my experiences.

Being a woman of color compounded some issues as I felt the typical frustrations of white feminism, intersectionality, and the burden of representation that Audre Lorde discusses at length. She notes that those of us who are understood as part of "some group defined as other, deviant, inferior, or just plain wrong," we are "expected to stretch out and bridge the gap between the actualities of our lives and the consciousness of our oppressor."[21] Further, "whenever the need for some pretense of communication arises, those who profit from our oppression call upon us to share our knowledge with them. In other words, it is the responsibility of the oppressed to teach the oppressors their mistakes."[22] I was lucky to have a faculty advisor who was also an Asian/Canadian woman writing about Asian/American and Asian/Canadian literature and the other woman of color in the department as part of my thesis committee. My supervisor herself reflects on the connections and differences in Asian/Canadian and Asian/American literary contexts, noting that in Canada, "We have been invisible, yet we have been branded as 'visible' and minor" through the catchall nomenclature of "visible minorityhood," whereas "in the United States, racial politics plays out slightly differently" insofar as, "up until recently, American media and culture tended to refer to white and black America, leaving Native Americans, people from the Middle East, Southeast Asia, South Asia, and Mexico out of the generalization about races."[23] Yet I still felt lonely and uncomfortable, like I was an annoyance, or curiosity, or poster child in the department. In fact, at one point during my studies, the university took formal photographs of me to use in their marketing. I reassured webpage visitors of campus diversity that I myself did not feel.

Now, five years after accepting a faculty position in a different Canadian university I still feel lonely. I have very supportive colleagues both within my department and across the university, but I am again the only person of color, and therefore also the only woman of color, in my department. I am thankful to be able to do the work that I do (I was hired specifically to teach critical race studies, which provides me with hope in some ways); however, I wish there was a more visible Ethnic Studies presence on campus. I wish that I didn't have to catch myself daily trying to locate other people of color at university events, counting us, sometimes being the only one. I wish that I wasn't always asked if I think Asian students are "taking over the university" due to the conflation of Asian/Canadians and Asian/Americans with people from overseas, or if they are making it too difficult for non-Asians because of a false model minority stereotype that discounts the diversity of Asian ethnic communities, experiences of immigration, and so forth.

When I was a student, I also turned to a group of people off campus who were active, mobilizing, and thinking about their identities, because my graduate school peers were privileged enough not to have to do this work. Mostly I worked in the restaurant industry where more racial and class diversity appears. I left my campus early in my PhD and moved to other places where I could build relationships with other women of color. My first stop was in Boston, where I lived with a woman whom I had known my whole life in southern Ontario. She was a recent graduate and was working at Harvard at the time. I spent my Fulbright linked to different departments at the university. Although we came from different disciplinary backgrounds and racial communities, we shared a common knowledge of what it felt like to be women of color in graduate school. Her informal mentorship was the greatest part of that sojourn. It is also in Boston that I met a series of Korean adoptees collaborating and working together for social justice and to build a visible community. This amazed me because until that point I had met so few people in the same circumstances as me. The interactions with other Korean adoptees underscored the commonalities between us—growing up in predominately white communities as one of the lone people of color.[24] They inspired me to travel to South Korea and challenge myself and I am thankful for them.

As a transnational adoptee, my racial context is always weighted with paradoxes of loss and gain, alienation and proximity, self-fashioning and imitation. Whiteness, for me, was normalized beyond the typical ways it impresses itself upon all of us. Without friends, family, or community of color, I was first encouraged to imagine myself as honorarily white and then disrupted by the realization, as an adult, that not only was this a fallacy, but that white approximation was not something I desired. I grew to be ashamed of my whiteness and white adjacency. I threw myself into critical race scholarship to address those anxieties, but here too I was left without grounding. These conundrums have been explored in meaningful ways in the United States, with scholars and writers, artists, and activists critically engaging with the racial discomfort many transnational and transracial adoptees experience. In Canada, where we are even more regionally segregated, where official multiculturalism often silences or dismisses resistant antiracist critiques, these conversations are not yet being had in a truly audible way. Unsurprisingly, therefore, transracial adoptee subjectivity is not fully attended to. I wrote about myself and people like myself in my thesis, which was uncommon in my program. It was challenging work. It was emotional and messy work because I underwent a birth search at the same time and reunited with my Korean family. But I had people around me by then, in Boston, in Seoul, and later in Montréal who held on to me and with whom I shared a knowledge that did not have to be spoken aloud. Of course, that doesn't work for everyone, and there were serious challenges involved. Reunion brings with it a host of other anxieties and griefs, some of which are exacerbated by the general tone of melancholia shared by many adoptee peers as they, too, struggle with birth searches and reunions.[25] The emotional labor of autocritical work can be stalling. I am also fully aware of the privilege that enabled these movements to different countries and spaces as well as maybe the personal circumstances that already made me feel disconnected from people and place and perhaps allowed this kind of movement in the first place. I had never felt anchored to any particular space but felt like I was floating amid various cultures and communities, none of which fully accepted me. But it is the people that I met on these travels and the work that I did while I was away from the institution that, in the long run, made it all worthwhile.

These days I've turned to other kinds of writing because scholarship about transnational and transracial Asian adoption still somehow feels empty or performative. My memoir, *Older Sister. Not Necessarily Related,* has become a venue to highlight my relationship with other Korean adoptees, with other Korean people, including my first family. Two beautiful things have emerged from this work. First, I've found an outlet for imagining my racial identity that complements my academic career (in the Department of English, creative writing qualifies as research at my institution) in a way that is more comfortable and allows me an open space for challenging systems and people that I feel do harm (including academe). Second, I've been embraced by a community of Black, Indigenous, and people of color (BIPOC) writers who, while they cannot relate to my position as an adoptee, validate and see my life and my work in ways I've never before experienced. This kind of work is still autocritical but recalibrating outside of more traditional forms of knowledge output has finally opened an opportunity for being a Korean adoptee in Canada outside of what was previously prescribed.

Conclusion

The things that have helped us through the challenges of being isolated in graduate school were relationships . . . and relationships that celebrate unconventional ways of learning. They are in contrast to the sterile, unmessy, nonemotional, rationalism of our peers that are often celebrated. To those watching, it might be questioned as non-rigorous, too personal, too subjective. But this is an important part, we think, of challenging the institution because academia has already proven itself to be dismissive of discomforting methods and ideas, and in its refusal to acknowledge and institutionalize Ethnic Studies it has somehow opened a door for these kinds of alternative forms of knowledge production. It is about taking control of our bodies, bodies that are watched so cautiously, and using them to prop up the other women of color we love, as visible markers of our collaborations and to hold on to one another. To hold on for a long, long time.

Notes

1. Karen Umemoto, "'On Strike!' San Francisco State College Strike, 1968–69: The Role of Asian American Students," *Amerasia* 15 (1989): 3.

2. Both the protestors and the police maintain that the other party was responsible for most of the damage, which included the destruction of the university's computer lab and fire.

3. Samah Affan, "Ethical Gestures: Articulations of Black Life in Montréal's 1960s" (Master's thesis, Concordia University, 2013), 113.

4. On April 19, 1969, members of the Afro-American Society at Cornell University occupied Willard Straight Hall (WSH) to protest the lack of Black Studies on campus and university responses to recent acts of on-campus racism (including the burning of a cross outside of the Black women's co-op building the night before). When members of a white fraternity tried to disrupt the protest by entering WSH, and after a physical confrontation, Black protestors elected to protect themselves from future attacks by arming themselves with rifles. Despite the success of negotiations in changing university policy and programming, images and rhetoric emerged framing protestors as aggressive, violent, and "uncivilized."

5. Critical Ethnic Studies Conference, "2013 Online Conference Schedule," *Critical Ethnic Studies Association*, September 11, 2013, https://www.criticalethnic studies.org/content/2013-online-conference-schedule.

6. See special issue of *Canadian Ethnic Studies* 44, 2 (2012): "Racialization, Race, and the University."

7. Johnnella Butler, Introduction, *Color-Line to Borderlands: The Matrix of Ameri-*

can Ethnic Studies, ed. Johnnella Butler (Seattle: University of Washington Press, 2001), xxii–xxiii.

8. See Eve Haque, *Multiculturalism within a Bilingual Framework: Language, Race, and Belonging in Canada* (Toronto: University of Toronto Press, 2012) for an excellent analysis of language and race in the development of Official Bilingualism and Canadian Multiculturalism.

9. Himani Bannerji, *Dark Side of the Nation: Essays on Multiculturalism, Nationalism, and Gender* (Toronto: Canadian Scholars' Press, 2000).

10. Eleanor Ty and Donald Goellnicht eds., *Asian North American Identities: Beyond the Hyphen* (Bloomington: Indiana University Press, 2004), 3.

11. Eleanor Ty, *The Politics of the Visible* (Toronto: University of Toronto Press, 2004), 8.

12. Alexis Pauline Gumbs, "The Shape of My Impact," *The Feminist Wire* (blog), October 29, 2012, http://www.thefeministwire.com/2012/10/the-shape-of-my -impact/.

13. Dragonroot Media, "Bring Black Studies to Concordia: Interview with Anthony Mclachlan and Shannon Gittens-Yaboa," *Dragonroot Media*, https://hannah besseau.wixsite.com/dragonrootmedia/single-post/2016/11/08/Bring-Black-Studies -to-Concordia.

14. Peter James Hudson, "The Geographies of Blackness and Anti-Blackness: An Interview with Katherine McKittrick." *The CLR James Journal* (20): 235.

15. Katherine McKittrick, *Demonic Grounds: Black Women and the Cartographies of Struggle* (Minneapolis: University of Minnesota Press, 2006).

16. Marie McAndrew's work, *Fragile Majorities and Education: Belgium, Catalonia, Northern Ireland, and Quebec* (Montréal: McGill-Queen's University Press, 2013) is an example of the white victimhood discourse prevalent about Québec.

17. Broadly stated, Québec politics since the 1960s have been profoundly influenced by the debates on the future of Québec's place in Canada. The option of seeking independence from the rest of Canada has been most popular with the white French-speaking population. That said, what remains across all political tendencies in the province is the idea that Québec is a distinct nation within Canada.

18. Patricia Hill Collins, "That's Not Why I Went to School," *The Disobedient Generation: Social Theorists in the Sixties*, ed. Alan Sica and Stephen P. Turner (Chicago: University of Chicago Press, 2005), 110.

19. Rachel Zellars, "Violence That Never Was: Black Organizing, Violence against Women, and Black Women's Activism," paper presented at the American Studies Association conference, October 8, 2015.

20. Vilna Bashi Treitler, *Survival of the Knitted: Immigrant Social Networks in a Stratified World* (Stanford: Stanford University Press, 2007).

21. Audre Lorde, "Age, Race, Class and Sex," *Race, Class, and Gender: An Anthology*, eds. Margaret Anderson and Patricia Hill Collins (Boston: Cengage, 2015), 15.

22. Ibid.

23. Eleanor Ty, *Politics of the Visible*, 4–5.

24. Eleana J. Kim, *Adopted Territory: Transnational Korean Adoptees and the Politics of Belonging* (Durham: Duke University Press, 2010); Kimberly McKee, *Disrupting Kinship: Transnational Politics of Korean Adoption in the United States* (Urbana: University of Illinois Press, 2019); and Kim Park Nelson, *Invisible Asians: Korean Adoptees, Asian American Experiences, and Racial Exceptionalism* (New Brunswick: Rutgers University Press, 2016).

25. Elise Prébin, *Meeting Once More: The Korean Side of Transnational Adoption* (New York: New York University Press, 2013).

CHAPTER 6

For Those Considering Medical School

A Black Queer Feminist Perspective

Nwadiogo I. Ejiogu

I've started and stopped writing about my medical school experiences several times over the last three and a half years, feeling the contradiction of desperately needing to express myself and share my story with the overwhelming fear of showing my vulnerabilities to those who decide to pick up this collection, flip through its pages, see my contribution, and decide to read it. But something about my journey to medicine felt special and unique, and perhaps represents a narrative that has yet to be offered; specifically, an experience yet to be made intelligible through an unapologetically black, queer, feminist lens. All the frustration and anger I felt in medical school had to be transformed into something new, beautiful, and generative. It couldn't all have been for nothing, right?

What made medical school different, and in some ways more difficult, than graduate school was how inaccessible it felt. When I considered medical school, I didn't know of any African, queer, femme, chronically ill, feminist, activist doctors. Don't get me wrong; I had great physician mentors, some of which were badass women of color doctors. And I had many relatives in my extended family who were doctors. But I never quite felt like I found what Laverne Cox calls my "possibility model"[1]—doctors who shared some of my identities and politics and commitments to love, manifested as social justice. This chapter came out of a desire to ensure that aspiring medical students with a radical perspective see themselves reflected within the medical profession. It's a piece that draws on several scholarly legacies. The title is a direct reference to Dean Spade's "For Those Considering Law School," which offers a critical perspective of graduate legal studies.[2] The content of this piece evokes sacred texts offered by black queer feminists, like Audre Lorde and Barbara Smith, with an accessible list format inspired by Crunk Feminist Collective's "Back-to-School Beatitudes: 10 Academic Survival Tips" and online magazine *Everyday Feminism.*[3] This essay focuses simply on tips for surviving. I can't discuss thriving because I was far from thriving in medical school. What I can talk about is how I survived, and I can invite folks who thrived throughout this process to share their experiences. Words strung together about my experiences in medical school, along with 15 lessons I've learned along the way. On paper. In print. Forever. Hope this is helpful!

1. Research financial support early and often.

A significant barrier to training in medicine for marginalized communities (black, indigenous folks, people of color, trans and queer folks, poor and working-class folks, disabled folks) is money. Capitalism is intrinsic to allopathic medicine. Western medicine is referred to as the medical-industrial complex (MIC), which speaks to how capitalism (in concert with white supremacy, ableism, and cisheteropatriarchy[4]) ensures that only certain kinds of people have access to healthcare, medical knowledge, and training.[5] An overwhelming number of medical students have class privilege and come from middle- to upper-class families.[6] Capitalism has been propped up by histories of enslavement, colonialism, and racist immigration practices. Statistics show that Black, Latinx, and indigenous communities, as well as white poor folks, are underrepresented in medicine.[7] These trends are in no way a coincidence but instead illustrate how systems of privilege and disadvantage are institutionalized and are as foundational to the practice of medicine as the patient history and physical.

Several resources available to help students navigate these financial barriers include:

- Federal Student Aid (FAFSA)—Find out more on how to navigate student loans by visiting the AAMC FIRST website for more resources and advice.
- National Health Service Corps (NHSC)—Offers annual Loan Repayment Programs and Scholarships for students and clinicians pursuing primary care fields.

- Internal School Scholarships—Most schools will offer scholarships internally to students. Make sure to check in with your Student Affairs office to learn more.
- Work-Study Positions—These positions allow medical students to gain some income tutoring, supporting ancillary staff, or conducting research.
- External Scholarships—These include the Indian Health Service Loan Repayment Program, Point Scholars Program, Women in Medicine Scholarships, AMA Foundation Scholarships.

2. Hold relationships, community gatherings, art, and practices that mirror and affirm your identities as sacred—they'll nourish you and take priority, always.

Emotional support throughout medical school is just as important as financial support because of the vast amount of focused attention, time, and energy required while immersed in a very conservative environment. Before I started on this journey, I wish I had reached out for emotional support to people I could envision holding me through the tougher times of my training. I regret not telling these close friends and family members about the rigorous demands of medical school and that I needed more support than usual. I regret not intentionally checking in with folks to see if they had capacity to take on a more supportive role within our relationship during medical school. Help prepare these loved ones by telling them that your relationship won't always be one-sided, but that you'll need extra love, care, and patience during the next few years as you adjust to the demands of this new academic endeavor.

This request for emotional support should be accompanied by a commitment to ensuring that these loved ones and community spaces take priority, no matter your schedule or how many exams you need to study for. The academic work will always be there, even after you carve out time to build meaningful relationships with those who sustain you. For me, this looked like skipping an afternoon of classes to attend the first black queer feminist event that I came across in my new city. After moving to a city unfriendly to queer people and people of color and adjusting to the shock of training in medicine, I desperately needed a space that saw me and, to a certain extent, got me. I didn't regret missing class. I was glad I prioritized connecting with like-minded folks. By playing hooky, I made important relationships and built communities outside of school. These communities felt more like home and helped keep me grounded and accountable to a larger dream for justice that connects us.

3. Try to conserve your energy and focus on the humanity of folks who replicate racist, sexist, fatphobic, transphobic, homophobic, ableist, or classist sentiments.

The thing that took me the longest to get acclimatized to during medical school wasn't the long hours of studying, the obnoxious smells in cadaver lab, or the wobbly transition into seeing patients in my third year. It was becoming accustomed to hearing folks say racist, classist, transmisogynist, ableist, fatphobic, and heteronormative things without, for the most part, being critiqued or challenged.

When I started, I made a vow to address every single statement: To speak up and try to make change, in hopes of helping my colleagues become more culturally competent doctors. I gently pushed back on a professor who argued for limited reproductive technologies for incarcerated women. I offered alternative perspectives on offensive terminology, such as the r-word and the use of the word *gay* as an insult by classmates. In an LGBT student group, I frequently brought up the importance of Kimberlé Crenshaw's theory of intersectionality, after several LGBT health panels composed of all-white and mostly cis gay male speakers.[8] This practice of addressing oppression and inequity at all times lasted for a little over a semester, until I noticed that this took a serious emotional toll while also distracting me from the reason I was there in the first place: to learn. I spent so much time teaching my classmates an Anti-Oppression 101 curriculum, I barely had enough time to work on memorizing the coagulation pathway or the roots, trunks, divisions, cords, and branches of the brachial plexus.

It was from this experience that I learned to pick my battles and conserve my energy. Survival *is* resistance. Just existing in these spaces not made with us in mind *is* radical. You might have this urge to respond to every offensive comment and change the minds of all your colleagues, professors, and administrators. But, make sure you're getting what you need from this experience. One of the other ways the white supremacist, imperialist, cis-heterosexist, ableist, transmisogynist MIC works is by asking marginalized communities to take on unpaid work. It's okay to take space and not engage with every problematic statement or practice. That being said, there are certain circumstances where silence is complicity in violence—violence being broadly defined to include the harm done by structural practices of social, political, and economic marginalization. For instance, I have class privilege and part of my responsibility is addressing classist attitudes, statements, practices, and policies at school. As a person who benefits from the marginalization of poor and working-class communities, engaging people with class privilege is an important act of solidarity. What I found the most difficult in these instances is ensuring that I'm not speaking on behalf of folks who are from a particular marginalized community. Folks who live the experiences often marginalized in dominant culture are always best to speak to these nuances of power. My role as an ally is to lift up these voices and help address harmful statements.

4. Some lectures/classmates/professors/ attendings/staff will be oppressive. Try your best to anticipate triggers and take care of yourself.

Many of us entering medical school are survivors of violence that is racialized, sexualized, transphobic, classist, ableist, or medicalized in nature. As students training to be physicians, we yield a considerable amount of privilege within the MIC. However, that doesn't mean we automatically become immune to the ways in which allopathic medical environments can trigger histories of individual or transgenerational trauma. It is for these reasons that I learned how to better take care of myself during these moments at school or in a clinical setting, so I could be present for folks seeking care. For instance, in my first and second years of medical school, I had a professor, Dr. Williams,[9] who taught a clinical skills course. After having several lectures and one-on-one encounters with him, I knew that we had very different perspectives on politics and disagreed on some fundamental aspects of approaching care work. He was the kind of professor who, when female students complained about getting sexually harassed by patients, would respond by telling us our skirts were too tight or our blouses were too low cut.

I was conflicted when I saw in the syllabus that he would teach us how to do a pelvic exam. While I hoped that it would be handled professionally, I made sure to put together a self-care plan, just in case it ended up being triggering. This care plan consisted of bringing a grounding object to help me stay in my body, sitting close to the door in case I needed to leave, writing down my feelings, and planning a debriefing session with a friend. I am glad I prepared this plan as the lecture was unprofessional, sexually inappropriate, and triggering. As the years in medical school passed, I became better at anticipating and preparing for tough and often traumatic situations with faculty or patients. This made my overall experiences at school much less distressing.

5. Self-care is not selfish.

Audre Lorde says, "Caring for myself is not self-indulgence, it is self-preservation, and that is an act of political warfare."[10] This quote is especially important within the context of medical school. In the culture of medicine, it's easy to believe that taking a break, using spare time to connect with friends, or missing a meeting means you're "lazy" or not "passionate enough." Not only is this work culture ableist, but it's also harmful and can lead to burnout. Carving out space to engage in rituals or practices that replenish you is essential. I took every opportunity I could to dance, experience art, travel to visit friends and family, write, binge-watch shows on Netflix, and prioritize pleasure. Developing these go-to self-care practices early on is important. Burnout is, unfortunately, a continuous and consistent threat to wellness throughout medical school and residency, and it can even reach into clinical practice as an attending.

6. If you have even the slightest curiosity about therapy—try it out!

After struggling through my first year of medical school with the support of well-intentioned but ill-equipped loved ones, I made the intentional decision to see a therapist at the beginning of my second year. I sought professional help for a number of reasons. One, I was terrified by statistics on high levels of depression, anxiety, and suicidal ideation in medical students and wanted to nip any buds of distress early.[11] Two, I knew the threat of burnout would be an ongoing issue in my career. I sought to build up my toolkit for resilience and regeneration. Third, as a rising second-year medical student, I knew the highest stakes exam of my medical career, the first United States Medical Licensing Exam (USMLE Step 1), was on the horizon.

With these factors in mind, I began the process of shopping for a therapist. I picked the brains of trusted friends who I knew were in therapy, and I determined what I was looking for in a therapist. The qualities and skills important to me were having a therapist of African descent or a therapist of color, one who understood Black queer and disability justice politics and had an overall anti-oppression framework, and someone who could hold me accountable without tearing me down. Simply put, I desired a therapist with a shared vision and commitment to radical social change.

I was lucky to find a therapist who fit these requirements. After the first Skype session, I immediately wished that I had started therapy earlier. I felt seen and that my therapist "got it." Got me. She understood my complaints about the MIC, experiences of femme-phobia, and worries of being accountable to community in my future role as a physician. During our sessions, little to no time was spent on educating her about terminology or anti-oppression theory. Instead, we invested our time in working through the myriad of issues medical education brings up, developing coping strategies, and affirming the validity of these experiences. Working with a therapist whom I trusted because she understood my cultural and political contexts made medical school much more manageable. I can't recommend it enough.

7. Since I brought it up, let's talk about it— USMLE Step 1.

Let me first start by saying: It's going to be ok. Step 1 is an eight-hour computer-based exam designed to test the knowledge of the basic science curriculum learned in the first two years of medical school. It is a high-stakes exam, as the results of this exam largely determine which medical specialties you can successfully match into for your residency training after graduating medical school. It is an important test, but it's not the only metric that matters. An early, strong USMLE Step 2 score can often compensate for a lower Step 1 score. Therefore, try to be gentle with yourself as you prepare for Step 1. While it seems like new resources come out for these board exams every year, the key resources that helped me through it were: Doctors In Training (DIT), Pathoma, Firecracker, First Aid, Practice NBME's, Goljan Audio, and UWorld. A study plan made at the beginning of the second year of medical school (MS2 year) was also helpful. Making this study plan early ensured that I could carve out at least two months of study time dedicated to Step 1.

To confirm that these resources are still relevant, make sure to check the USMLE forums on Studentdoctornetwork.com. This site can be overwhelming, as most folks on it are anxious med and pre-med students; however, it's one of the most up-to-date and helpful resources out there. Those are my key pieces of advice for this exam, and I wish you all the best in getting over one of the major hurdles of medical school.

8. "Pimping" is mistreatment.

Within the Western medical world, pimping is an extreme form of the Socratic method. It's the archaic practice of singling out a medical student in front of their peers to ask them a tough, stump-worthy clinical question. It's a controversial learning strategy in medicine that was popularized in a 1989 *JAMA: The Journal of the American Medical Association* article by Frederick L. Brancati.[12] Some physician-educators view pimping as a valuable learning tool whereby the application of stress deepens medical knowledge of medical students and residents.[13] Others see the practice as outdated and a "primary driver of student humiliation" and mistreatment.[14] Some physicians also take a more balanced stance on the issue and call for the end of malignant forms of pimping while preserving the use of the Socratic method to diagnose learners, teach, and emphasize important clinical points.[15]

The medical term *pimping* has been traced to a German word *Pümpfrage*, which loosely means "to question." However, this derivation is not widely known. The word is commonly associated with sex work. Consequently, the ways medical students, residents, and physicians talk about pimping often parallel negative stereotypes about sex work, sex workers, and agency. Harmful and discriminatory attitudes toward folks engaging in sex work are pervasive in clinical environments. Needless to say, this term makes me uncomfortable, so I will be referring to it from now on as "grilling."

In my experience, grilling is not only hierarchical and outdated, it also creates an environment of fear, competition, and shame. This environment is counterproductive to learning and can be harmful to the well-being of students and residents. It's a practice that often gives attendings permission to express their biases. Medical students who are introverted, struggle academically, or hold marginalized identities tend to be singled out more often and experience a more virulent form of teasing if they don't know the answer.

I remember my first experience of the confluence of grilling and systems of oppression. It was during rounds on my surgery clerkship. We were following up on patients who were either being evaluated and optimized for an upcoming surgical procedure or were being monitored post-operation. I made a mistake in listing off fluid ins and outs for a patient who was on postoperative day one after a laparoscopic appendectomy. The attending physician was infamous for using a particularly malignant form of grilling. He asked me for the ins and outs again. Not realizing I had made a mistake in recording the units, I repeated the same values. In response, he scoffed and asked me if I thought the nurses were trying to kill the patient. Realizing I had made an error, I replied, "Of course not. Let me double check the patient's chart." In a squeaky, exaggeratedly high-pitched voice, the attending physician mockingly repeated, "*Of course not. Let me double check the patient's chart.* It's stupid mistakes like these that get patients killed." I immediately shut down. I went to the protective place every survivor has inside themselves that allows them to disconnect from a harmful environment. I couldn't hear what he was saying anymore. I was floating outside of my body and witnessing what was happening from a safe distance above. Luckily, two classmates started the process of looking up the correct values, shortening the time we sat in awkward silence. For the rest of the afternoon rounds, I was partly in and out of my body. The times when I was in my body, I concentrated on not crying or yelling or doing a bizarre combination of both. I was scared and no longer open to learning.

I know grilling is mistreatment, based on this experience and the countless other times I witnessed my classmates abused in the name of medical education. Naming this practice as abusive allows us to resist internalizing the feelings of shame or embarrassment and instead understand it as a problem within medical education that needs to be changed.

9. Note all the times you've witnessed physicians working cooperatively or hierarchically with nurses, staff, and other healthcare providers.

I started this practice of professional self-awareness in my third and fourth years of medical school. These are the years when medical students spend the majority of their time in clinical settings. During this period, I started writing down moments when I felt proud to be among physicians who took seriously an egalitarian approach to patient-centered care. I also made note of moments when doctors reproduced medical hegemony and perpetuating legacies of medicalized violence and domination (i.e., stereotypical attitudes and bias in medicine, inadequate informed consent, histories of medical experimentation and forced sterilization) toward marginalized communities. My intention was/is to capture some of my thoughts and feelings about the culture of medicine before it became "natural." Ideally, before I was indoctrinated into the cultural norms of the MIC.

I remember working with another attending physician during my Obstetrics and Gynecology rotation at an affiliated hospital. While working with him, I added extensive notes to my list of what *not* to do as a physician. I remember distinctly feeling like he was a walking, talking example of all the things I did not want to replicate as a physician. He was insensitive. He mocked patients outright. Without consent or explanation, he ignored a patient's questions to him in favor of teaching medical students about clinical presentations of chronic illnesses. He was overtly offensive. For example, statements like "an overcorrection of perineal lacerations incurred during childbirth will lead to happier husbands" reflected a misogynist outlook that centered male pleasure over the well-being of a woman postpartum.

Suffice it to say, I considered this attending to be everything antithetical to a good, competent clinician. The exception, however, was when it came to taking care of one specific patient. Let's call her Ms. Jones. This patient was unique. She and her mother were both delivered by this attending. Since then, he delivered all three of her children and was scheduled to deliver her fourth child. I noticed immediately that their relationship was different. It was a peculiar mix of unprofessionalism and decades of built-up trust and rapport. Every offensive or crude statement uttered by him received an equally harsh and insensitive comment from Ms. Jones. After a rally of condescending comments, mixed in with sound medical recommendations, the pair shared laughter, a hug, and a mutual contentment with how the appointment went. To Ms. Jones, this doctor was a good—scratch that—great doctor. His style worked for her, and she trusted him. Now this didn't erase all of the ways I felt that he lacked compassion and reproduced potentially harmful power dynamics in his interactions with patients, but it did make me see the model he provided as complex. The clinical vignettes I witnessed during my time with him were not *all* bad. I was able to appreciate and take note of moments of true, meaningful connection.

Ultimately, it's my hope that as my complicated list of clinical dos and do nots grows, I will take the time every year to revisit these reflections and try my hardest not to replicate interactions that feel classist, ableist, fatphobic, or otherwise oppressive, while also modeling my clinical encounters after the moments I saw physicians doing the most good for the people in their care.

10. Ignore folks who swear the only way you can be a *true* activist physician is by specializing in certain fields, such as family or internal medicine.

First, I want to be clear: I'm not throwing shade at primary care physicians (PCPs). The PCP has a vibrant and important role within healthcare. The field attracts folks who have a more social justice–based framework in comparison to those who choose other specialties because primary care doctors often have an analysis that explores health inequities as they relate to access to care. However, I want to push back against the assumption that the only way you can have any kind of activist credibility as a physician is by specializing in primary care. Training in a surgical subspecialty, pathology, or radiology does not automatically put you in the category of a problematic capitalistic healthcare provider. At the same time, specializing in a field like family medicine does not automatically absolve you from replicating hierarchical power dynamics. I didn't realize these views were out there until I started hearing comments like "the more you specialize, the further you are from doing community-based transformative work" and "make sure you become a family doctor and not one of those doctors who overly specializes and becomes out of touch with community organizing work." I heard these and similar statements so frequently that I internalized them and often felt hesitant telling folks in activist spaces that I wanted to go into a surgical subspecialty.

This changed when I met a brilliant trauma surgeon who worked and lived in Oakland. I asked her how she found ways to make her commitments to social justice matter in her everyday work as a surgeon. She talked to me about her involvement in community organizing efforts to stop gun violence and how her activism was informed by the number of times she performed life-saving procedures on young black and brown youth with gunshot wounds. To her, the connection between social justice and her career as a surgeon was obvious. She performs critical surgical procedures on young healthy black and brown boys because of the high rates of gun violence in Oakland. It only made sense, she said, to get involved in changing the need for her services in the first place.

Meeting her and other social justice–minded doctors helped me push back against the many colleagues, mentors, and acquaintances who were telling me that my background in health equity research and community organizing meant that I was destined for primary care. It allowed me to pursue *all* my interests, while also dreaming of ways to make social justice matter in seemingly "bias-immune" medical and surgical subspecialties.

11. Your suspicions of medical mission trips are valid.

Missionary medicine is ubiquitous. When I was in medical school, it felt like medical or dental students were crowdfunding every month for an upcoming mission trip to Uganda, Guatemala, or another country in the Global South. However, I went to a historically black college (HBCU), so medical mission trips took on a different meaning. Mission trips were a way for many second-generation children of African immigrants, African Americans, and other folks of African descent to explore a uniquely diasporic sense of home. For example, on a mission trip to Kenya, one of my classmates had the opportunity to reconnect with extended family for the first time. This mission trip allowed her to reverse the familial fracturing caused by histories of colonialism and present realities of global capitalism. Systems that make traveling across continents to often unwelcoming environments one of the few viable options for economic stability for black and brown people. It was within this context that I saw medical mission trips as beautifully subversive—a way for African diasporic subjects to use a seemingly innocuous Western phenomenon to heal wounds caused by global inequities.

It was only when I began interviewing at predominantly white institutions that I was repeatedly confronted with the ways that medical mission trips are made possible by colonial tropes of a white savior amid backward, diseased, racialized Others. Most interviews had a PowerPoint slide dedicated to "Global Health" opportunities. On display were usually pictures of smiling white residents surrounded by black and brown children. It was the image that haunted many folks of African descent, including myself growing up. This image is a shorthand explanation of, and excuse for, histories of colonialism.

And while it's more complicated than a simple dichotomy of "mission trips organized by Black providers equals good" and "those organized by white providers equals bad," we know that relationships across privilege are complex and can be both problematic and transformative. Projects that resemble an international development model, such as medical mission trips, tend to socially and economically benefit folks with the most access to power. It allows folks from the Global North to ease any guilt they have about economic inequities. When added to one's curriculum vitae, these international health experiences can translate into new employment opportunities. While unskilled, unprepared healthcare providers are developing their social and professional capital, these medical mission trips further deplete the resources available to those who are most marginalized, by redirecting services and jobs to orient short-term volunteers to their new vacation spot. For all these reasons, and more, medical mission trips remain an ineffective way to bring about real structural and long-term social change.[16]

12. Resist the urge to diagnose everyone (including yourself).

Medicine encourages us to use a medical framework to understand the world. Often, this comes from a well-intentioned love of putting medical knowledge to use. Clinical diagnoses can be used as a type of conversational shorthand. And sometimes, use of this diagnostic framework can stem from an honest fear of losing clinical acumen if we don't apply it at every opportunity. Regardless of the underlying impetus, many medical students develop a reflex of diagnosing people. Friends, family, and strangers are all fair game. We base these diagnoses on anything we can observe: verbal expressions, character traits, social interactions, the way people walk, how someone holds a cup, anything we can readily appreciate. We do it, often, without thinking. It's an unconscious reflex. And if we're among folks with a similar medical background, we share and discuss these reflex diagnoses. We agree, disagree, or offer an alternative diagnosis, saying things like, "No, I actually don't think it's Graves disease because his adrenergic symptoms aren't paired with exophthalmos. I'm more suspicious of cocaine use." It's like a game. A game that we play with each other—frequently. It often leads to laughs, debates, and an overall sense of camaraderie and shared understanding.

But this unwarranted application of our diagnostic skills is not useful, and more importantly, it can replicate harmful viewpoints. This practice reproduces what critical disability studies scholars name "the medical model."[17] It represents a way of legitimizing normal and constructing disability as an individual "problem" with a disabled person's body that needs to be cured, fixed, or managed by medical providers. Disability justice activists have instead critiqued societal norms that marginalize, devalue, and stigmatize sick and disabled folks, especially those from a cash-poor background, from trans and queer experiences, and from communities of color. The act of pathologizing folks at any and every chance further solidifies a colonial medical framework that experiences people primarily as a laundry list of clinical problems. It doesn't allow room for a critique of ableism, centering decolonial perspectives on the body and healing, or understanding sick and disabled people of color as fully human.

So how do we shift this prevalent habit? What has worked for me is first becoming aware of this diagnostic reflex and why it's problematic. Instead of relying on this medical shorthand, I consider whether my observations are relevant in the first place, and if they are, whether I can describe personality traits, behavior, or movement instead of using a diagnosis. Additionally, at the core of this change is an understanding of medical knowledge not as "truth" but as a language. This is a different language that I can utilize when I'm in the medical provider role, but also a language I can put away when it no longer serves me or the folks around me. I'm intentional about drawing a line between the medical provider role and the personal because I feel that diagnosing within a clinical setting allows people to choose whether to take on the role of patient. Consent is important, especially for multiply marginalized folks who often experience violence while navigating the MIC and relying on Western medicine to access life-saving resources and care. In summary, be critical of preemptive or unwanted diagnoses and the ways this practice maintains medical hegemony.

13. Aggressively challenge feelings of being an imposter.

Imposter syndrome is a term popularized by clinical psychologists Pauline Clance and Suzanne Imes.[18] The term refers to the inability of high-achieving people to internalize their successes. Instead, these people are in constant fear of being exposed for who they think they really are: a fraud. Accomplishments are often dismissed as luck or good timing. While this term initially did not consider how forms of internalized oppression intersect and amplify feelings of self-doubt, some theorists have since drawn attention to how this phenomenon becomes one disproportionally experienced by people from marginalized communities.[19] The brilliance of Black and Indigenous communities, women of color, sick and disabled folks, poor and working-class communities, and trans and queer folks of color is consistently devalued. Critical race scholars and psychologists use the term *microaggression* to describe the subtle everyday manifestations of oppression that have detrimental long-term effects on the well-being of people from marginalized communities.[20] While these marginalized communities employ many ways to resist and affirm their inherent value, the harmful stereotypes are internalized.

Those of us who experience multiple forms of marginalization are forced not only to fight our own feelings of being an imposter but also other people's disbelief in our abilities. For example, when I started to revisit my dream of going to medical school, I faced my own feelings of self-doubt. What if I fail organic chemistry? What if I'm one of those people who will just never be able to do well on the MCAT? I don't have a science background; how can I expect to get competitive scores in my prerequisite science courses? These doubts were amplified by some not-so-micro aggressions I experienced when telling people I was applying to medical school. "You know medical school is really hard, right?" "Are you sure you don't want to just marry a doctor?" "Don't be discouraged when you don't get into medical school." When I got into medical school, there were new, yet familiar, sets of doubts internally and externally hurled at me. "I wish *I* was Black so I could get into an HBCU medical school." "Are you going to medical school to become a nurse?" "How do you expect to be a doctor if you can't cook/drive/(insert any random nonmedical skill here)?" "Isn't doing anesthesia really, *really* hard?" "Don't be discouraged if you don't match into your specialty of choice; there are always spots in (insert here an imagined less competitive specialty)." "You got an interview there? Wow, they must be trying to recruit underrepresented minorities." I know these are doubts that my white cis straight male counterparts are not experiencing as frequently.

What helped me dismiss these kinds of statements is acknowledging where they come from. Being able to name moments of self-doubt and external microaggressions as manifestations of the white supremacist, capitalist, ableist, cisheteropatriarchy helps me resist internalization. Additionally, I've made a conscious decision to highlight moments where I feel intelligent, clinically competent, and even like a good doctor in training. I've had mentors, friends, family members, and strangers along every part of this path through medical school who have told me repeatedly that I *can* do this. I listen to the voices that tell me that not only am I more than equal to the task, but that the medical field needs perspectives like my own.

14. Hold ourselves and our colleagues accountable for medicalized violence.

When we don the white coat and take on the privileged socioeconomic identity of a physician, it is important that we remember the harm done in the name of Western medicine. In the blog, "Leaving Evidence," writer and community educator, Mia Mingus, fleshes out the ways in which Western medicine has played a central role in creating and perpetuating *all* forms of oppression. She powerfully states:

> Oppressed communities have had long and complicated histories with the MIC. From the continued targeting of disabled bodies as something to fix, to the experimentation on black bodies, to the pathologized treatment of and violent attempts to cure queer and trans communities. From the humiliating, lacking or flat-out denial of services to poor communities, to forced sterilization and dangerous contraceptives trafficked to young women of color. From the forced medicalization used in prisons today, to the days when the mental institutions used to be the jails, and the ways that "criminal" and "mentally disabled" are still used interchangeably. From the lack of culturally competent services, to the demonization and erasing of indigenous healing and practices. From the never-ending battle to control populations through controlling birth, birthing and those who give birth in this country, to the countless doctors and practitioners who have raped and sexually assaulted their patients and the survivors who never told a soul. From all the violence that was and is considered standard practice, to the gross abuses of power.[21]

This is the legacy of Western medicine. And while many of us are from communities that have experienced medicalized violence, we need to hold ourselves accountable for the power we are now able to access as we carve out contentious, yet privileged, space within the MIC. We now gain access to power that is a direct result of the histories of violence described by Mingus.

So what can accountability look like? Well, let me start by saying what accountability does not look like—guilt. Guilt is useless and works to center the feelings of folks in positions of power. Instead, a more useful approach is to focus on *contributing* to social change efforts led by folks most impacted by the MIC. Also, *following* the lead of folks who are surviving the MIC means *listening*. For instance, I offer to listen to friends vent about their horrible experiences before, during, and after a doctor's appointment. I listen without offering unwanted explanations or excuses on behalf of healthcare providers. Lastly, one of the ways the MIC maintains power is by making clinical knowledge inaccessible. When asked, I'm eager to *share* what I've learned in medical school, in hopes of decreasing the knowledge gap that further entrenches power imbalances between healthcare provider and patient.

15. Remind yourself (or have people remind you) of why you went into medicine in the first place.

Maybe you dreamed of being a doctor since you were a child. Maybe you wanted to love on your community by creating alternative healing spaces within the MIC. Maybe you feel like you can make a unique contribution to clinical research and the way we practice medicine. Maybe you're in love with the idea of being a radical healer when the revolution or apocalypse comes. Perhaps you're interested in finding ways of using allopathic medical knowledge to complement indigenous healing traditions. Maybe it just feels right in your body to be in an operating room or taking care of people in the emergency department. Whatever the reasons are that called you to medicine in the first place, return to these reasons as often as possible. They will act as both an anchor and a guide—making sure your present is aligned with your initial vision for the future, while holding yourself accountable throughout your journey in medicine. Safe journey.

Resources:

White Coats for Black Lives—http://www.whitecoats4blacklives.org/
Philadelphia Trans Health Conference—https://www.mazzonicenter.org/trans-health
81 Awesome Mental Health Resources When You Can't Afford a Therapist—http://greatist.com/grow/resources-when-you-can-not-afford-therapy

Notes

1. Mey Valdivia Rude, "Flawless Trans Women Carmen Carrera and Laverne Cox Respond Flawlessly to Katie Couric's Invasive Questions," *Autostraddle* (blog), January 7, 2014, http://www.autostraddle.com/flawless-trans-women-carmen-carrera-and-laverne-cox-respond-flawlessly-to-katie-courics-invasive-questions-215855/.

2. Dean Spade, "For Those Considering Law School," *Dean Spade* (blog), November 1, 2010, http://www.deanspade.net/wp-content/uploads/2010/10/For-Those-Considering-Law-School-Nov-2010.pdf.

3. Audre Lorde, *Sister Outsider: Essays and Speeches* (New York: Ten Speed Press, 1984); Barbara Smith, "Toward a Black Feminist Criticism," *The Radical Teacher* 7 (1978): 20–27; Crunk Feminist Collective, "Back-to-School Beatitudes: 10 Academic Survival Tips," *Crunk Feminist Collective* (blog), August 25, 2011, http://www.crunkfeministcollective.com/2011/08/25/back-to-school-beatitudes-10-academic-survival-tips/.

4. *Cisheteropatriarchy* is a political, cultural, and socioeconomic system that privileges men who were assigned male at birth while marginalizing queer and trans folks, women, femmes, and girls.

5. Mia Mingus, "Medical Industrial Complex Visual," *Leaving Evidence* (blog), February 6, 2015, https://leavingevidence.wordpress.com/2015/02/06/medical-industrial-complex-visual/; bell hooks, *Feminism Is for Everybody: Passionate Politics* (Cambridge: South End Press, 2000).

6. Paul Jolly, "Diversity of U.S. Medical School Students by Parental Income," *Analysis in Brief* 8, no. 1 (2008): 1–2.

7. Douglas Grbic, Gwen Garrison, and Paul Jolly, "Diversity of U.S. Medical School Students by Parental Education," *Analysis in Brief* 9, no. 10 (2010): 1–2.

8. Kimberlé Crenshaw, "Demarginalizing the Intersection of Race and Sex: A Black Feminist Critique of Antidiscrimination Doctrine, Feminist Theory and Antiracist Politics," *The University of Chicago Legal Forum* 140 (1989): 139–167.

9. This is a pseudonym.

10. Audre Lorde, *A Burst of Light: Essays* (Ann Arbor: Firebrand Books, 1988), 131.

11. Liselotte N. Dyrbye et al., "Burnout among U.S. Medical Students, Residents, and Early Career Physicians Relative to the General U.S. Population," *Academic Medicine* 89, no. 3 (2014): 443–451.

12. Frederick L Brancati, "The Art of Pimping," *JAMA* 262 (1989): 89–90.

13. Neil Chanchlani, "Being PIMPed Ain't Easy: Neil Chanchlani Defends a Dying Teaching Method," *Medscape*, January 1, 2013, http://www.medscape.com/viewarticle/781525; Katherine D. van Schaik, "Pimping Socrates," *JAMA* 311, no. 14 (2014): 1401–1402.

14. Brian Mavis, Aron Sousa, Wanda Lipscomb, and Marsha D. Rappley, "Learning about Medical Student Mistreatment from Responses to the Medical School Graduation Questionnaire," *Academic Medicine* 89, no. 5 (2014): 705–711; Naif

Fnais, Charlene Soobiah, Maggie H. Chen, Erin Lillie, Laure Perrier, Mariam Tashkhandi, Sharon E. Straus, Muhammad Mamdani, Mohammed Al-Omran, and Andrea C. Tricco, "Harassment and Discrimination in Medical Training: A Systematic Review and Meta-analysis," *Academic Medicine* 89, no. 5 (2014): 817–827; Cian McCarthy and John McEvoy, "Pimping in Medical Education: Lacking Evidence and under Threat," *JAMA* 314, no. 22 (2015): 2347–2348.

15. Robert Oh and Brian V. Reamy, "The Socratic Method and Pimping: Optimizing the Use of Stress and Fear in Instruction," *Virtual Mentor* 16, no. 3 (2014): 182–186.

16. Sharon McLennan, "Medical Voluntourism in Honduras: 'Helping' the Poor?" *Progress in Development Studies* 14, no. 2 (2014): 163–179.

17. Michael Oliver, *Understanding Disability: From Theory to Practice* (New York: St. Martin's Press, 1996).

18. Pauline R. Clance and Suzanne A. Imes, "The Imposter Phenomenon in High Achieving Women: Dynamics and Therapeutic Intervention," *Psychotherapy: Theory, Research and Practice* 15, no. 3 (1978): 241–247.

19. David J. Leonard, "Impostor Syndrome: Academic Identity under Siege?" *The Chronicle of Higher Education*, February 5, 2014, http://chronicle.com/blogs/conversation/2014/02/05/impostor-syndrome-academic-identity-under-siege/; bell hooks, *Teaching Community: A Pedagogy of Hope*, (New York: Routledge, 2003), 128.

20. Chester M. Pierce, Jean V. Carew, Diane Pierce-Gonzalez, and Deborah Wills, "An Experiment in Racism: TV Commercials," *Education and Urban Society* 10 (1977): 61–87; Jioni A. Lewis, Ruby Mendenhall, Stacy A. Harwood, and Margaret B. Huntt, "Coping with Gendered Racial Microaggressions among Black Women College Students," *Journal of African American Studies* 17 (2013): 51–73.

21. Mingus, "Medical Industrial."

CHAPTER 7

Finding Grace

An Asian American Womxn's Counterstory to Graduate School Racial Microaggressions

Aeriel A. Ashlee

Settling into my seat, I retrieve a brand-new notebook and my favorite poppy red pen from my bag. I choose this pen on purpose, because the brightly colored ink reminds me to be confident and I have a feeling that I am going to need all the confidence I can muster as I embark on this next academic endeavor. Doodling in the margins, I wait for the classroom to fill. As the moments pass and my doodles sprawl down the side of the page, I let my mind wonder about the ideas and opinions that I will write in this, and the many other notebooks sure to come. Before I wander too far into my own thoughts, I bring myself back to the present. I return to this day, to the start of my next big adventure. My last first-day of school; the beginning of my doctoral education.

Today is new student orientation and my first day as a full-time student after a six-year hiatus of working full-time. Feeling emboldened by my new school supplies (even as a thirty-year-old I cannot resist the rush of optimism and giddy anticipation that accompanies back-to-school shopping) I eagerly await my formal induction into doctoral student life. When the current doctoral students and program faculty file into the classroom and take their seats for the orientation program to begin, I feel my previous sense of confidence and optimism slowly retreat. As each person takes turns introducing themselves and their research interests, my stomach starts to churn with self-doubt; not because of the words they say, but because of the faces I see. At least twenty minutes pass by before I realize that my new notebook and poppy red pen lay untouched on the desk in front of me. Shocked into a silent stupor, I am overcome by the stark observation that none of the eleven scholars representing my new academic community—five doctoral students and six faculty members—look like me.

This opening vignette is my most salient memory from the first day of my doctoral education and, unfortunately, not an isolated incident in my graduate school experience nor to the reality of Asian American students more broadly. In fact, it is well documented that despite popular post-racial rhetoric, racism and racial microaggressions continue to be an insidious part of American history, society, and education.[1] While overt and covert forms of prejudice and discrimination targeting African Americans and Latinx/Hispanic Americans are generally recognized, Asian Americans are commonly viewed as a model minority who have made it in society and therefore experience little in the form of racism.[2] This frequently held belief—and problematic racial stereotype—runs counter to a long history of racism toward Asians in America and serves to uphold systems of anti-Black racism and white supremacy.[3] Indeed a study of Asian American history reveals patterns of systemic racism ranging from the denial of citizenship, to the prohibition of land ownership, and incarceration in prison camps.[4] Yet much of the existing scholarship on race and racism in U.S. society and American education does not include the experiences of Asian Americans. Not seeing myself represented in the scholars of my academic program at new student orientation was just one of many racial microaggressions I have endured in my graduate education.

Racial microaggressions are everyday forms of systemic racism used to keep those at the racial margins in their place.[5] Defined as subtle, stunning, and often unconscious exchanges and insults directed toward people of color, microaggressions are invalidating and have been proven to take a toll on people of color's self-esteem and psychological well-being.[6] Critical race scholars contend that the cumulative effects of racial microaggressions can be quite devastating, going so far as to assert that "this contemporary form of racism is many times over more problematic, damaging, and injurious to persons of color than overt racist acts."[7] However, because microaggressions are often covert and innocuous, they are regularly overlooked such that well-intended individuals may engage in these biased acts without knowledge or even recognition of their discriminatory actions.[8] The pervasiveness of the aforementioned model minority myth—the racial stereotype that generally defines Asian Americans as a monolithically hardworking and successful racial group—further obscures the microaggressive racist realities experienced by Asian Americans in educational settings.

Sharing my truths is an act of resistance, a refusal to acquiesce to the perpetual exclusion and minimization of my experience with racism and racial microaggressions as an Asian American doctoral student. Following the call of Sara Ahmed[9] and other feminist killjoys who have come before me, this narrative—the exercise of my voice—is an enactment of my belief that my experience and writing can and should transform academia. Rooted in a critical race perspective, this chapter draws from Critical Race Theory (CRT), an outgrowth of critical legal studies, which has been extended to the field of education.[10] CRT privileges the experiences of people of color in opposition to normative White standards and has been described as a movement comprised of "activists and scholars engaged in studying and transforming the relationship among race, racism, and power."[11] CRT is an explanatory framework used in research on the experiences of people of color in education as they navigate and resist racial microaggressions.[12] While there has been some scholarly variance in the defining principles of CRT, there are consistently five basic tenets that guide the use of the framework; these include: (1) centrality and intersectionality of race and racism; (2) challenge to dominant ideologies and deficit perspectives; (3) centrality of experiential knowledge, (4) interdisciplinary analyses; and (5) explicit commitment to social justice.[13]

By recounting some of the racial microaggressions I experienced in my doctoral studies, I demonstrate the perceived normalcy and ordinariness of everyday manifestations of racism in higher education. Additionally, to illuminate the intersectional nature of race and racism, I center not only my racialized experience as an Asian American doctoral student, but specifically explore the intersection of multiple oppressions (namely racism and sexism) that I experience as an Asian American womxn of color. It is important to note, that I intentionally use "womxn" as a form of resistance to patriarchy. By rejecting the traditional spelling, I along with other scholar-activists assert that "womxn are their own free and independent persons, separate of men."[14] The "x" in the spelling I use throughout this chapter is formed by two intersecting lines, which represent the intersections of the many different identities and experiences embodied in womxnhood; most salient in this chapter is that of my race and gender as an Asian American womxn. My story is just one among the many voices of womxn of color graduate students who are speaking up and writing down our stories; unafraid of being academic killjoys.[15] Dominant ideologies of meritocracy and colorblindness that prevail in education have not translated to my lived experience as womxn of color in graduate school. Therefore, in accordance with my commitment to social justice, I offer this chapter as a counterstory, a method of centering my lived experience as a person of color who has been forced to exist at society's margins.[16] I write this manuscript as a tool for exposing, analyzing, and challenging systemic racism in education.[17]

It is important to situate my counterstory within my field of study, which is higher education. The decision to reflect on these racial microaggressions is informed by both my lived experience as a womxn of color in graduate school and by my academic interests as a higher education critical race scholar. There is a gross underrepresentation of Asian American scholars in the field of higher education even though Asian Americans are one of the fastest growing racial demographics in the United States and one of the largest college-going populations of any racial group.[18] According to the National Center for Education, less than 1% of doctoral degrees conferred in higher education go to Asian American womxn. This discrepancy between Asian American undergraduate student enrollment and Asian American graduate student degree completion demonstrates a problematic incongruence and palpable need for more Asian Americans in higher education graduate programs, given research on the importance of role models and mentors to the success and persistence of students of color.[19]

Within the field of higher education, diversity, inclusion, and social justice are espoused core values.[20] Yet minimal research explores the racialized experiences of graduate students of color in higher education programs specifically.[21] While scholars have theorized graduate school experiences for students of color as generally oppressive and dehumanizing,[22] further research into the nuanced experience of specific racial and ethnic groups is needed.[23] Unfortunately, some of the existing scholarship that claims to study the experiences of graduate students of color, actually omits Asian Americans from their samples altogether.[24] In fact, while preparing to write this chapter, I encountered books, like the autoethnographic anthology *Tedious Journeys*,[25] which claim to feature narratives of diverse womxn of color in the academy, only to discover the text includes only the voices of Black and Latina womxn in higher education. As an Asian American womxn of color, the realization that my community's voice is excluded from community of color scholarship is infuriating. This empirical microaggression is not only invalidating to the lived experiences of Asian

American graduate students, it dangerously contributes to the erasure of Asian Americans' racialized experiences as people of color.

I have been a student of higher education for over a decade. In that time, I held many roles, from undergraduate student, to master's student, and now as a doctoral student and emerging scholar-activist. Yet in all that time, I have had the opportunity to explicitly study Asian Americans only when I created the assignment or course curriculum myself; and that has not come without costs. In mid-November of my first year in my doctoral program, I found myself needing to register for spring classes. Only three months into the program, I felt utterly overwhelmed and uninspired. Those first few months had been difficult for me. As it turned out, my undergraduate and master's education had not adequately prepared me for the barrage of microaggressions that awaited me at my doctoral institution; a rurally located, affluent, predominantly white institution.

Daily in those first few months I was bombarded by messages that I did not belong and was not welcome; except perhaps for the fetishized pleasure of my White male counterparts. Regarding the latter, for example, while walking in town adjacent to my university—in pursuit of a quiet study spot—I was regularly cat-called, objectified, and reduced to eye-candy for the consumption and enjoyment of White men. Every time I commuted to campus, I drove past a Confederate flag. On more than one occasion a student asked me, "Where are you from?" Implicit in their question was the assumption that because I am Asian, I could not possibly be from or belong here. Even in class discussions about systems of power and oppression, if I did not bring up the implications of white supremacy and patriarchy for Asian American womxn, the issue was not broached at all.

Discouraged and depressed by these experiences, I was uncertain if I would continue pursuing my PhD and so the prospect of choosing spring semester classes felt trite. In search of inspiration and encouragement, I turned to a book my partner had given me as a gift, Grace Lee Boggs's autobiography *Living for Change*. Within reading the first few chapters, I felt seen. I underlined whole paragraphs and read aloud multiple passages, resonating with much of Grace's story. Early in the book, Grace writes:

> It used to infuriate me when not only my peers but my teachers and other adults would ask me, "What is your nationality?" I would reply patiently, as if giving them a civics lesson that my nationality was American because I was born in the United States but that my parents were Chinese. But no matter how often or how carefully I explained, I would be asked the question again and again . . . [26]

Yes! I knew this annoyance and exhaustion all too well, as the perpetual foreigner[27] stereotype is just one of the microaggressions that greets me with unfailing regularity. In ways I did not expect, Grace's story spoke to my heart and breathed life into my soul. Rather than feeling invisible or invalid as I had during much of those initial months in my doctoral studies, I felt affirmed reading Grace's story.

This was just the antidote I needed to the *imposter syndrome*—the persistent feeling of inadequacy and deeply held fear of being unmasked as a fraud at any moment; irrespective of one's accomplishments or evidence to the contrary[28]—that had begun to set in. Imposter syndrome, a common affliction among academics, is more prevalent in womxn than in men.[29] Characterized as a very real and specific form of intellectual self-doubt, new graduate students are particularly susceptible to imposter thinking. According to a recent study, Asian Americans are more likely than their African American or Latinx peers to experience imposter feelings.[30] When layered with an internalization of the model minority myth, imposter syndrome becomes particularly dangerous as Asian Americans aim for unrealistic expectations to be consistently high-achieving and high-performing.[31] A confluence of these factors resulted in my own self-doubt about my place and potential in the academy. These insecurities were exacerbated by strong feelings of shame for my struggles as I wrestled with not measuring up to my own high expectations.

Holding Grace's self-authored story in my hands, I felt hopeful. She helped me understand that ideas that matter are created by individuals who explain, cope with, and resist their sociohistorical circumstances.[32] I was inspired to follow Grace's lead in navigating and coping with my own graduate school conditions. As painful and challenging as those initial months had been, I resolved to make meaning and heal from those experiences by naming my oppression and aligning with other fierce Asian American womxn of color scholar-activists. In that moment, I decided to design an independent study purposefully centering the voices of Asian American womxn activists like Grace Lee and Yuri Kochiyama. In crafting the independent study, I had the opportunity to intentionally reflect upon and begin to construct my own story as an Asian American womxn, facilitating my own agency and emergence as a scholar-activist by learning about the legacies of those who came before me. Heartened by Grace's connections between her own personal experiences with racial microaggressions and her lifelong commitment to transcending racial and class boundaries, the independent study proposal flowed out of me. As I typed each word, I felt more sure, more confident, and more fired up than I had about anything to date in my doctoral education. Rather than relegating the stories of Asian American womxn to my own personal or recreational reading, I determined to root my academic endeavors in studying their narratives and lived experiences.

The creation of this independent study was a defining moment of my graduate education and my development as an Asian American scholar-activist. Prior to this, I felt my racial identity excluded me from, or at least served as a liability to, my career in academia. I was regularly the only Asian American face in the room, whether that be academic classrooms or departmental meetings. In my many years of postsecondary education (undergraduate, master's, and now doctoral studies), I had only one Asian American faculty member (during my master's program). How isolating! Unfortunately, this is congruent with national numbers, which indicate that less than 6% of college faculty are Asian American.[33]

Relatedly, in my years of study, I rarely encountered academic content that extended beyond a superficial account of Asian Americans. For instance, in my master's program I recall spending about half of one class meeting to the discussions of Asian American students in higher education. How is it sufficient to spend a mere 70 minutes out of an entire semester on one of the fastest growing college demographics in the country? This sort of marginal acknowledgment of Asian Americans in higher education brutally truncates the complexities of this population and forces the discourse to remain surface-level. It is no surprise then, that many educators continue to focus on the model minority myth as the most salient issue facing Asian Americans in higher education today, rather than delving into the invisibility of disparate ethnic groups' needs when aggregating data or exploring the intricacies of intersections of identity (e.g., considering the multiple forms of oppression and marginalization experienced by trans, queer, and low-income Asian Americans).

My independent study inspired by Grace Lee Boggs led to a profound intellectual, political, and deeply personal journey. Spending time reading and thinking with brilliant Asian American womxn scholar-activists like Grace and Yuri, Mari Matsuda and Cheryl Matias, was my saving grace in an otherwise painfully bleak first year of doctoral studies. I used my graduate coursework to find reprieve and to resist rather than surrender to the white supremacist and patriarchal norms of my campus that insisted I was not welcome. To be sure, this was not an easy endeavor. Nonetheless, I tenaciously carved out a space for myself in an institution that was not built for me. While my mere presence in the academy was a direct challenge to white supremacy and patriarchy, my emerging research interest in empowering womxn of color through critical race counterstorytelling was likely an additional antagonizing factor. And yet somehow, perhaps strengthened by the community and solidarity I felt with the Asian American womxn scholar-activists I studied, I felt a surge of conviction, a spark of hope. I can and I will persevere. Although I am currently the one Asian American in my doctoral program, I will not be the only.

According to Grace Lee Boggs, "revolutionists have a responsibility to create strategies to transform ourselves as well as the victims of oppression."[34] This was not in my consciousness when I first started my doctoral studies. I did not realize I was embarking on a revolution, one that would prove to be both emotionally taxing and healing. I did not anticipate that I would find empowerment through naming and resisting racial microaggressions. Certainly, I experienced anger, isolation, and depression in my first semester of my doctoral studies. However, I also experienced a revolutionary awakening. By finding grace—literally in Grace Lee Boggs's autobiography and figuratively in seeing my experience reflected in the narratives of the Asian American womxn scholar-activists I read—I began to discover authentic and radical ways of being in the academy. Through resistance pedagogy, radical self-love, and critical race praxis, I uncovered new hope in working toward my own liberation and that of other womxn of color in higher education.

Perhaps there are still risks as I pursue this work: risks to my future in the field; risks to my physical, mental, and spiritual wellness; risks to suggesting that there is no single right (read White) way to author a book chapter or pursue a doctoral degree. But staying silent, enduring and accepting racial microaggressions as a normative part of graduate school for Asian American womxn of color, is also risky. Therefore, I do as Grace Lee writes,

> To make a revolution, people must not only struggle against existing institutions. They must make a philosophical/spiritual leap and become more *human* beings. In order to change/transform the world, they must change/transform themselves.[35]

I make space for my voice, finding a way to exist and persist despite the skepticism of others. I write my truth unapologetically and I hold space for my sisters, other Asian American womxn graduate students as they make their way to the academy.

To be clear, my intent in sharing this counterstory is not only to encourage Asian American womxn graduate students, but also to provide recommendations and reflections that may help deepen and expand the discussion of diverse womxn of color's experiences in graduate school. First, education that focuses on raising awareness of microaggressions and their impact within higher education institutions is needed given that racial microaggressions largely operate outside of people's conscious awareness. Additionally, culturally relevant counseling to help Asian Americans womxn (and other racially marginalized groups) name and thus not internalize the microaggressive messages they receive is essential to these communities' wellness and persistence.[36] Moreover, the creation of counter-spaces, curricular and cocurricular contexts that enable Asian American womxn to foster their own learning in supportive environments where their experiences are validated and viewed as important knowledge is essential to reducing the harmful effects of racial microaggressions.[37]

Second, the systemic silencing of Asian American voices in higher education, by their consistent exclusion from literature about communities of color, must end. Positioning Asian Americans as the model minority is a tool of white supremacy, meant to breed fear, scarcity, and competition for limited resources between communities of color. If Asian American womxn doctoral students are expected to live in the margins—neither included in majority research nor included in counter-narrative anthologies—the field of higher education is actively, if not intentionally, contributing to the erasure of this community. The responsibility to remedy this injustice cannot and should not fall solely upon shoulders of Asian American scholars themselves; as there are currently so few of us represented in academia. Graduate school educators need to develop their own critical consciousness and recognize that by playing into the model minority myth and continuing to exclude Asian Americans from research on communities of color they are colluding with white supremacy. Therefore, regardless of their own racial/ethnic identities, graduate faculty must engage diverse perspectives in all curriculum and research. To offer research or readings on communities of color representing only the experiences of Black and Latinx populations is dangerous and demeaning not only to Asian Americans but also Native/Indigenous communities as well as multiracial people. Relatedly, Critical Race Theory should be an integral element in all higher education graduate programs because of its theoretical and methodological implications for those who have been historically and systemically silenced and oppressed.

Finally, broader acceptance of personal narrative as relevant and valid knowledge is needed if we are to continue to make advancements in higher education with a critical race lens. It is through counterstorytelling—the promotion and sharing of personal narratives from people of color—that CRT features the subjective perspectives of people of color to counter pervasive stereotypes and hegemonic viewpoints rooted in white supremacy.[38] Critical race scholars can begin to combat racial exclusion and oppression in higher education by legitimizing the voices and lived experiences of people of color.[39] This chapter is an embodiment of this third recommendation. In sharing my counterstory as an Asian American womxn in a higher education doctoral program, I challenge the intersectional oppression of white supremacy and patriarchy that is so pervasive in U.S. higher education. I speak truth to power by documenting the racial microaggressions I have sustained in my graduate education. By finding grace and authoring this chapter, I assert my place, my voice, and my value in higher education.

A final thought for all the future Asian American womxn graduate students. You matter. You belong. You may be excluded from research or isolated at your institution, but you are not alone. I see you. I hear you. I am with you.

Notes

1. Derald Wing Sue, Jennifer Bucceri, Annie I. Lin, Kevin L. Nadal, and Gina C. Torino, "Racial Microaggressions and the Asian American Experience," *Cultural Diversity and Ethnic Minority Psychology* 13, no. 1 (2007): 72.

2. Ibid.

3. OiYan Poon, Dian Squire, Corinne Kodama, Ajani Byrd, Jason Chan, Lester Manzano, Sara Furr, and Devita Bishundat, "A Critical Review of the Model Minority Myth in Selected Literature on Asian Americans and Pacific Islanders in Higher Education," *Review of Educational Research* 86, no. 2 (2016): 469.

4. Shelley Sang-Hee Lee, *A New History of Asian America* (New York: Routledge, 2014).

5. Lindsay Pérez Huber and Daniel G. Solórzano, "Racial Microaggressions as a Tool for Critical Race Research," *Race Ethnicity and Education* 18, no. 3 (2015): 298.

6. Sue et al., "Racial Microaggressions," 73.

7. Derald Wing Sue, *Overcoming Our Racism: The Journey to Liberation* (San Francisco: Jossey Bass, 2003), 48.

8. Daniel Solórzano, Miguel Cejas, and Tina Yosso, "Critical Race Theory, Racial Microaggressions, and Campus Racial Climate: The Experiences of African American College Students," *The Journal of Negro Education* 69 (2000): 61.

9. Sara Ahmed, *The Promise of Happiness* (Durham: Duke University Press, 2010).

10. Gloria Ladson-Billings, "Just What Is Critical Race Theory and What's It Doing in a *Nice* Field Like Education?" *Foundations of Critical Race Theory in Education*, eds. Edward Taylor, David Gillborn, and Gloria Ladson-Billings (New York: Routledge, 2009), 17–36.

11. Richard Delgado and Jean Stefancic, *Critical Race Theory: An Introduction* (New York: New York University Press, 2017), 3.

12. Daniel Solórzano, "Critical Race Theory, Race and Gender Microaggressions, and the Experiences of Chicana and Chicano Scholars," *Qualitative Studies in Education* 11, no. 1 (1998).

13. Pérez Huber and Solórzano, "Racial Microaggressions," 300–301.

14. Southeast Asian Retention through Creating Hxstory, "What Does the 'X' in Hxstory Stand For?" *Southeast Asian Retention Through Creating Hxstory*, last modified Spring 2014, https://searchuci.wordpress.com/about/what-does-the-x-in-hxstory-stand-for/.

15. Ahmed, *Promise of Happiness*, 50–87.

16. Daniel Solórzano and Tina Yosso, "Critical Race Methodology: Counter-Storytelling as an Analytical Framework for Educational Research," https://journals.sagepub.com/.

17. Edward Taylor, "The Foundations of Critical Race Theory in Education: An Introduction," in *Foundations of Critical Race Theory in Education*, eds. Edward Taylor, David Gillborn, and Gloria Ladson-Billings (New York: Routledge, 2009), 7–8.

18. Pew Research Center, *The Rise of Asian Americans*, Washington, D.C.: Pew Research Center, 2013, http://www.pewsocialtrends.org/files/2013/04/Asian-Americans-new-full-report-04-2013.pdf.

19. Rowena Ortiz-Walters and Lucy L. Gilson, "Mentoring in Academia: An Examination of the Experiences of Protégés of Color," *Journal of Vocational Behavior* 67, no. 3 (2005): 471.

20. American College Personnel Association and National Association of Student Personnel Administrators, "Professional Competency Areas for Student Affairs Educators," last modified August 2015, http://www.naspa.org/images/uploads/main/ACPA_NASPA_Professional_Competencies_FINAL.pdf.

21. Chris Linder, Jessica C. Harris, Evette L. Allen, and Bryan Hubain, "Building Inclusive Pedagogy: Recommendations from a National Student of Students of Color in Higher Education and Student Affairs Graduate Programs," *Equity & Excellence in Education* 44, no. 2 (2015): 180.

22. Geneva Gay, "Navigating Marginality En Route to the Professoriate: Graduate Students of Color Learning and Living in Academia," *International Journal of Qualitative Studies in Education* 17, no. 2 (2004): 267.

23. Kevin L. Nadal, Stephane T. Pituc, Marc P. Johnson, and Theresa Esparrago, "Overcoming the Model Minority Myth: Experiences of Filipino American Graduate Students," *Journal of College Student Development* 51, no. 6 (2010): 694.

24. Ryan Evely Gildersleeve, Natasha Croom, and Philip L. Vasquez, "'Am I Going Crazy?': A Critical Race Analysis of Doctoral Education," *Equity & Excellence in Education* 44, no. 1 (2011): 93; and Ortiz-Walters and Gilson, "Mentoring in Academia," 459.

25. Cynthia C. Robinson and Pauline Clardy, *Tedious Journeys: Autoethnography by Women of Color in Academe* (New York: Peter Lang Publishing Inc., 2010).

26. Grace Lee Boggs, *Living for Change: An Autoethnography* (Minneapolis: University of Minnesota Press, 1998), 10.

27. Que-Lam Huynh, Thierry Devos, and Laura Smalarz, "Perpetual Foreigner in One's Own Land: Potential Implications for Identity and Psychological Adjustment," *Journal of Social and Clinical Psychology* 30, no. 2 (2011): 133.

28. Kirsten Weir, "Feeling Like a Fraud?" *gradPSYCH Magazine*, November 2013, http://www.apa.org/gradpsych/2013/11/fraud.aspx.

29. Scarlette Spears Studdard, "Adult Women Students in the Academy: Imposters or Members?" *Journal of Continuing Higher Education* 50, no. 3 (2002): 24.

30. Kevin Cokely, Shannon McClain, Alicia Enciso, and Mercedes Martinez, "An Examination of the Impact of Minority Status Stress and Imposter Feelings on the Mental Health of Diverse Ethnic Minority College Students," *Journal of Multicultural Counseling & Development* 41, no. 2 (2013): 82.

31. Samuel D. Museus and Peter N. Kiang, "Deconstructing the Model Minority Myth and How It Contributes to the Invisible Minority Reality in Higher Education Research," in *Conducting Research on Asian Americans in Higher Education*, ed. Samuel D. Museus (San Francisco: Wiley Periodicals, 2009), 6.

32. Boggs, *Living for Change*, 45.

33. Howard Wang and Robert T. Teranishi, "AAPI Background and Statistics: Perspectives of the Representation and Inclusion of AAPI Faculty, Staff, and Student Affairs Professionals," *Asian Americans and Pacific Islanders in Higher Education: Research and Perspectives on Identity, Leadership, and Success*, eds. Doris Ching and Amefil Agbayani (Washington D.C.: NASPA, 2012), 15.

34. Boggs, *Living for Change*, 152.

35. Ibid., 153.

36. Gloria Wong-Padoongpatt, Nolan Zane, Sumie Okazaki, and Anne Saw, "Decreases in Implicit Self-Esteem Explain the Racial Impact of Microaggressions Among Asian Americans," *Journal of Counseling Psychology* 64, no. 5 (2017): 581.

37. Solórzano et al., "Critical Race Theory, Racial Microaggressions, and Campus Racial Climate," 70.

38. Amy Liu, "Critical Race Theory, Asian Americans, and Higher Education: A Review of Research," *InterActions: UCLA Journal of Education and Information Studies* 5, no. 2 (2009): 2.

39. Edward Taylor, "A Primer on Critical Race Theory," *The Journal of Blacks in Higher Education* 19 (1998): 122.

CHAPTER 8

How to Help

Learning the Legacy of the Social Work Professional

Arianna Taboada

I had never heard of a social work career before the age of 20. During a summer health administration internship program, I was placed at a community health center that was led by a public health-trained social worker. The Chief Executive Officer (CEO) of the health center, let's call him Mr. G, reminded me of my dad in many ways. He was outspoken, passionate about his work, and a living legend in both his local community and on the national community health center scene. He was a proud social worker. The first one I had ever met.

Part of the internship involved weekly meetings with Mr. G, where we debriefed about the week's progress, and he shared examples from his professional trajectory. I learned that his social work credentials were rooted in social justice and Chicano rights issues. A former member of the Brown Berets, Mr. G spent his youth working in the steel plants in a large Midwestern city, and then, as he became more politicized, he and his friends began to organize the steel worker community. Given his organizing and advocacy acumen, the Master's of Social Work (MSW) program at a local university recruited him. Mr. G's professional social work training and community-based background culminated in his running one of the country's most respected Federally Qualified Health Centers (FQHC).

As I spent the summer learning from Mr. G and his staff I remember thinking, "I don't know what this social work profession is about, but if it involves getting paid and respected for working on community health issues and organizing alongside marginalized population, I should definitely look into it!" At the time, I was an undergraduate at the University of California, Los Angeles, minoring in Chicana/o Studies. I was a proud member of the Movimiento Estudiantil Chicana/o de Aztlán (MEChA), a student movement founded in the 1960s wave of advocacy for access to education and self-determination for marginalized communities, particularly racial/ethnic minorities. While I headed into my last year of college, I realized how much that summer's internship and exposure to the field of social work shaped my own career trajectory.

My commitment to social justice and interest in culturally and linguistically tailored services peppered my applications to graduate schools. I accepted and enrolled in an MSW program, nearly 3,000 miles away from home. To be honest, I knew little about social work history or the current state of the profession when I landed at my new university to begin graduate school. But I felt strongly that a profession built around advocating on behalf of others and empowering others to advocate for themselves was a good fit. Indeed, I learned that social work as a field is considered a "helping profession" deeply rooted in and committed to social justice and underserved communities.[1] However, I also learned that the profession is rooted in a legacy of mostly white, middle- and upper-class professionals who serve mostly poor, marginalized communities. This legacy is apparent in the predominantly white enrollment and teaching faculty in social work programs.

My reflections on this legacy use the lens of Critical Race and LatCrit theories to share my experience. Within the context of higher education, and graduate school in particular, both theories have been used to develop a nuanced conceptual, methodological, and pedagogical strategy for understanding and addressing the role of race and racism in U.S. graduate school programs; LatCrit has particularly centered on Chicana/Chicano graduate school experiences. Furthermore, both theories acknowledge the intersection of a racialized experience in graduate school with other factors at play, such as gender, citizenship, and class identity.[2] While this chapter is about the experience of one individual, the vignettes will sound familiar to anyone who has shared the experience of attending a predominantly white institution or program. It tells the story of learning on the margins, of deconstructing an inherently racist curriculum, and of forging a way forward for Chicana social workers—even when our education was not designed with us in mind. The stories I share of (mis)representation, otherness, and racial battle fatigue were painful to write about; the memory of constantly wondering "how will I make it?" was still fresh. However, it is important to make these struggles visible. To speak them, to write them, to hold space for them. They inevitably contributed to a more resilient version of myself, and I was also able to relive those people and safe spaces as I wrote. I could remember what it felt like in those instances where I was seen or listened to and met with compassion, mentorship, and support.

Setting the Stage for Social Workers as "Helpers"

During my first semester in particular, I struggled with the tension of trying to merge my sociopolitical and ethnic identity as a bilingual, bicultural Chicana with the identity of a "professional helper" that I was expected to adopt as a social worker. This social worker identity carries a certain connotation in the U.S. context that reads as "gatekeeper" of public resources and services. One of the most widely heard public assumptions about social workers is that they work for Social Services, and if they arrive at your house, they are there to remove your children. This anecdote is particularly common among women of color who are criminalized for social conditions and behaviors related to poverty. In fact, many communities' experiences with social workers negate the identity of social workers as "professional helpers." I assumed that the social work classroom would be the natural place to discuss this illustrative example of structural and professional power, privilege, and oppression, and related examples. However, I found little space for such discussions with peers or faculty.

This was, in part, due to the reality of racial/ethnic diversity—or lack thereof—in social work education. As of 2010, when I matriculated into my MSW program, full-time enrollment of Latino students in MSW programs nationally was 10.2%, with Chicano/as accounting for 1.8% of these. This was the equivalent of 529 individuals spread across the country.[3] Not many were sitting alongside me in my new program. Full-time social work faculty nationally were 72.7% white at that time, with part-time faculty following closely behind at 69.2%. Only 4.8% of full-time faculty and 5.8% of part-time faculty identified as Latino. And, only 1% and 1.9%, respectively, considered themselves Chicana/o.[4] Needless to say, none of my professors were quite like Mr. G. In fact, I did not have a single professor who identified as Chicano/Latino and had a background in community-based political organizing.

148

Even beyond national statistics and the makeup of my specific program, the gap between who social workers tend to be and who they tend to serve is vast. In her article, "Innocence Lost and Suspicion Found: Do We Educate for or against Social Work?" Amy Rossiter describes this dissonance:

> I want my students to recognize that social work is a problem for identity. To do social work in capitalist, imperialist countries is to occupy a place of pain and doubt. There is no theory that can shield us from the complexity of the gesture of a white middle-class woman giving an alcoholic Native homeless man a bowl of soup. It is a gesture that is overdetermined by my history of ancestors who landed in the New World, and great aunts who were missionaries, and great grandparents who were farming folks who moved West and destroyed his linguistic and cultural heritage in order to cover up the theft. We are helping out of this history, not apart from it, and this necessarily troubles the act of helping and thus our identity as helpers.[5]

Rossiter illustrates the complexity of adopting a professional identity and delivering services under the umbrella of social justice when these acts are inextricable from systemic and personal injustices. She posits that social workers must deploy a critical analysis of our inherent complicity with social structures that determine who helps and who receives help. Nevertheless, this reality is infrequently discussed in depth at the classroom level among social work students or faculty. Often these differentials in privilege and life experiences are overlooked or ignored.

The historical themes of community trust/distrust, self-help, self-determination, and community organizing that I brought with me from my academic background in ethnic studies were at the forefront of my mind as I entered the field. While I did not anticipate a historically and predominantly white graduate school program to necessarily center these narratives, I did expect that they would be addressed as relevant topics for consideration in our professional development. Instead, I found that, despite these themes being the driving force in my decision to become a social worker, they were left unaccounted for and largely unaddressed in my social work program. The few experiences where issues of power and privilege emerged were pivotal turning points, central to my professional training and development as a social worker. While each situation at the time felt like a negative experience, they all created room for developing coping strategies I then utilized to critically analyze my experience, build a community of allies, and engage in institutional and professional change.

These defining moments helped me forge my own way through graduate school and adopt a professional identity that made me feel proud. However, it is important to highlight that the lessons learned that resulted from these difficult moments by and large happened on the margins. At the time that these experiences occurred, any processing, individually or in community, happened outside of the class, outside of my formal education, and even outside of the formal supervision I received as a social work trainee. As the time of this writing, in hindsight, I am able to engage storytelling as a LatCrit technique to challenge the dominant discourse.[6] I center my narrative, making the counterstory the focal point, instead of a marginalized response.

The Representation of Racial/Ethnic Minority Communities in the Coursework

As part of a required course on oppression and diversity, all MSW students had to individually complete an online overview of racial/ethnic minority history. The purpose behind the online pre-course activities was to ensure that all students had basic knowledge about major historical moments related to communities of color in the United States. The online resources included nine videos ranging from 12 minutes to 33 minutes in length. These videos covered historical events specific to marginalized communities (e.g., the Tuskegee Syphilis Experiment, the Farmworker Movement, and the Holocaust) and more conceptual issues such as white privilege and social stigma associated with living in poverty. From my perspective, for students who identified with those communities, had previously studied the communities, or had any knowledge above basic Civil Rights history, the content grossly underrepresented the multifaceted, complex historical context and contemporary lives of those communities.

Essentially, each video contained decades of history compressed into a clip that was void of any nuance. I questioned whether these snapshots of isolated events without proper contextualization were educational or damaging, especially for students who had no other formal or experiential connection with minority populations, and there were quite a few of those students present. As I watched the short clip on the Farmworker Movement, used to discuss and represent not only Mexican American history, but also the sociohistorical context of Latinos in the United States, I began to wonder if I was at the right school or even in the right profession. What about the active collaboration and partnership between Filipino American and Mexican American communities during the Farmworker Movement? No mention of it. What about the student-led movements happening during the 1960s in Latino communities throughout the country that provided a backdrop for community-level organizing? No mention of it. What about the self-help organizations that tirelessly fought to ensure that communities of color had access to services that mainstream service organizations did not provide them? No mention of it. As I painfully made my way through the online course material, I couldn't help wondering why no one had warned me that graduate school could be like this. I was frustrated and disappointed.

This is not to say that my mentors failed to prepare me for the realities of graduate school. They went to great lengths to teach me about micro-aggressions from peers, navigating programs with little to no faculty of color, and building cross-discipline camaraderie. Yet, none of my previous mentors specifically discussed what attending graduate school in the U.S. South would hold for me, specifically in a region of North Carolina where a recent influx of migrant families created a landscape where nativism and legality went hand in hand with discussions on race and community-building.

Despite being an incredibly well-educated academic community, there was limited knowledge of the historical context of Chicano/Latinos in this country, particularly given very recent and rapid demographic shifts. Consequently, issues of "diversity" that included Chicano/Latinos were often boiled down to an immigration debate. When I sparked a critical dialogue about the problematic nature of these videos, I soon realized that only a handful of my peers understood why such a one-dimensional representation of any community is dangerous. Imagine a classroom discussion where students who self-identify as progressive refer to Latino communities as "illegals," without knowing why or how that would be offensive. For example, when I brought up how the Treaty of Guadalupe Hidalgo impacted legal status and likely impacted access to social services at that time, I received blank stares from most of the classroom.[7]

The few affirmative head nods became my anchors—the classmates with whom I could relate both personally and professionally. In our mutual outrage about the pre-course videos, we found each other quickly and learned what spaces on campus and which professors were our allies. We met, discussed, vented, and supported each other—on the margins. On our own time and with our own resources, we sought to learn some of the institutional history about why these pre-course activities were in place.

In doing so, we also learned about the great lengths many of the faculty and staff representatives had made to make sure that any inclusion of these topics was required. Clearly, we were not the first cohort to draw attention to this. Still, I was angry. I was disappointed, frustrated, and upset to learn that a profession committed to social justice was training future social workers whose only exposure to racial/ethnic minority communities before they entered their field education experience may very well have been those videos.

Field Education and Racial Battle Fatigue

In addition to course work, fieldwork is a central component of social work curricula.[8] Each social work program organizes the field experience a little differently, but all social workers-in-training spend significant time practicing what they are learning in the classroom with real people at real agencies. In a white paper published by the Council on Social Work Education, Dean Pierce describes the hallmark of social work education as synergy between classroom-based learning and field-based learning, writing:

> The intent of field education is to connect the theoretical and conceptual contribution of the classroom with the practical world of the practice setting. It is a basic precept of social work education that the two inter-related components of curriculum—classroom and field—are of equal importance within the curriculum, and each contributes to the development of the requisite competencies of professional practice. Field education is systematically designed, supervised, coordinated, and evaluated based on criteria by which students demonstrate the achievement of program competencies.[9]

During our field education and training, we are expected to apply the social work concepts learned in the classroom to the clients we serve at our host organizations. Field education is an essential aspect of learning how our skills are applied, challenged, and refined in real-life settings. Nine hundred hours are required by the Council on Social Work Education (CSWE) for masters-level students to graduate.[10] This requirement ensures that we learn not only from our professors, but also from the clients we interact with and the organization where we worked. In the MSW program I enrolled in, students contribute the equivalent of $1.2 million worth of service hours to government, nonprofit, and other social service agencies.[11]

My university and field placement were located in a state in the middle of a demographic shift, particularly with regard to the Latino immigrant population. Therefore, as part of my field education, I was immediately thrust into the social and organizational tensions around race and ethnicity. The Federally Qualified Health Center (FQHC) I was placed in was in Durham, North Carolina, known colloquially as the "Black Wall Street" of the South. The city is notorious for its financial and educational institutions that produced some of the wealthiest and well-educated local leaders, all within the context of the Jim Crow South. The Center was previously the Black hospital during segregation, left vacant after Watts, the white hospital, was integrated. The empty building became a health center run by and for the Black community, built on the premise that Watts (now Durham Regional Hospital) remained racist in its administration and delivery of services. Many of the staff members had been there for decades and shared with me upon my arrival that, previously, the community served was reflective of Durham—a Black population that was economically powerful, well educated, and of course, steeped in the context of Southern race politics.

When I began, 86% of patients lived below the Federal Poverty Level (FPL) and 34% were immigrants best served in a language other than English. This is not uncommon of FQHCs. These institutions are the country's safety net system for the most vulnerable populations. However, the racial and ethnic shifts for the community were significant. From 1990 to 2000 the state boasted the fastest growing Latino population in the nation.[12] From 2000 to 2010, the Latino population continued to grow, increasing from 378,963 in 2000 to 800,120 in 2010—a dramatic increase of 111%.[13] With more than 800,000 Latinos living in North Carolina, this group accounted for approximately 8% of the state's current population[14] in the year I relocated there. More than half of North Carolina Latinos were foreign-born,[15] and 35% reported limited or no English proficiency.[16] One third are estimated to be undocumented,[17] adding an additional element of social vulnerability.

The pediatrics department of the FQHC represented the most visible shift in patient population, with the U.S.-born children of Latino immigrants, mostly monolingual Spanish speakers, accounting for 80% of the patients. However, the organizational shifts in providers who could meet the needs of this population moved quite slowly in comparison. Not a single provider on the pediatric staff spoke Spanish, and the first bilingual nurse was hired around the same time I started. There were two full-time interpreters and, due to patient volume, most providers relied on a telephone interpreting system called Rosario. The patient comes in, the provider picks up the phone, and an interpreter is on the line. The appointment is carried out as a three-way conversation with speaker phone.

Coming from FQHC settings in California where most staff were bilingual and bicultural, and Latino-serving clinics were the norm, I was shocked. After my first week, I was convinced that the accrediting body must have made a mistake, mixed up the paperwork, and accidently signed off that the clinic met the national cultural and linguistic competency standards. I actually looked into it. I learned they did indeed meet all four standards for culturally and linguistically competent services that are required of agencies receiving federal funds.[18] These include:

> Standard 1. Health care organizations should ensure that patients/ consumers receive from all staff members effective, understandable, and respectful care that is provided in a manner compatible with their cultural health beliefs and practices and preferred language.
>
> Standard 2. Health care organizations should implement strategies to recruit, retain, and promote at all levels of the organization a diverse staff and leadership that are representative of the demographic characteristics of the service area.
>
> Standard 3. Health care organizations should ensure that staff at all levels and across all disciplines receive ongoing education and training in culturally and linguistically appropriate service delivery.
>
> Standard 4. Health care organizations must offer and provide language assistance services, including bilingual staff and interpreter services, at no cost to each patient/consumer with limited English proficiency at all points of contact, in a timely manner during all hours of operation.

There are 10 other standards that are recommended, but not required, by the Office of Minority Health.[19] These standards include important steps such as letting patients know they have the right to receive services in their preferred language, ensure the quality of interpreting (not using family or friends), ensuring there is signage in multiple languages, and develop a strategic plan for organizational policy, operations, and management accountability to the topic, among other standards. Given that these were not required, there was simply no attempt to address them, as far as I could tell.

Those first few weeks of field education were a powerful opportunity to step outside of what I naively assumed was standard access to care and service delivery for Spanish-speaking immigrant communities. However, it was also emotionally exhausting. Every day I witnessed microaggressions, lack of empathy, and structural barriers to quality care. I arrived back at my house sobbing after field placement multiple times. While at my placement, I began feeling tremendous pressure and anxiety to do as much as I possibly could, such as ensuring that patients received referrals to the right services and obtaining their preferred appointment time. To ensure they got what they needed, I went beyond my scope of practice. It was exhausting. We were over capacity and I was burning out before I even completed my program.

These psychological stress responses (e.g., anxiety, disappointment, fear, frustration, shock, and so forth) have been well-documented in the literature of higher education as the symptoms of racial battle fatigue.[20] They are tied to the "battle" of navigating spaces where subtle, institutional racism and microaggressions are constant and unrelenting (including, but not limited to graduate school). These symptoms often go undiagnosed and untreated.[21] Now, reflecting back on the nuances of the stress I was experiencing, I am able to analyze the role that both racism and sexism played in the symptoms I experienced. The feminization of helping, including the dominant cultural narrative of women of color singlehandedly lifting their communities and families up, played a significant role in the pressure I put on myself to live up to my perceived expectation of a professional helper—no matter what. In retrospect I can see that that narrative is written and engrained through a dominant, majority lens. The reality of being a female helping professional is so much more nuanced, and that unraveling of the truth can happen only through counter-narratives that explore the complexity entailed.

For my own mental health, I learned how to leave my field experience at the field placement. I needed to figure out ways to bring my time with patients to a healthy close at the end of my day at clinic, so I could recharge for the next day and, ultimately, make it through graduate school. Designing end-of-the-day rituals to transition out of my professional role was an important component to my self-care. Simply bringing my awareness to literally closing the office door and saying my goodbyes to the staff made a difference. Instead of absentmindedly wandering out to my car or checking my cell phone as I locked the door to the office, I simply focused on shutting down for the day. Once sitting in my car, a quick body scan helped me assess. I had left the building, but was I carrying some tension out with me? More often than not, the answer was yes. I began diligently doing a few neck rolls, taking deep breaths, and literally shaking it off when I had a particularly challenging client. Upon reflection, these are some of the exact mindfulness techniques I shared with clients, but practicing them myself was an added layer of professional development that yielded a personal benefit.

There were, of course, some client cases so horrifying that I could not leave them behind at the end of the day. The cases of depression so severe that I became depressed too. Or, the small child so severely traumatized that I would wake up at night thinking about her. With those instances, my best coping mechanism was to get the case out of my mind and onto paper or into a discussion. Those cases would be the examples for my classroom presentation on treatment planning, or it would be the case I went over in depth with my supervisor. When I verbally processed these cases with someone else, it felt like I was able to handle it, instead of emotionally drowning in it. The value of a formal, supported structure for exploring how cases affected both personal and professional resilience was one of my most significant lessons learned.

The Historical Engagement of Social Workers with Immigrant Communities

One faculty member in particular was my sounding board through my first year as I navigated feelings of overwhelming frustration and disappointment. She made herself available to listen, was willing to have the hard discussions that didn't happen in the classroom, and eventually became a mentor. My mentor gave me a book that would change my life, *Social Services and the Ethnic Community* (2010).[22] The book discusses the history and evolution of social service delivery to multiple ethnic communities with detail. The authors elaborate on exclusionary practices from mainstream services, self-help organizations, ethnic-specific agency development, and the important role of self-determination and social justice. In that book I found exactly what was missing from the diversity and oppression pre-course activities—discussion of the complex reality of ethnic minority communities and the challenge of providing services given that sociopolitical complexity.

The book also contextualized social work's historical engagement with immigrant communities. Given my introduction to social work as a field that advocated for and served these communities, I was appalled to discover the historical reality of the profession's role in serving immigrants.

Racism and exclusion within early social work institutions such as settlement houses and charity organizations were rampant.[23] This declaration by a settlement house director, "You can Americanize the man from southeastern and southern Europe, but you can't Americanize a Mexican," exemplifies a dominant and professionally acceptable perspective at the turn of the nineteenth century.[24]

The professionalization of social work and the creation of formal social service organizations rarely met the specific needs of immigrants.[25] Services thought to be "culturally neutral" often reflected the values and beliefs of dominant White culture, excluding ethnic and linguistic minority groups from mainstream formal services.[26] Therefore, ethnic service agencies, often without trained social workers on staff, took responsibility for providing the organizational structure and services to ethnic and linguistic minority groups.[27] The more I learned, the more shame I felt about the profession. I became increasingly aware that my decision to become a social worker would involve more than finishing my training and going back out into the world. I was motivated to contribute toward the paradigm shifts within the profession that impact how we are trained and how we serve. In particular, the need to change how social workers of color, specifically women social workers, are recruited, represented, trained, and treated, was cemented into my work moving forward. Driving this motivation was my personal experience in learning how to deal with racial battle fatigue tied to my education—both in the classroom as well as the field—and the realization that resilience and fortitude would be key ingredients in navigating my chosen profession of social work beyond graduate school.

Upward and Onward: Future Direction and Next Steps

In what follows I offer specific strategies that could make a difference in how the field of social work unpacks and addresses privilege and oppression, both among the professionals trained, and the communities we serve. Changes at both the macro and micro level are significant. At the macro level, updating language and policies in professional standards plays an important role. For example, the National Association of Social Workers (NASW) Code of Ethics has recently reframed standards for professional practice with immigrants in its sections on culturally competent practice.[28] NASW recently added *immigration status* as an explicit category of people for whom social workers should oppose discrimination.[29] Similarly, the Council on Social Work Education (CSWE) Educational Policy and Accreditation Standards speak to the importance of preparing culturally competent students for practice in global societies.[30] Given social work's historical assimilationist stance toward immigrants, these are important steps.

These changes in macro frameworks led to more micro changes as social work educators sought to better prepare students to work with an increasing number of clients who are immigrants settling into new communities.[31] For example, schools of social work have developed concentrations and certificate programs related to immigration and transmigration.[32] These programs are designed to better prepare future social workers for the critical analysis required to effectively work with diverse groups of immigrants and the myriad of social, economic, political, legal, and psychological issues associated with immigration.[33] Understanding the historical reality of social workers engaging with immigrant communities is an important element of these ongoing curricular changes.

At the micro level, there are also three interpersonal strategies that could make a significant impact on the resilience for social work students themselves, with the intention of curbing racial battle fatigue and providing support that meets the unique needs of female social workers of color during graduate training:

AFFINITY GROUPS

These groups inevitably form as de facto groups, as was the case at my social work program. Students of color created spaces to discuss issues relevant to their experience in graduate school, and in the field as well. It is worth noting that affinity groups serve a different function than student groups, which are often expected to put on events and educate the dominant group about issues relevant to their population. Affinity groups benefit the attendees, first and foremost, and are facilitated by members of the group themselves.

MENTAL HEALTH SUPPORT

While affinity groups provide a space for social support, combatting racial battle fatigue may require psychological resources beyond the required professional supervision that social work programs offer. Providing mental health resources, at no cost to students of color in particular, sends the message that our resilience and psychological well-being is important.

Finally, the burden of educating social workers on privilege and oppression should fall on the institution, not on students of color. Social work programs should consider adopting antiracist coursework that goes beyond profiles of communities of color and cover topics such as white privilege, structural racism, and systematic oppression in detail.

Concluding Reflections

Prior to my having stepped foot at a School of Social Work, I learned about the field from a well-regarded community leader and was motivated to become a social worker based on my own commitment to political activism and social justice. I went into graduate school ready to focus my studies on self-determination and community-led action for culturally and linguistically competent service. The reality I faced was quite unexpected, with my first academic social work experience undermining the complexity and context of communities of color.

Throughout graduate school, I learned more about what the predominantly white profession has meant both historically and contemporarily. Although I certainly learned useful skills in the classroom, it took strong mentorship, meaningful peer interaction, and challenging field experiences to develop a deeper understanding of how social justice can not only be conceptualized in social work education but also applied in practice. I was frequently surprised, and even disappointed with, what I learned about how communities of color and social workers of color were marginalized even within the context of a profession that claimed to serve these very populations with dignity and respect. However, these experiences are embedded into the profession's history and need to be acknowledged. Knowing this history was instrumental in my developing a more critical stance as a social worker.

Social work as a discipline is characterized for being both action- and value-based.[34] However, this focus has not been equivalent to a critical stance. During my graduate school experience, I grappled with the rapid depoliticization of the field and figured out what social justice meant in this context. My identity and experiences entering the social work field inherently and repeatedly brought up the question: Can you have a social worker identity without wholeheartedly adopting the profession's critical social justice underpinnings? For myself, my personal politics and lived experience as a Chicana social worker were intertwined with and affected how I aimed to serve my clients and my expectations while practicing the profession. During my graduate school training, I discovered that this identity also affected my interaction with classmates, professors, and those who would ultimately become my colleagues. While I came into the professional hypersensitive to the racialized nature of the institutions that house social work services (e.g., health centers, state institutions, municipal and local social services), I was unaware of how racism and sexism would operate in the very institutions and programs that trained and supervised emerging social workers. The degree to which microaggressions and the privileging of certain kinds of knowledge were present in my graduate school training, as well as the overall lack of critical dialogue, surprised me. Perhaps it was naive to assume otherwise, but I entered the program based on the assumption that social work education did not exist without a social justice framework.

During graduate school I learned, however, that for many of my class-mates and professors, the question of a social work professional identity simply nodded to social justice roots, without a genuine adoption of critical social justice principles. The question that I posed about whether one could become a social worker without adopting social justice under-pinnings foundational to the field was in fact not a question that came up frequently during coursework or supervised clinic work. Instead it was left to office hours with trusted professors and after-hours conversations with fellow women of color classmates.

The conversations I assumed would be happening about power privi-lege, race, gender, and class were not at the core of my education. Instead, they were happening on the margins, fueled by my need to find those allies and mentors who could help me navigate and make sense of my new professional identity. Those opportunities to be in community with other students and professors who could provide what was not available to be in the classroom were central to my resilience and persistence. In good company, I realized that what the profession means to me as a Chicana social worker may very well never be the same as what it means to my colleagues who do not feel the need to keep the profession's social justice principals at the center of their work. That has been both a source of frustration—in realizing how complacency in the face of injustice has and will continue to operate—as well as inspiration for centralizing the often marginalized role of the female social worker of color. Although the communities we come from are not always given their due complexity, our stories are not always in the textbooks, and our legacy is not always spoken of, they do exist. We do exist. We serve, we teach, we fight. We keep social work professionals accountable to a critical approach to working with communities. Our contribution to the field matters.

Notes

Sections of this chapter have been adapted from the author's 2013 article, "Carolina del Norte and the New South: Social Work Practice with New Latino Immigrant Communities," *Journal Advances in Social Work*.

1. Harold Lewis and Jayne Silberman, *Intellectual Base of Social Work Practice: Tools for Thought in a Helping Profession* (New York: Routledge, 2012).

2. Daniel G. Solórzano and Tara J. Yosso, "Critical Race and LatCrit Theory and Method: Counter-storytelling," *International Journal of Qualitative Studies in Education* 14, no. 4 (2001): 471–495.

3. Council on Social Work Education, "2010 Statistics on Social Work Education in the United States," *Council on Social Work Education*, last edited 2011, http://www.cswe.org/File.aspx?id=52269.

4. Ibid.

5. Amy Rossiter, "Innocence Lost and Suspicion Found: Do We Educate for or against Social Work?" *Critical Social Work* 2, no. 1 (2001): 2.

6. Richard Delgado, "Storytelling for Oppositionists and Others: A Plea for Narrative," *Michigan Law Review* 87, no. 8 (1989): 2411–2441.

7. The Treaty of Guadalupe Hidalgo was signed February 1848 by the governments of Mexico and the United States, marking the end of the Mexican American War. The Treaty ceded roughly half of Mexico's national territory (present-day California, Nevada, and Utah, as well as portions of Arizona, New Mexico, Colorado, and Wyoming) to the United States. As a result, Mexican citizens living in those states were now considered Mexican Americans and became ethnic minority U.S. citizens. See Richard Griswold Del Castillo, *The Treaty of Guadalupe Hidalgo: A Legacy of Conflict* (Norman: University of Oklahoma Press, 1992).

8. Julianne Wayne, Marion Bogo, and Miriam Raskin, "Field Education as the Signature Pedagogy of Social Work Education," *Journal of Social Work Education* 46, no. 3 (2010): 327–339.

9. Dean Pierce, "Field Education in the 2008 EPAS: Implications for the Field Director's Role," *Council on Social Work Education*, last modified 2008, http://www.cswe.org/File.aspx?id=31580.

10. Council on Social Work Education, "Educational Policy and Accreditation Standards," *Council on Social Work Education*, last modified 2012, http://www.cswe.org/File.aspx?id=13780.

11. UNC School of Social Work, "Field Education Program," *UNC School of Social Work*, http://ssw.unc.edu/programs/masters/fieldeducation.

12. H. Nolo Martinez and Andrea Bazán Manson, "Health Disparities among North Carolina's Latinos: Our Point of View," *North Carolina Medical Journal* 65, no. 6 (2003): 356–358.

13. Pew Hispanic Center, "Census 2010: 50 Million Latinos: Hispanics Account for More than Half of Nation's Growth in Past Decade," *Pew Hispanic Center*, last modified 2011, http://www.pewhispanic.org/files/reports/140.pdf.

14. U.S. Census Bureau, "2010 Census: State Population Profile Maps," *U.S. Census Bureau*, last modified 2010, http://2010.census.gov/2010census/.

15. Sejal Zota, "Immigrants in North Carolina: A Fact Sheet," *Popular Government* 74, no. 1 (2008): 38–44.

16. "U.S. Census Bureau, American Community Survey Five Year Estimates 2005–2009," last modified 2010, http://factfinder.census.gov/servlet/DatasetMain PageServlet.

17. Jeff Popke, "Latino Migration and Neoliberalism in the U.S. South: Notes toward a Rural Cosmopolitanism," *southeastern geographer* 51, no. 2 (2011): 242–259.

18. U.S. Department of Health and Human Services, "Office of Minority Health. National Standards for Culturally and Linguistically Appropriate Services in Health Care," *U.S. Department of Health and Human Services*, last modified 2001, http://minorityhealth.hhs.gov/assets/pdf/checked/finalreport.pdf.

19. Ibid.

20. William A. Smith, Walter R. Allen, and Lynette L. Danley, "'Assume the Position . . . You Fit the Description,' Psychosocial Experiences and Racial Battle Fatigue among African American Male College Students," *American Behavioral Scientist* 51, no. 4 (2007): 551–578.

21. Tara Yosso, William Smith, Miguel Ceja, and Daniel Solórzano, "Critical Race Theory, Racial Microaggressions, and Campus Racial Climate for Latina/o Undergraduates," *Harvard Educational Review* 79, no. 4 (2009): 659–691.

22. Alfreda P. Iglehart and Rosina M. Becerra, *Social Services and the Ethnic Community: History and Analysis* (Long Grove: Waveland Press, 2010).

23. Lisa de Saxe Zerden, Arianna Taboada, and Quentin Joshua Hinson, "Carolina del Norte and the New South: Social Work Practice with New Latino Immigrant Communities," *Advances in Social Work* 14, no. 1 (2013): 260–275.

24. Iglehart and Becerra, *Social Services*, 5.

25. Ibid.; Michael B. Katz, *In the Shadow of the Poorhouse: A Social History of Welfare in America* (New York: Basic Books, 1996).

26. Tricia B. Bent-Goodley, "Culture and Domestic Violence Transforming Knowledge Development," *Journal of Interpersonal Violence* 20, no. 2 (2005): 195–203; Katz, *In the Shadow*.

27. Iglehart and Becerra, *Social Services*.

28. National Association of Social Workers, "Code of Ethics: Section 1.05 Cultural Competence and Social Diversity," *National Association of Social Workers*, last edited 2008, http://www.socialworkers.org/pubs/code/code.asp.

29. National Association of Social Workers, "Immigration and Refugee Resettlement," *National Association of Social Workers,* last edited 2012, http://www .socialworkers.org/practice/intl/issues/immigration.asp.

30. Council on Social Work Education, "Educational Policy and Accreditation Standards."

31. Rich Furman and Nalini Negi, *Social Work Practice with Latinos* (Chicago: Lyceum Books, 2010); Nalini Negi and Rich Furman, *Transnational Social Work Practice* (New York: Columbia University Press, 2013).

32. Universities that include an explicit focus on immigrants include: Arizona State University, Chicago School of Professional Psychology, New Mexico Highlights University, Saint Joseph College—Connecticut, University of Denver, University of Houston, Columbia University, Loyola University—Chicago, and University of Maine.

33. Mary Nash, John Wong, and Andrew Trilin, "Civic and Social Integration A New Field of Social Work Practice with Immigrants, Refugees and Asylum Seekers," *International Social Work* 49, no. 3 (2006): 345–363.

34. Robert P. Mullaly, *Challenging Oppression: A Critical Social Work Approach* (Oxford: Oxford University Press, 2002).

Epilogue

Kimberly D. McKee and Denise A. Delgado

When we conceived of this project more than five years ago, we were in graduate school together. We faced the same challenges encountered by many graduate students: the struggle to balance our personal and professional lives, the stress caused by living far from family and loved ones, and the pressure to excel in an environment that is often competitive even when it should be more cooperative. However, most of our conversations, both with each other and other women of color, had to do with our gendered and racialized experiences in graduate school. We shared advice on how to deal with racism in the classroom, how to handle microaggressions from members of our program and/or cohort, what to do about professors that mocked and ridiculed accents in the classroom, and the struggle to make time for our intellectual work while still trying to mentor other marginalized students.[1] We gave suggestions on how to answer emails and questions that were racially problematic, and we created roundtable discussions on how to better incorporate the work of women of color and Indigenous women in the classroom. When we gathered together, many spoke of their struggles with partners that expected full-time domestic duties in addition to graduate work, with family that worried what impact education would have on a woman's marriage prospects, and with sexism experienced in the classroom, whether it was in their position as an instructor or a student.

While our white and/or male colleagues had some of the same issues that we did, it seemed exacerbated for women of color and Indigenous women—many graduate students struggle to find their place in graduate school, but nonwhite women graduate students seemed far more likely to feel like imposters and wonder if a mistake was made in letting them in, even when their scholastic achievements clearly indicated their fitness. While first-generation college students are not only from communities of color or Indigenous communities, many of us were the first ones to attend college and graduate school, giving us less knowledge of the process and what to expect from the experience.[2] Coming from poor or working-class families unable to contribute financially is an additional struggle for many women of color and indigenous women graduate students. At the same time, even if one was not a first-generation student, it became evident that there was a shared reality of different expectations and treatment experienced by nonwhite women as a whole. In order to negotiate these issues, we read books and blogs specifically aimed at people of color and Indigenous people in academia, joined groups and led roundtable discussions with other women of color, and tried to create our own communities and support groups, often relying on women only a year or two further in the process for advice and assistance. This cooperative community became the inspiration for this book. We envisioned bringing together these voices to tell our truths and address the hidden, and not so hidden, subtleties of navigating higher education. *Degrees of Difference: Reflections of Women of Color on Graduate School* reflects this commitment to unabashedly share what it means to be one of the few nonwhite women in a program or department or the only woman of color or Indigenous woman in a cohort. Women have testified to their experiences, their struggles, their triumphs, and their methods for navigating this space.

Contributors illuminate what is at stake when we speak out and push back against gendered, racialized, sexualized harassment and microaggressions as well as negotiate relationships with faculty and peers who fail to understand the unique ways women of color and Indigenous women experience graduate school and how they may be complicit in the marginalization of nonwhite women. In sharing their experiences, these women embody the feminist killjoy, pushing back against an academy that expects a particular level of gratefulness that we were even let into the door, let alone the room. These women interrupt and disrupt notions of what higher education *is* by offering reflections on what it *should be* to allow them, and other women of color and Indigenous women, to thrive in the academy. They give voice to countless other women who may be unable to speak up and speak out due to constraints out of their control. The realities disclosed contribute to a growing movement of women of color and Indigenous women's counterstories to the academy and what it means to challenge institutionalized norms. And, we may encounter resistance even in spaces that might seem to be more welcoming to us—minority serving institutions and ethnic studies departments or programs.[3]

Collectively, *Degrees of Difference* contributors understand the value in sharing their experiences and claiming space. They are not wallflowers waiting to be heard. Many of them pushed back while in graduate school and challenged the status quo to make space for the realities of marginalized communities. For some, this work resulted after identifying mentors, sponsors, and other supporters who helped empower these women to make particular choices. For others, their speaking out was rooted in an internal desire to ensure what happened to them would not happen to others. Whether it includes a graduate student group pushing for a change in curriculum for issues related to diversity and inclusivity or creating an organization meant to address the issues of women of color and Indigenous women, women like ourselves participate in these activities to ensure that the women that come after us are better prepared for the reality of graduate school and have more support from faculty, staff, and peers. We also call for faculty and staff who see themselves as mentors or sponsors of women of color and Indigenous women in graduate school, or even postdoctoral fellows or junior faculty, to amplify the work of those women. By calling attention to the labor and efforts of nonwhite women, these gatekeepers can open doors or hold others accountable in ways that women of color and Indigenous women graduate students cannot due to their positions in the academy.

We want more voices. Our contributors are from different fields and different universities, with different cultural, familial, religious, and linguistic backgrounds. This diversity of experience demonstrates both the unique experience of each contributor and the similarities found in their narratives. For example, Carrie Sampson discusses the struggle of parenting and familial illness and challenges the microaggressions she experienced in her personal and professional life, and Soha Youssef reflects on the gender and religious microaggressions she confronts within the academy and critiques familial and religious practices affecting her experiences. The authors, in both of these instances, highlight not only their professional struggles, but how women of color must also confront *and* navigate gendered labor and expectations.

Moreover, discussions of microaggressions and the struggle to maintain a good work/life balance appear in many of the chapters with authors also elucidating the importance and value of community and strong mentorship to support successful completion of their graduate degrees. These networks provide effective emotional and professional support. Delia Fernández emphasizes the role of the Robert E. McNair program in graduate school preparation as she forged relationships with supportive mentors. Similarly, Regina Idoate considers the importance of mentors and community for Native scholars and the value of mirrors for underrepresented scholars. And, Jenny Wills and Délice Mugabo make clear the significance of cultivating intentional interracial and interdisciplinary communities, in their discussion of Canadian higher education. These essays provide women of color and Indigenous women graduate students a roadmap to multiple ways to create and find communities and the types of mentorship that provide much needed support.

Finally, *Degrees of Difference* focuses on specific steps that can be taken by graduate students to fight back against microaggressions and bias in their own fields and departments. Nwadiogo Ejiogu discusses the particular concerns and struggles faced by medical students of color and how she fought against marginalization within her own department. Building on the ways that nonwhite women can combat stereotyping and assert oneself is Aerial Ashlee's discussion of the specific issues facing Asian American women in graduate school. Arianna Taboada echoes these reflections as she explores the role of implicit bias and its impact on low-income communities of color in the field of social work. All three authors come from different departments and branches of intellectual thought, but all discuss the impact of academic culture, gender, and racial bias, and microaggressions within these fields. They give specific advice on how to combat these issues, some particular to the discipline being discussed, but also other advice that can work for graduate women of color in a variety of fields.

What is important to recognize, however, is that we did not create this collection to discourage nonwhite women from contemplating graduate school. *Degrees of Difference* is constructed to serve as a mechanism for women of color and Indigenous women as well as their allies and mentors to contextualize their experiences within a broader community. Each chapter provides helpful tips and experiences that support nonwhite women as they resist being shut out of the academy. Existing in isolation only perpetuates feelings of imposter syndrome and alienation. The contributors underscore the importance of community building—from building a community of other women of color and Indigenous women graduate students, or graduate students outside of your particular program or cohort, to engaging the local community of your university to find strength.

Articulating the benefits and limits of intentionally creating a space for graduate students of color in her discussion of the Mentoring Future Faculty of Color Project at the City University of New York Graduate Center, Melissa Phruksachart writes: "For scholars whose work is informed by interdisciplinary fields like black studies, ethnic studies, queer studies, and decolonial thought, part of intellectual life is the constant struggle for legitimacy and institutional access. Minoritized graduate students understand all too well that their topics, modes of analysis, physical appearance, or personal experiences can *a priori* prevent their work from being taken seriously. . . . By intentionally fostering community, life can be found in the academy outside the *curriculum vitae*."[4] And, it is our hope that readers of this collection will see the importance of investing in building networks across disciplines and departments.

At the same time, this community does not need to be limited to real-life interactions. Online communities and friendships through social media support women of color and Indigenous women as they seek advice or feedback about an incident or, more positively, celebrate a success. For Kimberly, engaging with colleagues in Asian American Studies and Adoption Studies frequently occurs on social media because so often these scholars are the only ones at their institutions. Digital networks become a way to supplement the face-to-face interactions at conferences. Cultivating a community nourishes the contributors precisely because it offers a space for them to engage in deep and intentional conversations about racism and misogyny, among other -isms, with folks who can empathize with a particular experience. We should see ourselves as colleagues of one another and celebrate the successes of everyone, because when one person succeeds, we all will.

We found intellectual communities to be one of the formative sites of resistance. Whether it was participating in the Association for Asian American Studies/East of California Junior Faculty Retreat or the National Women's Studies Association Women of Color Leadership Project, Kimberly benefited from the formal and informal conversations with a range of senior and junior faculty. These spaces facilitated connections and reflection on her teaching, research, and service.[5] Kimberly also took advantage of the myriad mentoring and professional development opportunities she encountered as an early career faculty member.[6] Participating in a variety of workshops, programs, and sessions allowed her to intentionally reflect on *who* she wanted to be in the professoriate.[7] This reflection resulted in an invitation to provide remarks at the National Women's Studies Association

Graduate Caucus Reception in November 2015,[8] where she shared the following tips for transitioning from graduate student to faculty member:

1. Be comfortable with sharing your writing early and often.
2. Writing groups are critical.
3. External funding is not you against the world.
4. The job market is not for the faint of heart.
5. Collegiality is key.
6. Building networks with one another is critical.
7. Don't be afraid to discuss rejection.

And while these tips are important, what's more significant is to remember that mentoring comes from multiple places and that there's no single mentor who will have all the answers. These mentors may be senior faculty, junior faculty, your peers in graduate school, staff, or administrators. To limit yourself to the one you think makes the "best" mentor will reduce your possibilities. One of the most valuable pieces of information Kimberly learned as she transitioned from graduate school to postdoctoral fellow to junior faculty was that not all mentors are direct mirrors. Yes, it's important to have mirrors and to see yourself represented; however, some of her most influential mentors have not been Asian American women or nonwhite women. To discount who could be a mentor does a disservice to you. Kimberly remembers having this conversation with one of her first undergraduate research mentees. This woman was initially skeptical of what Kimberly could offer her, a Black woman, because she held onto the idea that mentors should align with one's racial or ethnic identity. Yet as they got to know one another, the undergraduate student realized that a good mentor is not about whether someone's identity neatly matches up with your identity.

As women of color and Indigenous women embark on their journeys as graduate students or transition into an alt-ac or faculty position, it's important to recognize the power of being strategic. From whether it's understanding the broad strokes of a way an institution operates to reflecting on the minutiae of a particular department or program, acknowledging how different strategies would benefit or hinder one's cause is critical. This does not mean one needs to acquiesce to the status quo. Instead, we should consider how one action will have a ripple effect tomorrow, the next month, the next year, and into the future. When is it most strategic to speak up and speak out? And, what is at stake if we remain silent? We know silence equals violence, so how can we work in coalitions, in collaboration, and with mentors and allies to enact change that has the most benefits possible to the largest group of people? The balancing act that we perform calls us to prioritize those who are the most marginalized or precarious, while also recognizing that not all battles can be fought due to time or mental and physical health. For us, this meant speaking up when we felt nonwhite women experienced marginalization within our graduate program. We sought to directly address what was occurring in order to enact change for future graduate students. At the same time, this is why we actively participated in graduate student organizations for Latino/a students and Asian American students, as well as worked in coalitions to engender change.

We embarked on *Degrees of Difference* in order to center the graduate school experiences of women of color and Indigenous women. Our perspectives are a critical piece to understanding the realities of nonwhite women in the professoriate. One cannot disentangle another without erasing how graduate school is a formative experience in shaping who we become as faculty and staff. This collection is meant to ignite conversation and spark change in the lives of women of color and Indigenous women, their mentors and allies, departments and programs, and campuses who want to commit and invest in shaping an academy that looks like the diversity of this world.

Notes

1. For additional examples of how women of color navigate the college classroom, see María Scharrnón-del Río, "Teaching at the Intersections: Liberatory and Anti-Oppressive Pedagogical Praxis in the Multicultural Counseling Classroom as a Queer Puerto Rican Educator," *Feminist Teacher* Vol. 23, Issue 2–3 (2017): 90–105; Imaani Jamillah El-Burki, "Contemporary Media Representations of Race and the Reshaping of the College Classroom Experience," *Feminist Teacher* Vol. 23, Issue 2–3 (2017): 106–116.

2. Donna J. Nichol and Jennifer A. Yee, "'Reclaiming Our Time': Women of Color Faculty and Radical Self-Care in the Academy," *Feminist Teacher* Vol. 23, Issue 2–3 (2017): 133–156.

3. S. Tay Glover, "'Black Lesbians—Who Will Fight for Our Lives but Us?': Navigating Power, Belonging, Labor, Resistance, and Survival in the Ivory Tower," *Feminist Teacher* Vol. 23, Issue 2–3 (2017): 157–175; B.A.L., "The Hidden Costs of Serving Our Community: Women Faculty of Color, Racist Sexism, and False Security in a Hispanic-Serving Institution," *Feminist Teacher* Vol. 23, Issue 2–3 (2017): 176–195.

4. Melissa Phruksachart, "On Mentoring Future Faculty of Color," *Feminist Teacher* Vol. 23, Issue 2–3 (2017): 117–118.

5. Kimberly McKee, "Reflections on the AAAS/EOC Junior Faculty Retreat," *Mckeekimberly.com*, May 1, 2015, https://mckeekimberly.com/2015/05/01/reflections -on-the-aaas-eoc-retreat/.

6. Kimberly McKee, "Reflections on Year One," *Mckeekimberly.com*, August 27, 2015, https://mckeekimberly.com/2015/08/27/reflections-on-year-one/;

Kimberly McKee, "The Benefits of Informal Mentoring," *Mckeekimberly.com*, February 20, 2015, https://mckeekimberly.com/2015/02/20/benefits-informal -mentors/.

7. Kimberly McKee, "Paying It Forward," *Mckeekimberly.com*, February 16, 2015, https://mckeekimberly.com/2015/02/16/paying-it-forward/.

8. Kimberly McKee, "NWSA Graduate Caucus Reception Remarks," *Mckee kimberly.com*, November 16, 2015, https://mckeekimberly.com/2015/02/16/paying -it-forward/.

Bibliography

Affan, Samah. "Ethical Gestures: Articulations of Black Life in Montreal's 1960s." Master's thesis, Concordia University, 2013.

Ahmed, Sara. "Feminist Killjoys (and Other Willful Subjects)," *The Scholar and Feminist Online* 8, no. 3 (2010): 1–8. http://sfonline.barnard.edu/polyphonic/ahmed_01.htm.

———. *The Promise of Happiness*. Chapel Hill: Duke University Press, 2010.

American College Personnel Association and National Association of Student Personnel Administrators. "Professional Competency Areas for Student Affairs Practitioners." Last modified August 2015. http://www.myacpa.org/professional competency-areas-student-affairs-practitioners.

Anzaldúa, Gloria. *Borderlands/La Frontera: The New Mestiza*. San Francisco: Spinsters/Aunt Lute, 1987.

Apugo, Danielle L. "'We All We Got': Considering Peer Relationships as Multi-Purpose Sustainability Outlets among Millennial Black Women Graduate Students Attending Majority White Urban Universities," *Urban Review* 49 (2017), 347–367.

Aryan, Bushra, and Fernando Guzman. "Women of Color and the PhD: Experiences in Formal Graduate Support Programs," *Journal of Business Studies Quarterly* 1, no. 4 (2010): 69–77.

B.A.L. "The Hidden Costs of Serving Our Community: Women Faculty of Color, Racist Sexism, and False Security in a Hispanic-Serving Institution," *Feminist Teacher* 23, no. 2–3 (2017): 176–195.

Bannerji, Himani. *Dark Side of the Nation: Essays on Multiculturalism, Nationalism, and Gender*. Toronto: Canadian Scholars' Press, 2000.

Barakat, Halim Isber. *The Arab World: Society, Culture, and State*. Berkeley: University of California Press, 1993.

Barnes, Samesha R. "McNair Scholars Program Prepares Students for the PhD Program in Materials Research," *MRS Bulletin* 40, no. 6 (2015): 470–472.

Bashi Treitler, Vilna. *Survival of the Knitted: Immigrant Social Networks in a Stratified World*. Stanford: Stanford University Press, 2007.

Basturk, Ramazan. "The Relationship of Graduate Record Examination Aptitude Test Scores and Graduate School Performance of International Students at the United States Universities," 1–15. Proceedings of Annual Conference of the Mid-Western Educational Research Association, Chicago. 1999.

Bell, Derrick. "Foreword to the First Edition," *Critical Race Feminism: A Reader*, ed. Adrien Katherine Wing. New York: New York University Press, 2003.

Bell, Nathan E. "Data Sources: Graduate Degree Attainment of the U.S. Population," *Council of Graduate Schools* (July 2009): 1.

Bent-Goodley, Tricia B. "Culture and Domestic Violence Transforming Knowledge Development," *Journal of Interpersonal Violence* 20, no. 2 (2005): 195–203.

Berry, Theodorea Regina, and Nathalie Mizelle, eds. *From Oppression to Grace: Women of Color and Their Dilemmas within the Academy*. Sterling, Va.: Stylus Publishing, 2006.

Bertrand Jones, Tamara, JeffriAnne Wilder, and La'Tara Osborne-Lampkin. "Employing a Black Feminist Approach to Doctoral Advising: Preparing Black Women for the Professoriate," *The Journal of Negro Education* 82, no. 3 (2013): 326–338.

Boggs, Grace Lee. *Living for Change: An Autobiography*. Minneapolis: University of Minnesota Press, 1998.

Brancati, Frederick L. "The Art of Pimping," *JAMA* 262 (1989): 89–90.

Brunsma, David L., David G. Embrick, and Jean H. Shin. "Graduate Students of Color: Race, Racism, and Mentoring in the White Waters of Academia," *Sociology of Race and Ethnicity* 3, no. 1 (2017): 1–13.

Burke, Kenneth. "Terministic Screens," *Language as Symbolic Action: Essays on Life, Literature, and Method*, 44–62. Berkeley: The University of California Press, 1966.

Butler, Johnnella. Introduction. *Color-Line to Borderlands: The Matrix of American Ethnic Studies*, ed. Johnnella Butler, xi–xxvii. Seattle: University of Washington Press, 2001.

Caldwell, Kia Lilly, and Margaret Hunter. "Creating a Feminist Community on a Woman of Color Campus," *Frontiers: A Journal of Women Studies* 25, no.1 (2004): 25–26.

Canadian Ethnic Studies 44, no. 2: *Racialization, Race, and the University* (2012).

Castañeda, Mari, and Kirsten Lynn Isgro. *Mothers in Academia*. New York: Columbia University Press, 2013.

Chacón, Maria, Elizabeth Cohen, and Sharon Strover. "Chicanas and Chicanos: Barriers to Progress in Higher Education." *Latino College Students*, ed. Michael A. Olivas, 296–324. New York: Teachers College Press, 1986.

Chanchlani, Neil. "Being PIMPed Ain't Easy: Neil Chanchlani Defends a Dying Teaching Method," *Medscape*, January 1, 2013. http://www.medscape.com/viewarticle/781525.

Chessman, Hollie, and Lindsay Wayt. "What Are Students Demanding?" *Higher Education Today*, American Council on Education, January 13, 2016. http://www.higheredtoday.org/2016/01/13/what-are-students-demanding/.

Chilisa, Bagele. *Indigenous Research Methodologies*. London: Sage Publications, 2011.

Chinn, Pauline W. U. "Multiple Worlds/Mismatched Meanings: Barriers to Minority Women Engineers," *Journal of Research in Science Teaching* 36, no. 6 (1999): 621–636.

Clance, Pauline R., and Suzanne A. Imes. "The Imposter Phenomenon in High Achieving Women: Dynamics and Therapeutic Intervention," *Psychotherapy: Theory, Research and Practice* 15, no. 3 (1978): 241–247.

Cokely, Kevin, Shannon McClain, Alicia Enciso, and Mercedes Martinez. "An Examination of the Impact of Minority Status Stress and Imposter Feelings on the Mental Health of Diverse Ethnic Minority College Students," *Journal of Multicultural Counseling & Development* 41, no. 2 (2013): 82–95.

The Combahee River Collective. "Black Feminist Statement," *The Second Wave: A Reader in Feminist Theory*, ed. Linda Nicholson, 63–70. New York: Routledge, 1997.

Comer, Debra R., and Susan Stites-Doe. "Antecedents and Consequences of Faculty Women's Academic-Parental Role Balancing," *Journal of Family and Economic Issues* 27, no. 3 (September 10, 2006): 495–512. doi:10.1007/s10834–006–9021-z.

Committee on Maximizing the Potential of Women in Academic Science and Engineering (U.S.), and Committee on Science, Engineering, and Public Policy (U.S.), eds. *Beyond Bias and Barriers Fulfilling the Potential of Women in Academic Science and Engineering*. Washington, D.C.: National Academies Press, 2007.

Council on Social Work Education. *2010 Statistics on Social Work Education in the United States*. 2011. http://www.cswe.org/File.aspx?id=52269.

———. "Educational Policy and Accreditation Standards," 2012. http://www.cswe.org/File.aspx?id=13780.

Crenshaw, Kimberlé. "Demarginalizing the Intersection of Race and Sex: A Black Feminist Critique of Antidiscrimination Doctrine, Feminist Theory and Antiracist Politics," *The University of Chicago Legal Forum* 140 (1989): 139–167.

Critical Ethnic Studies Conference. "2013 Online Conference Schedule," Critical Ethnic Studies Association, September 11, 2013. https://www.criticalethnicstudies.org/content/2013-online-conference-schedule.

Crunk Feminist Collective. "Back-to-School Beatitudes: 10 Academic Survival Tips," *Crunk Feminist Collective* (blog), August 25, 2011. http://www.crunkfeminist collective.com/2011/08/25/back-to-school-beatitudes-10-academic-survival-tips/.

C-Span. "McNair Program Cuts." *C-SPAN.org*. https://www.c-span.org/video/?c4671411/mcnair-program-cuts.

Dace, Karen L, ed. *Unlikely Allies in the Academy: Women of Color and White Women in Conversation*. New York: Routledge, 2012.

Davidson, Martin N., and Lynn Foster-Johnson. "Mentoring in the Preparation of Graduate Researchers of Color," *Review of Educational Research* 71, no. 4 (Winter 2001): 549–574.

Davis, Angela Y. *Women, Race & Class*. New York: Vintage Books, 1983.

DeCuir-Gunby, Jessica T., and Dina C. Walker-DeVose. "Expanding the Counter-story: The Potential for Critical Race Mixed Methods Studies in Education," *Handbook of Critical Race Theory in Education*, eds. Marvin Lynn and Adrian Dixson, 248–259. New York: Routledge, 2013.

Del Castillo, Richard Griswold. *The Treaty of Guadalupe Hidalgo: A Legacy of Conflict*. Norman: University of Oklahoma Press, 1992.

Delgado, Richard. "Storytelling for Oppositionists and Others: A Plea for Narrative," *Michigan Law Review* 87, no. 8 (1989): 2411–2441.

Delgado, Richard, and Jean Stefancic. *Critical Race Theory: An Introduction*. New York: New York University Press, 2017.

Deloria Jr., Vine, and Daniel R. Wildcat. *Power and Place: Indian Education in America*. Golden, Colo.: Fulcrum Publishing, 2001.

de Saxe Zerden, Lisa, Arianna Taboada, and Quentin Joshua Hinson. "Carolina del Norte and the New South: Social Work Practice with New Latino Immigrant Communities," *Advances in Social Work* 14, no. 1 (2013): 260–275.

Dragonroot Media. "Bring Black Studies to Concordia: Interview with Anthony Mclachlan and Shannon Gittens-Yaboa." *Dragonroot Media*. https://hannahbesseau .wixsite.com/dragonrootmedia/single-post/2016/11/08/Bring-Black-Studies-to -Concordia.

Duncan, Patti. "Hot Commodities, Cheap Labor: Women of Color in the Academy," *Frontiers: A Journal of Women's Studies* 35, no. 3 (2014): 39–63.

———. "Outsiders, Interlopers, and Ingrates: The Tenuous Position of Women of Color in Women's Studies," *Women's Studies Quarterly* 30, no. 3/4 (Winter 2002): 155–168.

Dyrbye, Liselotte N., Colin P. West, Daniel Satele, Sonja Boone, Litjen Tan, Jeff Sloan, and Tait D. Shanafelt. "Burnout among U.S. Medical Students, Residents, and Early Career Physicians Relative to the General U.S. Population," *Academic Medicine* 89, no. 3 (2014): 443–451.

Eagan Jr., M. Kevin, and Jason C. Garvey. "Stressing Out: Connecting Race, Gender, and Stress with Faculty Productivity," *The Journal of Higher Education* 86, no. 6 (Nov./Dec. 2015): 923–954.

El-Burki, Imaani Jamillah. "Contemporary Media Representations of Race and the Reshaping of the College Classroom Experience," *Feminist Teacher* 23, no. 2–3 (2017): 106–116.

Finkelstein, Martin J., Valerie Martin Conley, and Jack H. Schuster. "Taking the Measure of Faculty Diversity," April 2016, Advancing Higher Education, TIAA Institute, New York, N.Y., 13.

Fnais, Naif, Charlene Soobiah, Maggie H. Chen, Erin Lillie, Laure Perrier, Mariam Tashkhandi, Sharon E. Straus, Muhammad Mamdani, Mohammed Al-Omran, and Andrea C. Tricco. "Harassment and Discrimination in Medical Training: A Systematic Review and Meta-Analysis," *Academic Medicine* 89, no. 5 (2014): 817–827.

Ford, Donna Y., and Janet E. Helms. "Overview and Introduction: Testing and Assessing African Americans: Unbiased Tests Are Still Unfair," *The Journal of Negro Education* 81, no. 3 (2012): 186–189. doi:10.7709/jnegroeducation.81.3.0186.

Freeman, Catherine, and Mary Ann Fox. "Status and Trends in the Education of American Indians and Alaska Natives. NCES 2005-108," *National Center for Education Statistics* (2005).

Furman, Rich, and Nalini Negi. *Social Work Practice with Latinos.* Chicago: Lyceum Books, 2010.

Gándara, Patricia. "Passing through the Eye of the Needle: High-Achieving Chicanas," *Hispanic Journal of Behavioral Sciences* 4, no. 2 (1982): 167–179.

Gardner, Susan K., and Karri A. Holley. "'Those Invisible Barriers Are Real': The Progression of First-Generation Students through Doctoral Education," *Equity & Excellence in Education* 44, no. 1 (2011): 77–92.

Garland-Thomson, Rosemary. "Misfits: A Feminist Materialist Disability Concept," *Hypatia* 26, no. 3 (Summer 2011): 591–609.

Gay, Geneva. "Navigating Marginality En Route to the Professoriate: Graduate Students of Color Learning and Living in Academia," *International Journal of Qualitative Studies in Education* 14, no. 2 (2004): 265–288.

Gildersleeve, Ryan Evely, Natasha Croom, and Philip L. Vasquez. "'Am I Going Crazy?!': A Critical Race Analysis of Doctoral Education," *Equity & Excellence in Education* 44, no. 1 (2011): 93–144.

Ginther, Donna K., and Shalamit Kahn. "Education and Academic Career Outcomes for Women of Color in Science and Engineering," *Seeking Solutions: Maximizing American Talent by Advancing Women of Color in Academia: A Summary of a Conference* (2013): 71–92.

Glover, S. Tay. "'Black Lesbians—Who Will Fight for Our Lives but Us?': Navigating Power, Belonging, Labor, Resistance, and Survival in the Ivory Tower," *Feminist Teacher* 23, no. 2–3 (2017): 157–175.

Goodstein, Lynne, and La Verne Gyant, "A Minor of Our Own: A Cause for an Academic Program in Women of Color," *Women's Studies Quarterly* 18, no. 1/2 (Summer 1990): 39–45.

Grbic, Douglas, Gwen Garrison, and Paul Jolly. "Diversity of U.S. Medical School Students by Parental Education," *Analysis in Brief* 9, no. 10 (2010): 1–2.

Grebler, Leo, Joan W. Moore, Ralph C. Guzman, *The Mexican American People.* New York: The Free Press, 1970.

Griffin, Kimberley A. "Reconsidering the Pipeline Problem: Increasing Faculty Diversity," *Higher Education Today*, American Council on Education, February 10, 2016. https://www.higheredtoday.org/2016/02/10/reconsidering-the-pipeline-problem-increasing-faculty-diversity/.

Gumbs, Alexis Pauline. "The Shape of My Impact," *The Feminist Wire*, October 29, 2012. http://www.thefeministwire.com/2012/10/the-shape-of-my-impact/.

Gutiérrez y Muhs, Gabriella, Yolanda Flores Niemann, Angela P. Harris, and Carmen G. González, eds. *Presumed Incompetent: The Intersections of Race and Class for Women in Academia.* Boulder: University of Colorado Press, 2012.

Haque, Eve. *Multiculturalism within a Bilingual Framework: Language, Race, and Belonging in Canada*. Toronto: University of Toronto Press, 2012.

Harris, Phillip, Bruce M. Smith, and Joan Harris. *The Myths of Standardized Tests: Why They Don't Tell You What You Think They Do*. Lanham, Md.: Rowman and Littlefield Publishers, 2011.

Haynes, Douglas M. "Always the Exception: Women and Women of Color Scientists in Historical Perspective," *Peer Review* 16, no. 2 (Spring 2014). https://www.aacu.org/publications-research/periodicals/always-exception-women-and-women-color-scientists-historical.

Hernández, Pilar, Mirna Carranza, and Rhea Almeida. "Mental Health Professionals' Adaptive Responses to Racial Microaggressions: An Exploratory Study," *Professional Psychology: Research and Practice* 41, no. 3 (2010): 202–209.

Hill Collins, Patricia. *Black Feminist Thought Knowledge, Consciousness, and the Politics of Empowerment*. New York: Routledge, 2002.

———. "That's Not Why I Went to School," *The Disobedient Generation: Social Theorists in the Sixties*, eds. Alan Sica and Stephen P. Turner, 93–114. Chicago: University of Chicago Press, 2005.

Hirschfield, Laura E., and Tiffany D. Joseph. "'We Need a Woman, We Need a Black Woman': Gender, Race, and Diversity Taxation in the Academy," *Gender and Education* 24, no. 2 (March 2012): 213–227.

Hirschfeld, Mary, Robert L. Moore, and Eleanor Brown. "Exploring the Gender Gap on the GRE Subject Test in Economics," *The Journal of Economic Education* 26, no. 1 (January 1, 1995): 3–15. doi:10.2307/1183461.

Hochschild, Arlie Russell, and Anne Machung. *The Second Shift*. New York: Penguin Books, 2003.

Hong, Grace. *Death beyond Disavowal: The Impossible Politics of Difference*. Minneapolis: University of Minnesota Press, 2015.

hooks, bell. *Ain't I a Woman: Black Women and Feminism*. Cambridge, Mass.: South End Press, 1991.

———. *Feminism Is for Everybody: Passionate Politics*. Cambridge, Mass.: South End Press, 2000.

———. *Talking Back: Thinking Feminist, Thinking Black*. Brooklyn: South End Press, 1989.

———. *Teaching Community: A Pedagogy of Hope*. New York: Routledge, 2003.

———. *The Will to Change: Men, Masculinity, and Love*. New York: Atria Books, 2004.

———. *Yearning: Race, Gender, and Cultural Politics*. Boston: South End Press, 1990.

Hudson, Peter James. "The Geographies of Blackness and Anti-Blackness: An Interview with Katherine McKittrick," *The CLR James Journal* (20): 240–253.

Huynh, Que-Lam, Thierry Devos, and Laura Smalarz. "Perpetual Foreigner in One's Own Land: Potential Implications for Identity and Psychological Adjustment," *Journal of Social and Clinical Psychology* 30, no. 2 (2011): 133–162.

Iglehart, Alfreda P., and Rosina M. Becerra. *Social Services and the Ethnic Community: History and Analysis*. Long Grove, Ill.: Waveland Press, 2010.

Johnson, Beverly. "Bill Cosby Drugged Me. This Is My Story," *Vanity Fair* (December, 2014).

Johnson, Gabrielle Vanessa Helene. *Time with College Graduates, Family Member Academic Level, and Time Spent in Federal Trio Programs as Predictive Factors of Higher GPA in Post-Secondary Education among Ethnic Minority College Students.* PhD diss., Oklahoma State University, 2015.

Jolly, Paul. "Diversity of U.S. Medical School Students by Parental Income," *Analysis in Brief* 8, no. 1 (2008): 1–2.

Joseph, Joretta. "From One Culture to Another: Years One and Two of Graduate School for African American Women in the STEM Fields," *International Journal of Doctoral Studies* 7 (2012): 125–142.

Journet, Debra. "Narrative Turns in Writing Studies Research," *Writing Studies Research in Practice: Methods and Methodologies*, eds. Lee Nickoson and Mary P. Sheridan, 13–24. Carbondale: Southern Illinois University Press, 2012.

Kachchaf, Rachel, Lily Ko, Apriel Hodari, and Maria Ong. "Career-Life Balance for Women of Color: Experiences in Science and Engineering Academia," *Journal of Diversity in Higher Education* 8, no. 3 (2015): 175–191.

Kadi, Joanna. *Thinking Class: Sketches from a Cultural Worker.* Boston: South End Press, 1996. Print.

Kafer, Alison. *Feminist, Queer, Crip.* Bloomington: Indiana University Press, 2013.

Kaplan and *Newsweek, Graduate School Admissions Advisor.* New York: Simon and Schuster, 2001.

Katz, Michael B. *In the Shadow of the Poorhouse: A Social History of Welfare in America.* New York: Basic Books, 1996.

Kelley Jr., Bill. "Reimagining Ceremonies: A Conversation with Postcommodity," *Afterall: A Journal of Art, Context and Enquiry* 39 (2015): 26–35.

Kelly, Bridget, Joy Gaston Gayules, and Cobretti D. Williams. "Recruitment without Retention: A Critical Case of Black Faculty Unrest," *The Journal of Negro Education* 86, no. 3 (2017): 305–317.

Keys, Alicia, Linda Perry, and Steve Mostyn. "Superwomen." Recorded 2005–2007. Track 3 on *As I Am.* Oven Studios, 2008, compact disc.

Kim, Eleana J. *Adopted Territory: Transnational Korean Adoptees and the Politics of Belonging.* Durham: Duke University Press, 2010.

Kovach, Margaret. *Indigenous Methodologies: Characteristics, Conversations, and Contexts.* Toronto: University of Toronto Press, 2011.

Kruse, Adam J. "Cultural Bias in Testing: A Review of Literature and Implications for Music Education." *Update: Applications of Research in Music Education* 35, no. 1 (Oct. 1, 2016): 23–31. doi:10.1177/8755123315576212.

Ladson-Billings, Gloria. "Just What is Critical Race Theory and What's It Doing in a *Nice* Field Like Education?" *Foundations of Critical Race Theory in Education*, eds. Edward Taylor, David Gillborn, and Gloria Ladson-Billings, 17–36. New York: Routledge, 2009.

Landau, Mark J., Jeff Greenberg, and Zachary K. Rothschild. "Motivated Cultural Worldview Adherence and Culturally Loaded Test Performance," *Per-*

sonality and Social Psychology Bulletin 35, no. 4 (April 1, 2009): 442–453. doi:10.1177/0146167208329630.

Lee, Shelley Sang-Hee. *A New History of Asian America*. New York: Routledge, 2014.

Lenning, Emily, Sara Brightman, and Susan Caringella. *A Guide to Surviving a Career in Academia: Navigating the Rites of Passage*. London: Routledge, 2011.

Leonard, David J. "Impostor Syndrome: Academic Identity Under Siege?" *The Chronicle of Higher Education*, February 5, 2014. http://chronicle.com/blogs/conversation/2014/02/05/impostor-syndrome-academic-identity-under-siege/.

Lewis, Harold, and Jayne Silberman. *Intellectual Base of Social Work Practice: Tools for Thought in a Helping Profession*. New York: Routledge, 2012.

Lewis, Jioni A., Ruby Mendenhall, Stacy A. Harwood, and Margaret B. Huntt. "Coping with Gendered Racial Microaggressions among Black Women College Students," *Journal of African American Studies* 17 (2013): 51–73.

Linder, Chris, Jessica C. Harris, Evette L. Allen, and Bryan Hubain. "Building Inclusive Pedagogy: Recommendations from a National Study of Students of Color in Higher Education and Student Affairs Graduate Programs," *Equity & Excellence in Education* 44, no. 2 (2015): 178–194.

Liu, Amy. "Critical Race Theory, Asian Americans, and Higher Education: A Review of Research," *InterActions: UCLA Journal of Education and Information Studies* 5, no. 2 (2009): 1–12.

Lorde, Audre. *A Burst of Light: Essays*. Ann Arbor: Firebrand Books, 1988.

———. "Age, Race, Class and Sex: Women Redefining Difference," *Race, Class, and Gender: An Anthology*, eds. Margaret L. Anderson and Patricia Hill Collins, 15–21. Boston: Cengage, 2015.

———. *Sister Outsider: Essays and Speeches*. New York: Ten Speed Press, 1984.

Mack, Dwayne, Elwood D. Watson, and Michelle Madsen Camacho, eds. *Mentoring Faculty of Color: Essays on Professional Development and Advancement in Colleges and Universities*. Jefferson, N.C.: McFarland and Company, 2012.

Mahmud, Yusr, and Viren Swami. "The Influence of the *hijab* (Islamic head-cover) on Perceptions of Attractiveness and Intelligence," *Body Image* (2010): 90–93. https://www.sciencedirect.com/science/article/abs/pii/S1740144509000953.

Mahtani, Minelle. "Mapping Race and Gender in the Academy: The Experiences of Women of Colour Faculty and Graduate Students in Britain, the US and Canada," *Journal of Geography in Higher Education* 28, no. 1 (2004): 91–99.

Mankiller, Wilma, and Michael Wallis. *Mankiller: A Chief and Her People: An Autobiography by the Principal Chief of the Cherokee Nation*. New York: St. Martin's Press, 1993.

Marbley, Aretha Faye, Aliza Wong, Sheryl L. Santos-Hatchett, Comfort Pratt, and Lahib Jaddo. "Women Faculty of Color: Voices, Gender, and the Expression of Our Multiple Identities within Academia," *Advancing Women in Leadership* 31 (2011): 166–174.

Margolis, Eric, and Mary Romero. "This Department Is Very Male, Very White,

Very Old, and Very Conservative": The Functioning of the Hidden Curriculum in Graduate Sociology Departments," *Harvard Educational Review* 68 (Spring 1998): 1–32.

Martin, Karen, and Booran Mirraboopa. "Ways of Knowing, Being and Doing: A Theoretical Framework and Methods for Indigenous and Indigenist Research," *Journal of Australian Studies* 27, no. 76 (2003): 203–214.

Martínez, Cristóbal, Randy Kemp, and Lisa Tolentino. "Radio Healer." *CHI'10 Extended Abstracts on Human Factors in Computing Systems*, 3113–3116. ACM, 2010.

Martinez, H. Nolo, and Andrea Bazán Manson. "Health Disparities among North Carolina's Latinos: Our Point of View," *North Carolina Medical Journal* 65, no. 6 (2003): 356–358.

Matthew, Patricia A. "What Is Faculty Diversity Worth to the University?" *The Atlantic*, November 23, 2016. https://www.theatlantic.com/education/archive/2016/11/what-is-faculty-diversity-worth-to-a-university/508334/.

Mavis, Brian, Aron Sousa, Wanda Lipscomb, and Marsha D. Rappley. "Learning about Medical Student Mistreatment from Responses to the Medical School Graduation Questionnaire," *Academic Medicine* 89, no. 5 (2014): 705–711.

Mayock, Ellen C., and Domnica Radulescu. *Feminist Activism in Academia: Essays on Personal, Political and Professional Change*. Jefferson, N.C.: McFarland and Company, 2010.

McAndrew, Marie. *Fragile Majorities and Education: Belgium, Catalonia, Northern Ireland, and Quebec*. Montreal: McGill-Queen's University Press, 2013.

McCarthy, Cian, and John McEvoy. "Pimping in Medical Education: Lacking Evidence and under Threat," *JAMA* 314, no. 22 (2015): 2347–2348.

McCaskill, Barbara, Julie Abraham, Barbara Becker-Cantarino, Kimberly Blockett, Dana Dragunoiu, Rosemary Feal, Jane Moss, Karen Shimakawa, Gerhard Sonnert, Karen Swann, Kimberly Wallace Sanders, and Monika Zagar. "Women in the Profession, 2000: MLA Committee on the Status of Women in the Profession," *Profession* (2000): 191–217.

McChesney, Jasper. *Representation and Pay of Women of Color in the Higher Education Workforce* (Research Report). CUPA-HR (May 2018). https://www.cupahr.org/wp-content/uploads/CUPA-HR-Brief-Women-Of-Color.pdf.

McGee, Rose, and Ann Fasco. *Story Circle Stories: Featuring Stories of Convening in Circle from 32 Diverse Voices and Visual Artists*. St Paul, Minn.: Belfry Books, 2014.

McKee, Kimberly. "Paying It Forward." *Mckeekimberly.com*. February 16, 2015. https://mckeekimberly.com/2015/02/16/paying-it-forward/.

———. "The Benefits of Informal Mentoring." *Mckeekimberly.com*. February 20, 2015. https://mckeekimberly.com/2015/02/20/benefits-informal-mentors/.

———. "Reflections on the AAAS/EOC Junior Faculty Retreat." *Mckeekimberly.com*. May 1, 2015. https://mckeekimberly.com/2015/05/01/reflections-on-the-aaas-eoc-retreat/.

———. "Reflections on Year One." *Mckeekimberly.com*. August 27, 2015. https://mckeekimberly.com/2015/08/27/reflections-on-year-one/.

———. "NWSA Graduate Caucus Reception Remarks." *Mckeekimberly.com*. November 16, 2015. https://mckeekimberly.com/2015/02/16/paying-it-forward/.

———. *Disrupting Kinship: Transnational Politics of Korean Adoption in the United States*. Urbana: University of Illinois Press, 2019.

McKee, Kimberly, and Adrienne A. Winans. eds. "Special Section of Women of Color in the Academy," *Feminist Teacher* 27, no. 2–3 (2017); Publication date winter 2019.

McKittrick, Katherine. *Demonic Grounds: Black Women and the Cartographies of Struggle*. Minneapolis: University of Minnesota Press, 2006.

McLennan, Sharon. "Medical Voluntourism in Honduras: 'Helping' the poor?" *Progress in Development Studies* 14, no. 2 (2014): 163–179.

Mingus, Mia. "Medical Industrial Complex Visual," *Leaving Evidence*, February 06, 2015. https://leavingevidence.wordpress.com/2015/02/06/medical-industrial-complex-visual.

Minikel-Lacocque, Julie. "Racism, College, and the Power of Words: Racial Microaggressions Reconsidered," *American Educational Research Journal* 50, no. 3 (2013): 432–465.

Moghadam, Valentine M. "Patriarchy in Transition: Women and the Changing Family in the Middle East," *Journal of Comparative Family Studies* 35, no. 2 (2004): 137–162. https://www.researchgate.net/publication/281510388_Patriarchy_in_Transition_Women_and_the_Changing_Family_in_the_Middle_East.

Moore, Mignon R. "Women of Color in the Academy: Navigating Multiple Intersections and Multiple Hierarchies," *Social Problems* 64, no. 2 (2017): 200–205.

Moraga, Cherríe, and Gloria Anzaldúa, eds. *This Bridge Called My Back: Writings by Radical Women of Color*. New York: Kitchen Table Women of Color Press, 1983.

Mullaly, Robert P. *Challenging Oppression: A Critical Social Work Approach*. Oxford: Oxford University Press, 2002.

Museus, Samuel D., and Peter N. Kiang. "Deconstructing the Model Minority Myth and How It Contributes to the Invisible Minority Reality in Higher Education Research," *Conducting Research on Asian Americans in Higher Education*, ed. Samuel Museus, 5–16. San Francisco: Jossey-Bass, 2009.

Nadal, Kevin L., Stephanie T. Pituc, Marc P. Johnston, and Theresa Esparrago. "Overcoming the Model Minority Myth: Experiences of Filipino American Graduate Students," *Journal of College Student Development* 51, no. 6 (November/December 2010): 694–706.

Nash, Mary, John Wong, and Andrew Trilin. "Civic and Social Integration: A New Field of Social Work Practice with Immigrants, Refugees and Asylum Seekers," *International Social Work* 49, no. 3 (2006): 345–363.

National Association of Social Workers. "Code of Ethics: Section 1.05 Cultural Competence and Social Diversity," 2008. http://www.socialworkers.org/pubs/code/code.asp.

———. "Immigration and Refugee Resettlement," 2012. http://www.socialworkers.org/practice/intl/issues/immigration.asp.

National Center for Education Statistics. "The Condition of Education—Post-secondary Education—Postsecondary Institutions—Characteristics of Postsecondary Faculty—Indicator May (2018)." *Revenues and Expenditures for Public Elementary and Secondary Education: School Year 2001–2002, E.D.* Tab. May 2018. https://nces.ed.gov/programs/coe/indicator_csc.asp.

Negi, Nalini, and Rich Furman. *Transnational Social Work Practice.* New York: Columbia University Press, 2013.

Nichol, Donna J., and Jennifer A. Yee. "'Reclaiming Our Time': Women of Color Faculty and Radical Self-Care in the Academy," *Feminist Teacher* 27, no. 2–3 (2017): 133–156.

Niemann, Yolanda Flores. "Lessons from the Experiences of Women of Color Working in Academia," *Presumed Incompetent: The Intersections of Race and Class for Women in Academia,* eds. Muhs, Niemann, Gonzalez, and Harris, 446–499. Logan, Utah: Utah State University Press, 2012.

Oh, Robert, and Brian V. Reamy. "The Socratic Method and Pimping: Optimizing the Use of Stress and Fear in Instruction," *Virtual Mentor* 16, no. 3 (2014): 182–186.

Okahana, Hironao, and Enyu Zhao. "Graduate Enrollment and Degrees: 2007–2017," Table B.10: First Time Graduate Enrollments by Citizenship, Race/Ethnicity, and Gender, Fall 2017, *CGS/GRE Survey of Graduate Enrollment and Degrees,* 2007–2017, 2018.

Oliver, Michael. *Understanding Disability: From Theory to Practice.* New York: St. Martin's Press, 1996.

Olmsted, Jennifer C. "Gender, Aging, and the Evolving Arab Patriarchal Contract," *Feminist Economics* 11, no. 2 (2005): 53–78. https://www.researchgate.net/publication/24080958_Gender_Aging_and_the_Evolving_Arab_Patriarchal_Contract.

Ong, Maria, Carol Wright, Lorelle L. Espinosa, and Gary Orfield. "Inside the Double Bind: A Synthesis of Empirical Research on Undergraduate and Graduate Women of Color in Science, Technology, Engineering, and Mathematics," *Harvard Educational Review* 81, no. 2 (2011): 172–208.

Ong, Maria, Janet M. Smith, and Lily T. Ko. "Counterspaces for Women of Color in STEM Higher Education: Marginal and Central Spaces for Persistence and Success," *Journal of Research in Science Teaching* 55, no. 2 (2018): 206–245.

Onwuegbuzie, Anthony J., Roslinda Rosli, Jacqueline M. Ingram, and Rebecca K. Frels. "A Critical Dialectical Pluralistic Examination of the Lived Experience of Select Women Doctoral Students," *The Qualitative Report* 19, no. 3 (2014): 1–35.

Ortiz-Walters, Rowena, and Lucy L. Gilson. "Mentoring in Academia: An Examination of the Experiences of Protégés of Color," *Journal of Vocational Behavior* 67 (2005): 459–475.

Park Nelson, Kim. *Invisible Asians: Korean Adoptees, Asian American Experiences, and Racial Exceptionalism.* New Brunswick: Rutgers University Press, 2016.

Pérez Huber, Lindsay, and Daniel G. Solorzano. "Racial Microaggressions as a

Tool for Critical Race Research," *Race Ethnicity and Education* 18, no. 3 (2015): 297–320.

Personal email, Denise Delgado and Kimberly McKee to Karen J. Leong, November 4, 2014.

Pew Hispanic Center. *Census 2010: 50 Million Latinos: Hispanics Account for More than Half of Nation's Growth in Past Decade.* 2011. http://www.pewhispanic.org/files/reports/140.pdf.

Pew Research Center. *The Rise of Asian Americans.* Washington, D.C.: Pew Research Center, 2013. http://www.pewsocialtrends.org/files/2013/04/Asian-Americans-new-full-report-04–2013.pdf.

Phruksachart, Melissa. "On Mentoring Future Faculty of Color," *Feminist Teacher* 23, 2–3 (2017): 117–132.

Pierce, Chester M., Jean V. Carew, Diane Pierce-Gonzalez, and Deborah Wills. "An Experiment in Racism: TV Commercials," *Education and Urban Society* 10 (1977): 61–87.

Pierce, Dean. "Field Education in the 2008 EPAS: Implications for the Field Director's Role," *Council on Social Work Education,* last modified 2008. http://www.cswe.org/File.aspx?id=31580.

Poon, OiYan, Dian Squire, Corinne Kodama, Ajani Byrd, Jason Chan, Lester Manzano, Sara Furr, and Devita Bishundat. "A Critical Review of the Model Minority Myth in Selected Literature on Asian Americans and Pacific Islanders in Higher Education," *Review of Educational Research* 86, no. 2 (2016): 469–502.

Popke, Jeff. "Latino Migration and Neoliberalism in the US South: Notes toward a Rural Cosmopolitanism," *southeastern geographer* 51, no. 2 (2011): 242–259.

Powell, Malea. "Stories Take Place: A Performance in One Act." *CCC* 64, no. 2 (2012): 383–406. http://www.ncte.org/library/NCTEFiles/Resources/Journals/CCC/0642-dec2012/CCC0642Address.pdf.

Prébin, Elise. *Meeting Once More: The Korean Side of Transnational Adoption.* New York: New York University Press, 2013.

Ramirez, Elvia. "'¿Qué Estoy Haciendo Aquí? (What Am I Doing Here?)': Chicanos/Latinos(as) Navigating Challenges and Inequalities during Their First Year of Graduate School," *Equity & Excellence in Education* 47, no. 2 (2014): 167–186.

Revilla, Anita T. "What Happens in Vegas Does Not Stay in Vegas: Youth Leadership in the Immigrant Rights Movement in Las Vegas, 2006," *AZTLAN—A Journal of Chicano Studies* 37, no. 1 (2012): 87–115.

Richards, Amy. *Opting In: Having a Child without Losing Yourself.* 1st ed. New York: Farrar, Straus and Giroux, 2008.

Robinson, Cynthia C., and Pauline Clardy. *Tedious Journeys: Autoethnography by Women of Color in Academe.* New York: Peter Lang Publishing Inc., 2010.

Robinson, William H., Ebony O. Mcgee, Lydia C. Bentley, Stacey L. Houston II, and Portia K. Botchway. "Addressing Negative Racial and Gendered Experiences that Discourage Academic Careers in Engineering," *Computing Science and Engineering* (March/April 2016): 29–39.

Rockquemore, Kerry, and Tracey A. Laszloffy. *The Black Academic's Guide to Winning Tenure—without Losing Your Soul.* Boulder: Lynne Rienner Publishers, 2008.

Romero, Mary. "Reflections on 'The Department Is Very Male, Very White, Very Old, and Very Conservative': The Functioning of the Hidden Curriculum in Graduate Sociology Departments," *Social Problems* 64, no. 2 (2017): 212–218.

Rossiter, Amy. "Innocence Lost and Suspicion Found: Do We Educate for or against Social Work?" *Critical Social Work* 2, no. 1 (2001).

Rude, Mey Valdivia. "Flawless Trans Women Carmen Carrera and Laverne Cox Respond Flawlessly to Katie Couric's Invasive Questions," *Autostraddle.* January 08, 2014. https://www.autostraddle.com/flawless-trans-women-carmen-carrera-and-laverne-cox-respond-flawlessly-to-katie-courics-invasive-questions-215855/.

Saldana, Lelliana Patricia, Felicia Castro-Villarreal, and Erica Sosa. "'Testimonios' of Latina Junior Faculty: Bridging Academia, Family, and Community Lives in the Academy." *Educational Foundations* 27, no. 2 (2013): 31–48.

Sánchez, Patricia, and Lucila D. Ek. "Before the Tenure Track: Graduate School Testimonios and Their Importance in Our Professora-ship Today," *Educational Foundations* (Winter 2013): 15–30.

Scharrnón-del Río, María. "Teaching at the Intersections: Liberatory and Anti-Oppressive Pedagogical Praxis in the Multicultural Counseling Classroom as a Queer Puerto Rican Educator," *Feminist Teacher* 23, Issue 2–3 (2017): 90–105.

Scripa, Allison J., Edward F. Lener, Cherly B. Gittens, and Connie Stovall. "The McNair Scholars Program at Virginia Tech: A Unique Model of Librarian Mentoring," *Virginia Libraries* 58, no. 3 (2012).

Simien, Evelyn M. "Gender Differences in Attitudes toward Black Feminism among African Americans," *Political Science Quarterly* 119, no. 2 (2004): 315–338.

Smith, Barbara. "Toward a Black Feminist Criticism," *The Radical Teacher* 7 (1978): 20–27.

Smith, Linda Tuhiwai. *Decolonizing Methodologies: Research and Indigenous Peoples.* London: Zed Books Ltd., 2013.

Smith, William A., Walter R. Allen, and Lynette L. Danley. "'Assume the Position . . . You Fit the Description' Psychosocial Experiences and Racial Battle Fatigue among African American Male College Students," *American Behavioral Scientist* 51, no. 4 (2007): 551–578.

Social Sciences Feminist Network Research Group. "The Burden of Invisible Work in Academia Social Inequalities and Time Use in Five University Departments," *Humboldt Journal of Social Relations* 39 (2017): 228–245.

Solórzano, Daniel. "Critical Race Theory, Race and Gender Microaggressions, and the Experiences of Chicana and Chicano Scholars," *Qualitative Studies in Education* 11, no. 1 (1998): 121–136.

Solórzano, Daniel G., and Tara J. Yosso. "Critical Race and LatCrit Theory and Method: Counter-storytelling," *International Journal of Qualitative Studies in Education* 14, no. 4 (2001): 471–495.

Solórzano, Daniel G., and Tara J. Yosso. "Critical Race Methodology: Counter-

Storytelling as an Analytical Framework for Education Research," *Qualitative Inquiry* 8, no. 1 (2002): 23–44.

Solórzano, Daniel, Miguel Ceja, and Tara Yosso. "Critical Race Theory, Racial Microaggressions, and Campus Racial Climate: The Experiences of African American College Students," *Journal of Negro Education* (2000): 60–73.

Southeast Asian Retention through Creating Hxstory. "What Does the 'X' in Hxstory Stand for?" *Southeast Asian Retention through Creating Hxstory*, last modified Spring 2014. https://searchuci.wordpress.com/about/what-does-the-x-is-hxstory -stand-for/.

Souto-Manning, Mariana, and Nichole Ray. "Beyond Survival in the Ivory Tower: Black and Brown Women's Living Narratives," *Equity & Excellence in Education* 40, no. 4 (2007): 280–290.

Spade, Dean. "For Those Considering Law School," *Dean Spade* (blog), November 1, 2010. http://www.deanspade.net/wp-content/uploads/2010/10/For-Those -Considering-Law-School-Nov-2010.pdf.

Spruill, Marjorie. "Women Unite! Lessons from 1977 for 2017," *Process: A Blog for American History*, Organization of American Historians, January 20, 2017. http://www.processhistory.org/women-unite-spruill/.

Squire, Dian D., and Kristen McCann. "Women of Color with Critical World Views Constructing Spaces of Resistance in Education Doctoral Programs," *Journal of College Student Development* 59, no. 4 (July–August 2018): 404–420.

Studdard, Scarlette Spears. "Adult Women Students in the Academy: Imposters or Members?" *Journal of Continuing Higher Education* 50, no. 3 (2002): 24–37.

Sue, Derald Wing. *Overcoming Our Racism: The Journey to Liberation*. San Francisco: Jossey Bass, 2003.

Sue, Derald Wing, Christina M. Capodilupo, Gina C. Torino, Jennifer M. Bucceri, Aisha M. B. Holder, Kevin L. Nadal, and Marta Esquilin. "Racial Microaggressions in Everyday Life: Implications for Clinical Practice," *American Psychologist* 62, no. 4 (2007): 271–286.

Sue, Derald W., Jennifer Bucceri, Annie I. Lin, Kevin L. Nadal, and Gina C. Torino. "Racial Microaggressions and the Asian American Experience," *Cultural Diversity & Ethnic Minority Psychology* 13, no. 1 (2007): 72–81.

Taylor, Edward. "A Primer on Critical Race Theory," *The Journal of Blacks in Higher Education* 19 (1998): 122–124.

———. "The Foundations of Critical Race Theory in Education: An Introduction." *Foundations of Critical Race Theory in Education*, eds. Edward Taylor, David Gillborn, and Gloria Ladson-Billings, 1–13. New York: Routledge, 2009.

Toastmasters International. "Where Leaders Are Made," *Toastmasters International*. http://www.toastmasters.org/.

Turner, Caroline Sotello Viernes. "Women of Color in Academe: Living with Multiple Marginality," *The Journal of Higher Education* 73, no. 1 (2002): 74–93.

Twale, Darla J., John C. Weidman, and Kathryn Bethea. "Conceptualizing Socialization of Graduate Students of Color: Revisiting the Weidman-Twale-Stein Framework," *The Western Journal of Black Studies* 40, no. 2 (2016): 80–94.

Ty, Eleanor. *Politics of the Visible in Asian North American Narratives.* Toronto: University of Toronto Press, 2004.

Ty, Eleanor, and Don Goellnicht, eds. *Asian North American Identities: Beyond the Hyphen.* Bloomington: Indiana University Press, 2004.

Umemoto, Karen. "'On Strike!' San Francisco State College Strike, 1968–69: The Role of Asian American Students," *Amerasia* 15, no. 1 (1989): 3–41.

UNC School of Social Work. "Field Education Program." http://ssw.unc.edu /programs/masters/fieldeducation.

University of Minnesota Women's Center. "Reflection: This World Is Ours to Build," *University of Minnesota Women's Center Blog,* The University of Minnesota, April 24, 2018. https://mnwomenscenter.wordpress.com/2018/04/24/reflection-this -world-is-ours-to-build/.

U.S. Census Bureau. "2010 Census: State Population Profile Maps," 2010. http://2010.census.gov/2010census/.

———. "Educational Attainment: Five Key Data Releases from the U.S. Census Bureau." U.S. Department of Census. https://www.census.gov/newsroom/cspan /educ/educ_attain_slides.pdf.

———. *American Community Survey Five Year Estimates 2005–2009.* 2010. http:// factfinder.census.gov/servlet/DatasetMainPageServlet?_program=ACS&_sub menuId=&_lang=en&_ts=.

———. *American Indian and Alaska Native Heritage Month: November 2011.* https:// www.census.gov/newsroom/releases/archives/facts_for_features_special_editions /cb11-ff22.html.

U.S. Department of Education. National Center for Education Statistics, Integrated Table 7–8: Doctorates Awarded to U.S. Citizens and Permanent Residents by Sex, Field, Ethnicity and Race, 2016 (NSF 19–304).

———. National Center for Education Statistics, Table 315.20. Full-time Faculty in Degree-granting Postsecondary Institutions, by Race/Ethnicity, Sex, and Academic Rank: Fall 2015, Fall 2016, and Fall 2017 (Table was prepared November 2018). https://nces.ed.gov/programs/digest/d18/tables/dt18_315.20.asp.

U.S. Department of Health and Human Services, "Office of Minority Health National Standards for Culturally and Linguistically Appropriate Services in Health Care," 2001. http://minorityhealth.hhs.gov/assets/pdf/checked/finalreport.pdf.

Vakalahi, Halaevalu F. O., Michelle Sermon, Andrea Richardson, Veronica Dillard, and Aryka Moncrief. "Do You See Me? The Complex Experiences of Women of Color MSW Students," *Intercultural Education* 25, no. 5 (2014): 418–427.

van Schaik, Katherine D. "Pimping Socrates," *JAMA* 311, no. 14 (2014): 1401–1402.

Vaughns, Katherine L. "Women of Color in Law Teaching: Shared Identities, Different Experiences," *Journal of Legal Education* 53, no. 4 (2003): 496–504.

Villanueva, Victor. "On the Rhetoric and Precedents of Racism," *College Composition and Communication* 50, no. 4 (1999): 645–661. https://wrd.as.uky.edu/sites /default/files/villanueva-racism.pdf.

Wallace, David. "Unwelcome Stories, Identity Matters, and Strategies for Engaging in Cross-Boundary Discourses," *College English* 76, no. 6 (2014): 545–561. https://

www.researchgate.net/publication/287711293_Unwelcome_stories_identity
_matters_and_strategies_for_engaging_in_cross-boundary_discourses.

Wang, Howard, and Robert T. Teranishi. "AAPI Background and Statistics: Perspectives of the Representation and Inclusion of AAPI Faculty, Staff, and Student
Affairs Professionals," *Asian Americans and Pacific Islanders in Higher Education:
Research and Perspectives on Identity, Leadership, and Success*, eds. Doris Ching
and Amefil Agbayani. Washington D.C.: NASPA.

Washington, Tanya. "Students' Demands for Diverse Faculty Is a Demand for
Better Education," *The Conversation*, The Conversation US, December 2, 2015.
https://theconversation.com/students-demand-for-diverse-faculty-is-a-demand
-for-a-better-education-50698.

Wayne, Julianne, Marion Bogo, and Miriam Raskin. "Field Education as the Signature Pedagogy of Social Work Education," *Journal of Social Work Education*
46, no. 3 (2010): 327–339.

Weir, Kirsten. "Feeling Like a Fraud?" *gradPSYCH Magazine* (November 2013).
http://www.apa.org/gradpsych/2013/11/fraud.aspx.

Williams, June. "The Invisible Labor of Minority Professors," *The Chronicle of Higher
Education*, November 8, 2015. http://www.chronicle.com/article/The-Invisible
-Labor-of/234098.

Williams, Patricia J. *The Alchemy of Race and Rights. Diary of a Law Professor.*
Cambridge: Harvard University Press, 1991.

Willison, Scott, and Emily Gibson. "Graduate School Learning Curves: McNair
Scholars Postbaccalaureate Transitions," *Equity & Excellence in Education* 44, no.
2 (2011): 153–168. doi:10.1080/10665684.2011.558416.

Wing, Adrien Katherine, ed. *Critical Race Feminism: A Reader*. New York: New
York University Press, 2003.

Withorn, Ann. "Dual Citizenship: (An interview with) Women of Color in Graduate School," *Women's Studies Quarterly* 25, no. 1/2 (Spring/Summer 1997):
132–138.

Wong-Padoongpatt, Gloria, Nolan Zane, Sumie Okazaki, and Anne Saw. "Decreases
in Implicit Self-Esteem Explain the Racial Impact of Microaggressions among
Asian Americans," *Journal of Counseling Psychology* 64, no. 5 (2017): 574–583.

Wood, Christine V., Patricia B. Campbell, and Richard McGee. "'An Incredibly
Steep Hill': How Gender, Race, and Class Shape Perspectives on Academic
Careers among Beginning Biomedical PhD Students," *Journal of Women and
Minorities in Science and Engineering* 22, no. 2 (2016): 159–181.

Yook, Eunkyong Lee. *Culture Shock for Asians in U.S. Academia: Breaking the Model
Minority Myth*. Lanham, Md.: Lexington Books, 2017.

Yosso, Tara J. *Critical Race Counterstories along the Chicana/Chicano Educational
Pipeline*. New York: Routledge. 2006.

Yosso, Tara J. "Whose Culture Has Capital? A Critical Race Theory Discussion
of Community Cultural Wealth," *Race Ethnicity and Education* 8, no. 1 (2005):
69–91.

Yosso, Tara, William Smith, Miguel Ceja, and Daniel Solórzano. "Critical Race Theory, Racial Microaggressions, and Campus Racial Climate for Latina/o Undergraduates," *Harvard Educational Review* 79, no. 4 (2009): 659–691.

Yunkaporta, Tyson. *Aboriginal Pedagogies at the Cultural Interface.* Unpublished doctoral thesis, James Cook University, Australia (2009).

Zaatari, Zeina. "In the Belly of the Beast: Struggling for Nonviolent Belonging," *MIT Electronic Journal of Middle East Studies* 5 (2005): 75–87.

Zellars, Rachel. "Violence that Never Was: Black Organizing, Violence Against Women, and Black Women's Activism," paper presented at the American Studies Association conference, October 8, 2015.

Zota, Sejal. "Immigrants in North Carolina: A Fact Sheet," *Popular Government.* Fall issues (2008): 38–44. http://sogpubs.unc.edu/electronicversions/pg/pgfal08/article4.pdf.

Contributors

AERIEL A. ASHLEE is an assistant professor of College Counseling and Student Development at St. Cloud University. Her research interests center around issues of race and racial identity in higher education, including womxn of color graduate students' empowerment and critical consciousness in the academy.

DENISE A. DELGADO received her PhD in Women's, Gender and Sexuality Studies from The Ohio State University and a BA in Women's Studies and Psychology from Arizona State University. She has published on a variety of topics, ranging from gentrification to women's body hair. She now works in the private sector, while occasionally adjuncting and mentoring students on applying for graduate school.

NWADIOGO I. EJIOGU is an activist scholar, community organizer, and healer-in-training. For over a decade she has been writing, serving, and organizing from the intersections of race, gender identity, class, disability, sexuality, criminalization, and healing justice. Currently, she is an Anesthesiology resident at Northwestern University Feinberg School of Medicine. She received her medical degree from Meharry Medical College.

DELIA FERNÁNDEZ is an assistant professor of History at Michigan State University. She is also a core faculty member in the Chicano/Latino Studies Program. Her current manuscript is on Latino labor migration, placemaking, and activism in West Michigan throughout the twentieth century. She is currently on the research team for the Humanities Without

Walls funded project, "Building Sustainable Worlds: Latinx Placemaking in the Midwest." Fernández also serves on the Historical Commission for the State of Michigan.

REGINA EMILY IDOATE, citizen of the Cherokee Nation of Oklahoma, comes from a family of strong Cherokee women. A descendant of Nanyehi Ward, Regina is the great-granddaughter of a teacher, granddaughter of an artist, and daughter of a nurse. Her research focuses on medical humanities and Native American health and wellness. Idoate currently serves as assistant professor in the Department of Health Promotion in the College of Public Health at the University of Nebraska Medical Center.

KAREN LEONG is an associate professor of women and gender studies and Asian Pacific American studies in the School of Social Transformation at Arizona State University. Leong is the author of *The China Mystique: Pearl S. Buck, Anna May Wong, Mayling Soong Chiang and the Transformation of American Orientalism* (University of California Press, 2005). She is currently working with JACL Arizona and members of the Japanese American community on an oral history project about Japanese Americans in Arizona.

KIMBERLY D. MCKEE is the director of the Kutsche Office of Local History and an associate professor in integrative, religious, and intercultural studies at Grand Valley State University. She is the author of *Disrupting Kinship: Transnational Politics of Korean Adoption in the United States* (University of Illinois Press, 2019). Her work also has been featured in *Journal of Korean Studies*, *Adoption & Culture*, *Feminist Formations*, and edited collections on transnational kinship and representations of Asian Americans.

DÉLICE MUGABO is a member of the Third Eye Collective, a group that focuses on gender violence within black communities and transformative justice. She is a PhD student at CUNY–The Graduate Center and researching violence against enslaved Black women in New-France. Her work focuses on the recorded cases of Black women freedom runners during the era of slavery in Quebec.

CARRIE SAMPSON is an assistant professor in the Division of Educational Leadership and Innovation at Arizona State University's Mary Lou Fulton Teachers College. She is a mother-scholar whose research and teaching focuses on educational leadership, policy, and equity from three interrelated strands—governance, community advocacy, and politics.

ARIANNA TABOADA is a public health social worker who specializes in participatory research and interdisciplinary collaboration for addressing health disparities. She holds a BA in Cultural Studies from UCLA and earned her Master of Social Work and Master of Science in Public Health from UNC–Chapel Hill. She has resided in Southeast Mexico since 2013, where she consults for NGOs and governmental reproductive health projects.

JENNY HEIJUN WILLS is associate professor of English at the University of Winnipeg. She is the author of *Older Sister. Not Necessarily Related. A Memoir* (Toronto: Penguin Random House, 2019).

SOHA YOUSSEF is an assistant professor of Writing and Rhetoric at Thomas Jefferson University. Her research interest centers around bridging the gap between the fields of composition/rhetoric and TESOL.

Index

The University of Illinois Press
is a founding member of the
Association of University Presses.

Composed in 11.25/13.5 Adobe Garamond Pro
with Rockwell display
by Jim Proefrock
at the University of Illinois Press
Cover designed by Jennifer S. Fisher
Cover illustration: GP Studio/Shutterstock.com
Manufactured by Sheridan Books, Inc.

University of Illinois Press
1325 South Oak Street
Champaign, IL 61820-6903
www.press.uillinois.edu